DATE DUE

OCT 3 0 2004		
NOV 0 8 2004		
DEC 0 8 2004		
JAN - 3 2005		
FEB 1 2 2005		
MAR 1 0 2005		
MAR 2 6 2005		
MAY 1 2 2005		
JUN 0 6 2005		
JUN 1 3 2005		
JUN 2 8 2005		
AUG 0 2 2005		

DEMCO 38-296

ORGANIZED CRIME

An Inside Guide to the World's Most Successful Industry

ORGANIZED CRIME

An Inside Guide to the World's Most Successful Industry

Paul Lunde

DK

LONDON, NEW YORK, MUNICH, MELBOURNE, DELHI

Produced for Dorling Kindersley by
The Brown Reference Group plc, 8 Chapel Place, Rivington Street, London, EC2A 3DQ

THE BROWN REFERENCE GROUP plc		DORLING KINDERSLEY	
Art Editor Stefan Morris	**Editorial Director** Lindsey Lowe	**Managing Art Editor** Louise Dick	**Production** Louise Daly
Editors Dennis Cove, Virginia Hill	**Managing Editor** Tim Cooke	**Managing Editor** Debra Clapson	**DTP Designer** John Goldsmid
Designers Thor Fairchild, Colin Tilleyloughrey	**Art Director** Dave Goodman	**Art Director** Bryn Walls	**Editorial Assistance** Victoria Heyworth-Dunne
Digital Illustrators Mark Walker, Thor Fairchild	**DTP Executive** Matthew Greenfield	**Editorial Director** Andrew Heritage	**Picture Researcher** Maria Gibbs

First American Edition, 2004
04 05 06 10 9 8 7 6 5 4 3 2 1
Published in the United States by DK Publishing, Inc.
375 Hudson Street, New York, New York 10014
Published in Great Britain by Dorling Kindersley Limited

Text copyright © Paul Lunde/James Morton
Compilation copyright © Dorling Kindersley Limited

A CIP catalog record for this book is available from the Library of Congress.
ISBN: 0-7894-9648-8

Reproduced by GRB, Italy
Printed and bound by Toppan, China
See our complete catalog at
www.dk.com

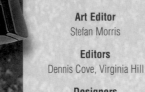

AUTHOR'S NOTE

This book could not have been written without the help of a number of people and institutions, some of whom have preferred to remain anonymous.

My debt to the works of academic criminologists such as Howard Abadinsky and Anton Blok, the starting points for all serious work on the complex phenomenon of organized crime in the United States, will be obvious. The history and study of organized crime is a relatively new discipline, and these two authors have laid the foundations for the serious study of a subject of increasingly compelling importance.

Herbert Asbury's vivid books on the gangs of Chicago and New York, written more than 50 years ago, are mines of fascinating information on 19th and early 20th century urban gangs, as are the many books of Carl Sifakis, whose *Mafia Encyclopedia* is a treasure trove of unusual information. Gus Russo's recent *The Outfit* is a passionate and detailed account of the growth and background of organized crime in Chicago. David E. Kaplan and Alec Dubro's wonderful book on Japanese organized crime, *Yakuza*, is a classic, and readers who wish to know more of this fascinating subject should buy it and read it. Giuseppe Carlo Marino and Salvatore Lupo's respective books on the Sicilian Mafia have still not been translated into English, but

are fundamental. Alexander Stille's *Excellent Cadavers* is the best book in English on the subject, beautifully researched and written. All these authors and many others too numerous to mention have been invaluable works of reference. None are responsible for errors of fact or interpretation.

The publications of the Drug Enforcement Agency, The Federal Bureau of Investigation, Department of Justice, and the various U.N. agencies have all contributed in many ways to make this a better book, and I would like to thank these agencies and the dedicated men and women who work for them for making their publications accessible.

I would like to thank James Morton, who collaborated in this book by writing the chapters on Outlaw Motorcycle Gangs, Organized Crime in Britain, the Yardies and Posses, the Mexican Cartels, and the Medellín and Cali Cartels, all of which were outside my competence. I would also particularly like to thank Caroline Stone for her chapters on the Yakuza and the Triad and Tongs.

I would also like to thank Sonny, Nick, Marty, Tony, and *gli amici* in Chicago and Rome.

Paul Lunde 2004

Contents

SURRAT.

BOOTH.

War Department, Washing

$100,000

WHAT IS ORGANIZED CRIME?

This section provides a number of ways of defining organized crime, and surveys historical patterns and precedents for underworld activities today.

Defining Organized Crime

Attempts by law enforcement and other agencies to provide a single definition of organized crime have been confounded by the fact that the activities of the criminal underworld are, by their nature, kaleidoscopic, constantly responding to shifts in market conditions and exploiting the myriad money-making opportunities provided by the legitimate overworld.

Some law enforcement agencies define organized crime as "a continuing and self-perpetuating criminal conspiracy, having an organized structure, fed by fear and corruption, and motivated by greed." Although suitably dramatic, this definition is inadequate from both the legal and the criminological viewpoint. The United Nations Convention against Transnational Organized Crime, signed in 2000, gives a very broad definition, defining organized crime as "structured groups of three of more people acting in concert to commit one or more serious crimes for material benefit." Jurists and criminologists have not so far been able to agree on a definition that pleases both, while police are impatient with definitions and want specific laws that will allow them to bring criminals to justice. Drafting effective laws to combat organized crime is only possible if there is a consensus about exactly what organized crime is, and how it differs from other criminal activities.

The doyen of U.S. criminologists, Howard Abadinsky, has given the most exhaustive and scrupulous definition: "Organized crime is a non-ideological enterprise involving a number of persons in close social interaction, organized on a hierarchical basis, with at least three levels/ranks, for the purpose of securing profit and power by engaging in illegal and legal activities. Positions in the hierarchy and positions involving functional specialization may be assigned on the basis of kinship or friendship, or rationally assigned according to skill. The positions are not dependent on the individuals occupying them at any particular time. Permanency is assumed by the members who strive to keep the enterprise integral and active in pursuit of its goals. It eschews competition and strives for monopoly on an industry or territorial basis. There is a willingness to use violence and/or bribery to achieve ends or to maintain discipline. Membership is restricted, although non-members may be involved on a contingency basis. There are explicit rules, oral or written, which are enforced by sanctions that include murder."

This, of course, is a description of the American Mafia, or La Cosa Nostra, and applies equally well to its Sicilian counterpart, but there are many effective criminal groups both in the United States and elsewhere that have different structures yet can be classified as "organized."

The more one considers the question of definition, the more one begins to sympathize with lawmakers faced with the challenge of coming up with a good, clear definition. Do the urban gangs of the United States, both past and present, qualify as "organized crime," or do they represent a stage in the development of true organized crime? Organized crime is an economic activity, and differs from street gangs like the Bloods and Crips, not just in the degree of organization and purpose, but

The Sicilian Mafia under fire
The unification of Italy in 1860 led to the first campaigns against the Mafia, as the government tried to establish its authority over the Sicilian countryside.

The face of organized crime: Al Capone
Media concentration on Al Capone's activities in Chicago in the 1920s deflected public attention from the causes and extent of organized crime in America.

Organized Crime In the European Union (EU)

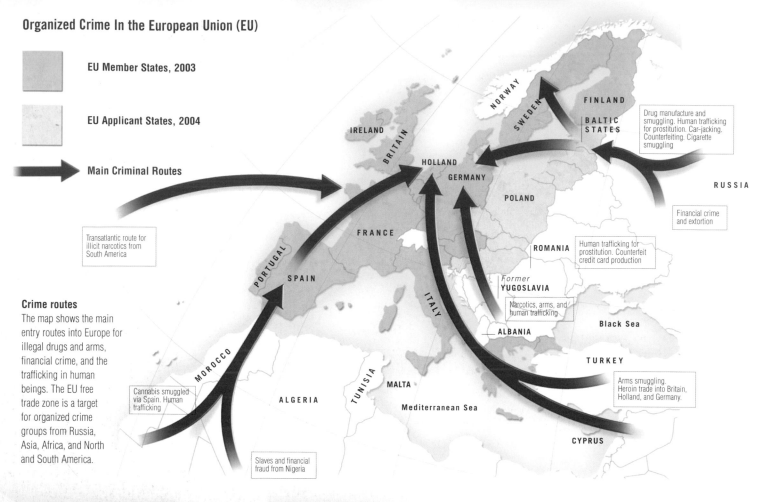

EU Member States, 2003

EU Applicant States, 2004

Main Criminal Routes

Transatlantic route for illicit narcotics from South America

Crime routes
The map shows the main entry routes into Europe for illegal drugs and arms, financial crime, and the trafficking in human beings. The EU free trade zone is a target for organized crime groups from Russia, Asia, Africa, and North and South America.

Cannabis smuggled via Spain. Human trafficking

Slaves and financial fraud from Nigeria

Drug manufacture and smuggling. Human trafficking for prostitution. Car-jacking. Counterfeiting. Cigarette smuggling

Financial crime and extortion

Human trafficking for prostitution. Counterfeit credit card production

Narcotics, arms, and human trafficking

Arms smuggling. Heroin trade into Britain, Holland, and Germany.

NORWAY · SWEDEN · FINLAND · BALTIC STATES · IRELAND · BRITAIN · HOLLAND · GERMANY · POLAND · RUSSIA · FRANCE · ROMANIA · Former YUGOSLAVIA · ITALY · ALBANIA · Black Sea · PORTUGAL · SPAIN · TURKEY · MOROCCO · TUNISIA · MALTA · ALGERIA · Mediterranean Sea · CYPRUS

---

because organized crime accumulates capital and reinvests it. It is this that differentiates organized criminal groups from street gangs and "unorganized" criminals. It is the accumulated capital of organized groups like the U.S.

Mafia and the Yakuza that enables them to buy the political protection that allows them to diversify and to respond to market shifts, such as the upsurge in demand for illicit drugs in the 1980s, and the growth in human trafficking in the 1990s.

White Collar Crime

At the other end of the spectrum from street gang crime is white collar crime. Do the conspiring executives of Enron qualify as "organized criminals?" Probably not, failing the tests of durability and use of violence, but it is not impossible to imagine longer lasting conspiracies to defraud that do verge on "organized crime."

American street gang member
American street gangs mimic the rituals and exclusivity of traditional organized crime groups.

On November 20, 2003, the Federal Bureau of Investigation (FBI) hit Wall Street, arresting 47 bankers, traders, and alleged members of organized crime groups for fraudulent foreign exchange dealings. The accused had been defrauding clients, including major banks, for 20 years, and there was evidence that violence and intimidation had been used. This fraud is closer to some definitions of organized crime, but should probably be classified as "a criminal conspiracy with organized crime links," but here the boundary separating the two is very porous, perfectly exemplifying the difficulties of definition.

The lack of consensus on a definition of organized crime has seriously hampered international law enforcement. National differences in judicial systems and police methods, plus a lack of information sharing, makes the formulation of a common international policy very difficult. These problems are made even more acute because organized crime groups frequently operate in many countries, each with their own legal and policing systems, and expertly exploit these asymmetries to their own advantage.

Common Characteristics

Organized crime, however defined, shares a few basic characteristics, whatever the differences among individual groups and the cultures that produced them. They have in common: durability over time, diversified interests, hierarchical structure, capital accumulation, reinvestment, access to political protection, and the use of violence to protect their interests. Successful organized crime groups each have their own mystique, ensuring solidarity and loyalty through shared ethnicity, kinship, or allegiance to a code of behavior.

Law enforcement agencies around the world agree that organized crime is on the rise, and that along with terrorism it poses a major threat to international order. In 2002, European law enforcement agencies identified 1,000 new organized crime groups operating in the European Union. Even with the use of varying definitions, this is still a remarkable number. Crime is booming.

The global profits of organized crime are difficult to assess. Figures of between $750 billion and a trillion dollars have been suggested, but the true amount is probably higher. In the Russian Federation, organized crime annually siphons off between 10 and 20 percent of the Gross National Product (GNP). The Australian government estimates that organized crime costs $20 billion a year, noting that all the major organized crime groups have lucrative operations in Australia. Canada and the United States estimate the gross profits of organized crime in their respective countries at 1 to 2 percent of the GNP. These huge sums of money are counted, laundered, banked, and invested by accountants, bankers, and investment houses worldwide. It is in the international finance system that underworlds and upperworlds unite and merge.

Main Organizations and Networks

The globalization of organized crime has occurred in tandem with the globalization of the world economy. In the 1970s most organized crime groups were still anchored in their countries of origin. However, in the 1980s traditional, culture-bound organizations like the Japanese Yakuza, the Chinese Triads, and the Sicilian Mafia went global, becoming increasingly sophisticated and diversifying into new markets.

In the early 1990s, the collapse of the Soviet Union created a situation that harks back to the late 19th century, with the reappearance of ethnic gangs on the international scene, many specializing in human trafficking. Trafficking on this scale had virtually disappeared and countries such as Italy have had to revive old laws to combat it. Legal penalties are still

Yakuza tattoo
Elaborate tattoos covering most of the body are a hallmark of the Japanese Yakuza. Traditional organized criminal groups, both East and West, create solidarity through shared myth, ritual, and outward signs.

Mafiya arrest
Russian police arrest a Tajik drug smuggler in the town of Yekaterinburg. Organized crime flourishes in the newly independent republics of the ex-Soviet Union.

Vice
A prostitute awaits her next client in the red light district of Birmingham, Britain. Organized crime controls the vice trade in major cities throughout the world, supplying services the legitimate economy cannot provide.

slight, making the trade even more attractive. The expansion of the European Union (EU) in 2004 means vast new markets are now open to organized criminals, who can move freely from Belarus to the Atlantic.

The European Crime Scene

Today there are around 4,000 organized crime groups operating in the EU, with an estimated total membership of 40,000. In addition to indigenous groups, Europe now hosts Chinese, Vietnamese, Colombian, Nigerian, North African, Caribbean, Russian, Turkish, and Albanian crime gangs. The major networks follow the ancient trade routes that have linked Europe to the East since classical times. For example, the "amber route" that linked the Black Sea to the Baltic is now a major channel for smuggling and human trafficking from China and Asia. The classical overland trade route from Byzantium (present-day Istanbul) to Rome through Greece and the Balkans now brings narcotics and arms into Germany, Holland, and Britain, while the sea route across the Adriatic from Albania to Italy brings illegal immigrants, white slaves, arms, and narcotics into Puglia and then north to the rest of Europe. Marijuana and illegal aliens from Africa flow from Morocco to Spain and then north, following routes dating back to Roman times. The major organized crime groups in Europe all arose at key points along these routes. The Baltic states are now the bases for counterfeiting and smuggling between Russia, Belarus, and Scandinavia. Lithuania specializes in drug and cigarette smuggling, illegal immigration and money laundering. Crime networks are based at points of entry, either by land or sea, and these points have scarcely changed over the centuries.

The Italy-based Sicilian Cosa Nostra, the Camorra, 'Ndrangheta, and Sacra Corona Unita are the best known organized crime groups operating in southern Europe. Although independent of each other, they share smuggling routes and often cooperate for specific ventures. The Sacra Corona Unita, based in Puglia, works with Albanian organized crime transporting illegal immigrants and arms from the Balkans and Nigeria to Italy. La Cosa Nostra has worked with the South American drug cartels since the 1970s, and they have formed links with organized crime groups in Turkey, Russia, and Asia, as well as with their U.S. counterpart. 'Ndrangheta groups have been found operating as far afield as Australia and Florida. The Camorra has established a virtual monopoly of illegal toxic waste disposal in Italy, in addition to its more traditional activities of extortion, narcotics, and prostitution, and also now operates in the United States. All of these groups have invested in real estate and casinos throughout Europe.

In the 1990s Albanian crime groups began working with their Chinese, Turkish, Italian, and British counterparts, supplying vice markets with East European prostitutes and handling illegal immigration into the EU.

Albanian organized crime is particularly interesting as an example of how men from a traditional society, long isolated from the rest of Europe under a repressive communist regime, have used the strong cohesiveness of their family clans and adherence to a code of traditional law as principles on which to base their groups. Another intriguing survival from the pre-modern period that has been shown to be extremely effective in the global economy is the old Asian method of informal banking called *hawala*, an Arabic term simply meaning "transfer." Money is deposited with

Upperworld and underworld
A police helicopter hovers over a Camorra stronghold in Naples. Ostensibly distant, upperworld and underworld are everywhere linked in symbiosis.

a trustworthy source in one country, and paid out in another by another member of the network. A similar system is used by the Chinese, who call it *fei ch'ien*, "flying money." These underground banking systems, based on trust and leaving no paper trail, makes tracing remittances almost impossible.

Mafiya, Yakuza, and Triads

The growth of Russian organized crime since the break-up of the Soviet Union has been extraordinarily rapid. Russian Mafiyas now operate in 60 countries in Europe, Asia, Africa, and the Americas. Well-armed, violent, and highly educated, Russian crime groups have affiliated themselves with the American Mafia and have invested heavily in Italy and Spain, specializing in extortion rackets, vehicle theft, smuggling, financial fraud, and the fur trade.

In Asia organized crime groups operate in Japan, China, Taiwan, and South East Asia, all of which are linked with organized crime in Europe and the Americas. The Japanese Yakuza and the Chinese Triads are the best known, and both operate in the United States and Canada, as well as in Europe. The mainland Chinese Big Circle Gang has cells operating worldwide. In the United States they are concentrated in Los Angeles, San Francisco, Seattle, Boston, and New York, specializing in high-tech crime, as well as people smuggling, drug trafficking, and vehicle theft.

In China itself the Triads from Taiwan, Hong Kong, and Macau are established in the Chinese capital Beijing, where they have

Triad bust
Young men between the ages of 18 and 25 fill the lower ranks of organized crime groups throughout the world and have the shortest life expectancy.

strong links with corrupt officials and in the business world. The 14 K Triad is involved in smuggling cigarettes and automobiles into China, where there is a booming market for illegal imports. In 1998 the Chinese government seized $650 million worth of illegal imports.

The Yakuza families of Japan, with an estimated annual revenue of $13 billion, form one of the world's most successful organized crime groups. There are more than 3,000 Yakuza families in Japan, with a total membership of 150,000, involved in arms trafficking, narcotics, prostitution, people smuggling, extortion, and gambling. They have established links with the Russian Mafiya, and obtain

Ripening opium in Pakistan
Farmers in poorer countries in Asia and South America respond to market forces by growing opium poppies and coca to supply internal and external demand. Both crops are labor intensive and prohibitions on cultivation result in poverty and dislocation for thousands of people.

heroin from Triad groups in Hong Kong and Taiwan. Yakuza groups are established throughout Europe, Asia, and Australia.

Organized Crime in Africa

The hub of African organized crime is Nigeria, until 1850 the world center of the black slave trade. Crime groups based in the capital Lagos have networks, reaching across Europe, Russia, Asia, Australia, and Africa. There are more than 500 Nigerian organized crime groups operating in 80 countries. Those that operate transnationally are the so-called "419" Syndicates, ironically named from the number of a government decree outlawing the transfer of money to foreign banks. The 419 Syndicates have branches worldwide and specialize in financial fraud, narcotics, vehicle theft, and the sale of children into prostitution and bonded labor. These syndicates are protected by corrupt politicians and police forces. South Africa hosts 200 organized crime groups, also specializing in narcotics, but with a sideline in smuggling endangered species.

South America

The only place where the coca plant grows is South America, and, as such, the continent is the source for the world

trade in cocaine. Colombia is the main exporter of the drug to the United States, while Peru and Bolivia service markets in Europe. Colombian cocaine traffickers also market counterfeit dollars and heroin to the United States, and work with the Sicilian and Amerian Mafias.

X-Ray drugs bust

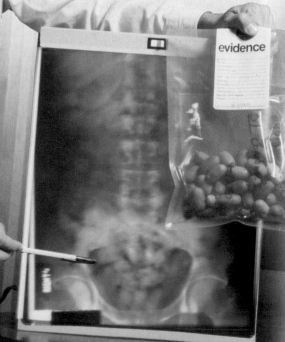

A New York customs officer displays an X-Ray image of a drug smuggler's stomach and the drugs that were recovered. Ingenious smugglers constantly experiment with new ways to elude discovery.

Illegal aliens on the Mexico–US border

Globalization coupled with economic asymmetries have led to a massive increase in migration toward richer countries and the involvement of organized crime in people smuggling.

Central America is the main base for people smuggling into the United States, an industry with an estimated $1 billion gross annual revenue. Around 100,000 migrants pass through the Central American corridor annually, and Central America is also a conduit for one-third of all cocaine shipments to the United States.

Mexican organized crime handles the export of heroin, cocaine, and marijuana, as well as illegal immigrants, into the United States. The tremendous level of legitimate commercial traffic across the Mexico–U.S. border makes control of illegal activities difficult, as does the porous border, more than 1,875 miles (3,000 km) long. Half the cocaine entering the U.S. comes via Mexico. In addition, the cross border trade in pirated and counterfeited goods has become extremely lucrative in recent years.

Mexican organized crime groups have corrupted and infiltrated the national police force, and the criminals operate with extreme violence, particularly those who are involved in the illicit narcotics trade, which was dominated for many years by the Arellano Felix organization and the Carillo Fuentes operation.

The Origins of Organized Crime

Both the Sicilian Mafia and the Neapolitan Camorra arose in pre-industrial societies and originally drew their strength from the countryside rather than from cities and towns. In postwar Sicily, the Mafia family of Lucciano Leggio from the small town of Corleone gained ascendancy in the capital Palermo over the more sophisticated urban Mafia families, evolving from rural banditry into leaders of an international organization. The Albanian Mafia, one of the most recent and effective organized criminal groups to reach across the world, is also the product of an agrarian society. The Italian crime groups 'Ndrangheta and Sacra Corona Unita, both recent formations, again are rural in origin and distinctly archaic in rituals and codes of behavior. Similarly, in Asia, the Triads and the Yakuza both emphasize links to a largely mythical heroic past. Even the American Mafia by its very

name (La Cosa Nostra) links itself to its origins in the poverty-stricken villages of Sicily rather than to its golden age in the 1920s during the Prohibition era in the United States, and has maintained its ethnic exclusiveness to the present day.

Piracy and banditry were to the pre-industrial world what organized crime is to modern society. Although neither fits modern definitions of organized crime, largely because the lives of individual bandit chieftains and pirate captains were notoriously short, the phenomena themselves endured for centuries.

Reading 17th-century Spanish complaints about English and Dutch pirates is curiously like reading accounts of modern reports on organized crime. They speak of pirate "brotherhoods" (Mafias), of tacit state support (political protection), the sale of plundered cargoes to legitimate businessmen (money laundering), and corruption of public officials (bribery). During the 17th and 18th centuries, pirates operated in international waters (globalization). Men like Edward Teach and Henry Morgan would pillage in the Pacific, Atlantic, and Indian Oceans.

The pirate republic of Salé on the Atlantic coast of Morocco would have gladdened the heart of U.S. Mafia boss Charles "Lucky" Luciano. Originally composed of *moriscos* (Moors converted to Christianity) who were expelled from Spain, and at first preying entirely on Spanish shipping, the pirate gang in Salé became multinational, accepting seaman of any nationality and attacking ships of all nations. The pirates of Salé had a written constitution regulating behavior and laying down rules for sharing in the plunder. The pirates elected their captain, and deposed him if he proved unsatisfactory. During the 17th century they raided London, Dublin, and Iceland. They were always open to negotiation, and wealthy ship owners could pay them not to attack their ships (protection). They are said to have been involved in insurance scams, allowing ship owners to collect insurance for lost cargoes, and then selling the cargo and splitting the take with the original owner.

Like slaving, piracy is once again on the rise. In the first nine months of 2003, there were 344 pirate attacks worldwide, a substantial increase over the previous year, with 271. The Malacca Straits in Southeast Asia are one of the most dangerous areas, with 24 pirate attacks, and have been a favorite hunting ground for pirates since the 16th century. Pirates armed with modern weapons think nothing of boarding oil tankers and cargo ships, killing anyone who resists and holding entire crews to ransom, exactly as their forebears did.

What pirates were to the sea, bandits were to the land. In the pre-industrial world, the

Pirate gold
Almost half the gold and silver produced in the New World in the 16th and 17th centuries was smuggled illegally into Europe and piracy flourished.

Sicilian Mafia on trial
Mafiosi held in a courtroom cage in 1928. Mass trials of Mafia suspects began in the late 19th century and continue today, yet the Mafia continues to operate and diversify.

countryside was a dangerous place. The only way to travel in safety was in convoy, preferably with armed guards. Banditry was endemic in much of Europe and Asia, in many places well into the 20th century. It was common in Sicily until the 1950s.

Today, crime is thought of as an urban phenomenon, but for most of human history it was the rural world that was crime-ridden. Pirates and bandits attacked trade routes, at times severely hampering commerce, raising costs, insurance rates, and prices to the consumer. One of the roles of the *gabbelotti*, forerunners of the Mafia in Sicily, was to control provisioning routes to towns and cities, either by killing the bandits or by paying them protection.

In Western Asia, even under powerful dynasties such as the Ottoman Turks, government control rarely extended into the

Blackbeard the pirate
Captain Edward Teach, better known as Blackbeard. Pirates were the terrorists of the 17th and 18th centuries, not only attacking ships, but sacking and burning port cities.

19th century stagecoach robbers
It was not until the late 19th century, and in some countries the mid-20th, that overland travel became safe. Carjacking and hijacking are the modern urban equivalents of rural banditry.

countryside, which was controlled by armed and dangerous tribesmen. These tribes demanded passage fees from any traveler who wanted to travel through their territory, and were expert at evaluating goods carried in caravans and charging accordingly. If unsatisfied, they simply took everything. The Ottomans were forced to pay tribes along the route to Mecca, the center of Islam, to guarantee safe passage for pilgrims. This system lasted until 1914, when the outbreak of World War I changed everything.

Barbarians and State Building

The early Christian world was dubious about the legitimacy of nation-states. In the 4th century, St Augustine famously defined them as what would now be called kleptocracies, states founded on theft. A later North African writer, Ibn Khaldun, observing the conquests of the Mongol leader Tamerlane in the 14th century, developed a theory of state formation based on the periodic conquest of civilized states by barbarians, who are quickly acculturated by urban life, lose their warlike qualities and

succumb in turn to conquest by yet another wave of barbarians. This model may not fit the modern world, but adequately described the foundation of many pre-modern states, including some of the early Greek city states. Barbarian conquerors, whether Vandals, Goths, Norsemen, Turks, or Mongols are not normally thought of as organized crime groups, yet they share many of the features associated with successful criminal organizations. They were for the most part non-ideological, predominately ethnically based, used violence and intimidation, and adhered to their own codes of law. All of them, with perhaps the exception of the Vandals, formed enduring states.

Although medieval feudal lords were not usually engaged in criminal activities, their hierarchical courts, monopoly of violence, extension of protection to their serfs in exchange for labor and a percentage of harvests and durability are structurally similar to classic organized crime groups like the Mafia. In the modern world, states controlled by family, political, or military cliques have proliferated. Essentially concerned with asset-stripping their own countries, or willing to let them be used as transit points for illicit trafficking, they are ideal allies for organized crime groups. In some cases, it is difficult to distinguish governments from organized crime gangs. These regimes, characteristic of some of the newly independent states of the former Soviet Union, use the state apparatus to control organized crime for their own ends.

European Traders

When the Portuguese reached India at the end of the 15th century, they established a "power syndicate" controlling all shipping on the Indian Ocean trade routes. The superiority of their warships and guns over the unarmed ships in the region allowed them to suppress piracy and collect "safe passage" money. They established a virtual monopoly over pepper export to Europe. In the 17th century, the Dutch followed their example, refining the method by controlling the supply of sought-after commodities like nutmeg and cloves by chopping down trees to keep the supply limited and the price high.

Without trying to retrospectively criminalize Portuguese and Dutch behavior in the age of European expansion, the organized crime model does suggest parallels. Tiny ethnic minorities operating outside their homelands

Chinese opium den
In the 19th century British merchants created a market in China for Indian opium, using it to pay for Chinese exports and creating more than 100 million addicts.

used violence to establish protection rackets and monopolies. Both the Dutch and the Portuguese saw that the key was control of transportation and ports, which in the modern world has been a preoccupation of organized crime groups.

In the 18th and 19th centuries, English and U.S. merchants created a market for Indian opium in China. By 1900 an estimated one-third of the population of China – 150 million people – were habitual users. This cynical development of a nation

"For what are states but large bandit bands, and what are bandit bands but small states?"

St Augustine of Hippo

of addicts, ensuring a constant and growing demand, would nowadays be classified as criminal, but at the time public opinion was only mildly aroused.

Human trafficking, now so much in the news, has only been criminalized since the mid-19th century. The economy of ancient Rome was founded on slavery and no Roman moralist inveighed against it. It was thought perfectly normal to traffic in women and children for sexual purposes, just as it was in later Islamic society, where the institution of slavery was

never questioned. It is now one of the major problems facing modern society, with an estimated 200 million people around the world who can be classified as slaves.

The Industrial Revolution

Extortion, protection rackets, narcotics, counterfeiting, smuggling, prostitution, theft, and murder have always existed. Rural banditry, piracy, and urban underworlds have existed for as long as we have historical records. Whether or not organized crime can be viewed as a specifically modern phenomenon depends on how we read the past and how we define it. What is beyond doubt is that the growth of cities during the 19th century, the flight of peasants from the country to urban areas, and the development of high-speed transportation coincided with the formation of durable organized crime groups of great efficiency, some of which have been able to adapt to rapidly changing markets, consolidate their power, accumulate capital, expand from their original bases, and continue to operate in the modern world.

GENUINE 19yrs
PRETTY BLOND

Hotel Vis
Open Early
GENUINE

Ravishing
Redhead
Brand New
In Town

ORGANIZED CRIME ACTIVITIES

The sheer range and variety of criminal enterprises in the modern world are examined under four principal headings in this section.

Genuine Photo

EUROPEAN COMMUNITY

UNITED KINGDOM OF GREAT BRITAIN AND NORTHERN IRELAND

PASS

0990 1

Exploiting the Human Condition

Trafficking in human beings is the most serious global crime problem facing the modern world. It covers everything from trafficking in women and children for sexual purposes to people smuggling, worker exploitation, debt bondage, slavery, and the trade in human organs. Transnational criminal organizations are involved in every step of these vicious trades, which generate billions of dollars annually.

The UN Protocol to Prevent Suppress and Punish Trafficking in Persons, Especially Women and Children, of November 2000, which supplements the UN Convention Against Transnational Organized Crime, Palermo December 2000 states in section 3a:

"The recruitment, transportation, transfer, harbouring or receipt of persons, by means of threat or the use of force or other forms of coercion, of abduction, of fraud, of deception, of the abuse of power or of a position of vulnerability or of the giving or receiving of payments or benefits to achieve the consent of a person having control over another person, for the purpose of exploitation. Exploitation shall include, at a minimum, the exploitation or the prostitution of others or other forms of sexual exploitation, forced labour or services, slavery or practices similar to slavery, servitude or the removal of organs."

As international law-enforcement puts more effort into preventing drug smuggling, and gambling and pornography are increasingly legalized or available on the Internet, human trafficking has become very attractive to organized criminal groups around the world. Overheads are low and penalties in most countries lacking or derisory, although this is beginning to change. In 2003, Britain sentenced an

Albanian asylum-seeker turned trafficker to 10 years in jail. Small-scale traffickers are increasingly being coopted by international gangs that possess the resources to bribe police and border guards and to organize long-distance transportation. Another attraction for organized crime is that people wear out quickly, particularly in the sex industry, where a worker may service some 40 clients a day, and need to be replaced after only a few years. Unlike cars or mobile phones, there is no danger of the market becoming saturated.

Vice

Since the 1990s, Europe, the United States, and Japan have been the preferred destinations for illegal immigrants from Eastern Europe, South East Asia, and South America. Organized criminal groups control this traffic, as well as the vice centers of major cities. Enticed by promises of work, money, and even marriage, thousands of women and girls from impoverished countries are duped into sex slavery. Heavily indebted to their traffickers, lacking knowledge of the local language, and afraid to go to the police, they are easy to control and exploit. They are at the mercy of their pimps, who are often cogs in a much larger machine, with bosses in Moscow, Albania, and elsewhere in the world.

Profits from the trade are channeled through bank accounts in the Caribbean, Switzerland, or Argentina. Local operations are now almost always linked to transnational organized crime.

The Exploitation of Children

The most notorious form of human trafficking is that of children for prostitution, particularly in South East Asia, where great

Workers in the Billion Dollar Industry
Prostitutes ply their trade in a London street. Prostitution has long been a major revenue source for organized crime groups and invariably involves coercion, threats, and enforced drug addiction.

Young girls in Moscow
Michel Lebed, Chief of Criminal Investigations for the Ukraine Ministry of the Interior has said that gangsters make more money from these women in a week than he has in his law enforcement budget for the whole year. Many Ukrainian girls have been forced, or tricked, into the sex industry by poverty.

poverty coincides with a lavish infrastructure, enabling sex tourists from Japan, the European Union, and the United States to indulge themselves in safety and comfort. As laws against pedophiles become more stringent in the developed world, the incentive for organized crime to exploit this massive low-risk source of income increases.

Although much of this traffic is small scale and local, organized crime is becoming increasingly involved, coordinating, taking orders, bribing authorities, and providing protection from "interference" by rival operators

Village women in South East Asia or parts of Africa are often approached directly by recruiters, usually a woman purporting to be connected to the area and prepared to offer the child an education in exchange for companionship or respectable work.

Child prostitute

A child prostitute in a bar in Bangkok in Thailand. In spite of government efforts at control, the availability of children makes Thailand a magnet to pedophiles from around the world.

She will exploit dire financial need or simple ignorance. Some of these children may end up on the international market, but many will remain within the area of origin: boys from Pakistan and India forced to work in carpet workshops; an estimated 1.3 million girls working as unpaid domestic and plantation workers in Kenya; and more than

> "The children tricked into prostitution are getting younger and younger. These are nine, ten, eleven year old kids."
>
> A Thai child prostitution specialist

a million women and children working as prostitutes in Thailand and Southeast Asia.

In poverty stricken areas like the highlands of South East Asia, Nepal, and Bangladesh, children are simply bought, usually for under $100, from parents who are often starving and hope this fate will be better for them than death. Not infrequently, the traffickers save themselves money by simply kidnapping the children, selling them wherever they can get a good price, to the notorious "Cages" of Mumbai [Bombay] with its more than 50,000

prostitutes, or the brothels of Bangkok or Tokyo. Others will end up in the Gulf, as domestic labor.

One of the largest-scale human trafficking operations takes place within Africa. Children and teenagers, acquired under false pretenses or for sums as low as $15–45, are sold as domestic labor, many ending in the sex industry. Boys are taken to the cocao plantations of the Ivory Coast, where they work under appalling conditions. The $13 billion chocolate industry represents one of the world's largest capitalist combines, driving the price of cocao so low that farmers find it impossible to pay wages of even $1 or $2 a day. Similar situations are customary in the mining and coffee industries, both in Africa and South America. Growing public awareness of these abuses, and organizations such as Anti-Slavery International, have led increasing numbers of retailers to stock Fairtrade products, which do not rely on what is essentially slave labor.

The New Slavers

In 2003 police in London and the south of England penetrated an organization running 15 or more brothels in a multi-million pound operation. When undercover officers entered several brothels, they were presented with a "bill of fare" listing the sexual services available, with prices. Further investigations led to the arrest of two Thai sisters in their forties, who were the masterminds behind an organization that shipped hundreds of young girls from Thailand into Britain to be used in the illegal sex industry. In the majority of cases the girls had been promised work as domestic servants. With such false promises the girls had traveled from their homes to Britain. The reality was very different. Instead of being placed

in legal employment, the girls were processed through a "finishing school" for prostitutes in a south London suburb, before being put to work full time in one of the organization's many brothels.

PREYING ON INNOCENCE

Each of the girls was "indebted" to the vice ring for the sum of £44,000, which was to be the total bill for board and lodging, travel, visas, and their training as prostitutes. Advertisements described the girls as "young, beautiful Oriental girls." One girl was advertised as "a rude girl who will do anything you want without a condom." The girls could only buy their freedom from the racket by performing between 500 and 1,000 sexual acts for between £50 and £100 a time. Both sisters were found guilty for their part in the network of brothels that generated some £1.1 million annually. One was sentenced to five years and the other to three and a half years in prison.

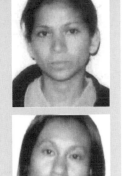

Convicted criminals
Monporn Hughes (top) and her sister Bupha Savada (below) were imprisoned for running a brothel network.

Prostitute's doorbell
A typical sign on the entrance to a prostitute's apartment (left). The establishment is probably run by criminals.

Traditional Slavery

On January 10, the UN declared 2004 the Year of the Abolition of Slavery, while Haiti, celebrating two centuries as the first republic founded by liberated slaves, battles with a growing internal slave traffic.

One reason that the West has been slow to respond to the sudden rise in human trafficking is that it is assumed that slavery, like piracy, is a thing of the past, so remote as to be almost picturesque. It is hard to accept the fact that both are with us again, slavery in a more virulent and inhumane form, since human beings have a lower market value than in the past, and rarely have personal relationships with their masters. Organized crime has learned from tradition: old trade routes for slaves or drugs are being reopened, while abuses are taking new forms in contact with transnational crime.

A few areas of traditional slavery survive, most notably in Sudan, where the nomadic Arab tribesmen of the north

have preyed for centuries on the black non-Muslim southerners, especially the Dinka. The imposition of the Shari'a (Islamic law) in 1991 coincided with an increase in slave-raids. The Koran forbids the enslavement of monotheists, but the animist populations of the south are vulnerable.

The slavers are drawn from Arab tribes, who have tacit government support to terrorize the southerners, whose homelands contain important oil and mineral reserves.

Slave raids follow the traditional pattern: villages are attacked, the men killed, and the women and boys led away in chains. Rape, branding, flogging, and even castration are not unusual, as the stories and scars of thousands of freed slaves bear witness. The slaves may be used by their captors or sold. The U.S. Embassy in the capital Khartoum believes that child slaves are being taken across the desert to Libya, and there is evidence of Sudanese being sold to Saudi Arabia and the Gulf. Sudanese women are also appearing much father afield, suggesting that some sales may be to purchasers from organized crime networks, now linking up with the traditional routes.

Debt Bondage

Debt bondage accounts for much of the slavery on the Indian subcontinent and elsewhere, and is one of the main reasons for the sale of children and organs. It is a classic form of slavery, usually associated with the

Sudanese slaves
A group of southern Sudanese slaves who have been freed after being bought from their slavers by an international anti-slavery charity. Even so, when they return home they will remain vulnerable to future slave raids.

The Balkan Connection

Prostitution in Britain is an attractive business because the penalties are low (pimping carries a sentence of two years) and the returns are high. Police have noticed that an increasing number of prostitutes working in London's Soho district are girls from Eastern Europe controlled by Albanian gangs. Why are Albanians so prominent in this shady world of vice in Britain's capital?

After emerging from more than 40 years of harsh totalitarian rule in 1991, Albania plunged into a period of economic uncertainty, weak government, and lack of law enforcement. Financial meltdown, caused by the collapse of several pyramid investment schemes in 1996, led to many ordinary people losing their life savings, and the country collapsed into chaos in 1997. The war in neighboring Kosovo in 1999 resulted in a huge increase in weapons in the region and a general increase in violence and gang rule. In the words of an Albanian lawyer now working in Italy, "the criminals have nothing to lose – no other jobs and no stable political situation to control them."

Unscrupulous procurers exploited the naïveté of many Albanians. Thousands of women and girls were lured out of Albania by offers of marriages or jobs in the West, or were simply kidnapped. For many, their final destination was a life of prostitution in the sleazy back rooms of Soho, London.

Albanian society is very traditional and made up of closeknit clans. The clans soon began to fight back against the criminals, so the traffickers looked further east, to Romania, Moldova, and Ukraine for their victims.

A STUDY IN HUMAN MISERY

One case is typical of the thousands of tragedies brought about by the traffickers. A 15-year-old Romanian girl was kidnapped by Albanians near the Romanian–Yugoslav border in 2001. She was taken to Albania, where she was sold for £150, then raped at gunpoint. Imprisoned for prostitution in the capital, Tirana, she was again sold on by her lawyer to a woman in Vlora on the Adriatic coast. From there she was taken to England via Italy and Holland, where she was given to an Albanian pimp called Stanislav.

Stanislav told her that she owed him £3,000 for the journey. Renamed "Angela" she was put to work as a prostitute earning £300 per day in various saunas and apartments. After a particularly brutal beating, "Angela" managed to escape from Stanislav and began working in a different part of London for another Albanian pimp.

Stanislav offered to pay £10,000 to anyone who killed "Angela." When he found out where she was, he dragged her from the sauna where she was working and beat and tortured her. He then fled to Manchester. "Angela" escaped again and sought help from social services. Stanislav was eventually arrested for burglary and "Angela" managed to escape to Holland.

Advertising cards
Examples of the cards prostitutes use to advertise their services.

Soho raid
Police lead away a suspect during a raid on more than 50 brothels in Soho, London, in 2001. Many of the prostitutes were illegal immigrants.

Trapped into prostitution
Eastern European women are lured to the West with promises of work. Once they arrive, they are forced into prostitution. As illegal immigrants, they are too afraid to go to the authorities.

village money-lender, rather than with organized crime. The original debt, which may have started out as a small and manageable one, through exorbitant interest or "extras" entangles the borrower in a way they never understood or foresaw. It is typologically similar to the sweat-shop or sex worker, whose earnings are withheld to repay their trafficker; the mule who is forced to carry drugs to repay a debt to underworld loan sharks; or the small Italian or Japanese business owners who are forced to borrow at impossible rates from the Mafia or Yakuza because bank loans are not available, and who eventually have to perform criminal "favors" in return.

People Smuggling

According to a United Nations' report published in 2000, smuggling people across international borders illegally generates profits for organized crime second only to those from the drug trade. The International Organization for Migration estimates that at any one time there are between 15 and 30 million illegal immigrants on the move. This includes people smuggled against their will, either by force or under false pretenses, ending up as virtual slaves in the country of their destination, as well as economic migrants who pay to be smuggled. This latter category includes those fleeing political repression, social and economic chaos, and poverty. They have little hope of emigrating through normal channels, so pay large sums to "Snakeheads" (specialists in illegal border crossing) to help them reach their destinations. The emigrants' desire for a better life, and the seemingly limitless market in wealthy nations for cheap domestic, agricultural, and manual labor, combine to produce a lucrative source of income for organized crime. Law enforcement in the receiving countries is generally lax, particularly in countries where illegal immigrants provide cheap labor to important industries. This is particularly true in the agricultural sector, whether within the European Union or in the United States. A lawyer in Miami, Florida, questioning a major orange grower, asked whether a particularly notorious and

> "On a good night, after I have paid all my costs, I can earn $10,000"
>
> People Trafficker

brutal people trafficker should be jailed. No, was the reply, such people were needed to keep the price of oranges down. In the long run it is the community at large that pays the price. Organizations that supply legal seasonal workers who work under reasonable conditions are undercut, law-abiding farmers and businessmen cannot compete, union efforts to obtain fair living wages for workers are undermined, and the state is defrauded of taxes. Large numbers of illegal immigrants with no stake in society and justifiable grudges against their treatment inevitably pose many problems, from health to crime, to their host country.

People smuggling is thus anything but the "victimless crime" it is sometimes seen to be. The cost in human suffering is high, and causes misery on a worldwide scale. Migrants are transported in inhuman conditions, as the 19 dead immigrants found in a crowded, overheated tractor-trailer in Texas, or the 58 suffocated immigrants found in a truck at Dover docks in Britain show, to say nothing of the thousands who are drowned each year making the dangerous crossing from Morocco to Spain, or Albania to Italy.

The Mexico–U.S. border is one of the most porous borders in the world. Organized gangs of smugglers have a sophisticated network to convey people into the United States. Recruiters prowl the border areas looking for would-be immigrants. They arrange for them to meet with guides known as "coyotes," who lead the immigrants across the border. In 1998 Operation Gatekeeper tightened up controls at the Texas–California border. Now the favored crossing is the far more dangerous border with Arizona.

Between 1997 and 2000, more than 700 migrants attempting this route died of drowning, dehydration in the deserts, or of hypothermia in the extreme cold of the mountains.

Sign warning
A sign on a highway near the Mexico–U.S. border warns drivers to watch out for illegal immigrants crossing the road. The 2,000-mile border between the countries is impossible to seal off completely.

Border guard
An officer of the U.S. Border Patrol searches a young would-be immigrant on the Mexican–U.S. border. The Border Patrol catches a fraction of the total number of illegal border-crossers each year.

CASE STUDY

Capture of a Snakehead

In London in 2003 Yong Zhang, a notorious "Snakehead," was tried and found guilty of conspiring to "assist illegal entry and grievous bodily harm." A "Snakehead" is a Chinese term for a people smuggler. Snakeheads smuggle people across borders for a fee, and usually have a good reputation with their clients. However, some, such as Yong Zhang, use the vulnerability of the new immigrants to extort extra money from them, or force them into sweated labor.

Yong Zhang had come to Britain as an illegal immigrant and worked in the black economy. It is believed that his gang was smuggling more than 20 illegal immigrants a month into Britain at £15,000 each. The gang made an estimated £11 million in three years. Zhang's role came to light when a client he had brutally attacked to get payment went to the police.

The client, farm laborer Li En Kai, and his family had contracted a Snakehead gang in China to smuggle him to Britain. Having paid a deposit, Kai set off on a four-month journey (with a fake Korean passport) from Asia via Africa to London. On arrival, Kai destroyed his false documents and claimed asylum. After a night in detention Kai was released. Zhang caught up with him and demanded that his family in China pay the rest of his "fare," a total of £15,000. Kai's mother took the money to the Snakeheads in China but refused to leave their premises until she heard her son's voice on the phone. At this point Zhang was beating Kai up with a baseball bat. He let Kai speak to his mother and assure her of his safety before continuing the beating, later letting Kai go.

Zhang was arrested and found to be in possession of a paper listing 20 Chinese names. Further investigation identified 16 of the 20 as illegal immigrants. Zhang and an accomplice were jailed in October 2003.

Yong Zhang
People traffickers like Zhang bring immigrants from mainland China into western countries.

Sweatshops
Traffickers often exploit new immigrants by making them work for slave wages in restaurants (below), hotels, and factories.

Routes into Europe

Albania, once again, is a major point for illegal entry into the European Union. In 1999 it was estimated that 10,000 people per month were smuggled into Europe via Albania. In response, the Albanian law enforcement agencies, in partnership with their Italian counterparts, mounted Operation Eagle to reduce the flow of illegal immigrants shipped across the Otranto Channel to Italy. Fifteen speedboats, 7 motorized rubber dinghies, 7 large ships, and 10 other vessels were seized. An Albanian speedboat owner interviewed in March 2001 described his business: "...On a good night, after I have paid all my costs, I can earn $10,000. I reckon that in Vlora [the main Albanian port for smugglers] there are 10 to 15 speedboats that leave nightly when the weather is good. On average, they carry between 30 and 40 passengers. Operation Eagle has made it harder for speedboat owners. But we pay the police to turn a blind eye and, although they have speedboats, you're never going to stop the activity. There is too much money involved."

Albania is both a sending country, with an estimated 25 percent of its population now working abroad, and also a transit country for immigrants from further east: Kurds, Iraqis, Afghans, Indians, and Chinese. Some illegal immigrants pay for the whole journey before they leave their homeland. The cost of transit from China to Europe can be as high as $20,000. Passage across the Adriatic typically costs $1,000 for adults, $500 for children. Trips from Albania to Britain are often accompanied by a guide.
The Sacra

Asylum seekers in Italy
Italian officials oversee the arrival of a ship crowded with asylum seekers in 2001. Italy's long coastline is difficult to police and thus is targeted by traffickers from Albania.

Selling Human Organs

The trade in human organs has grown rapidly since the introduction of cyclosporine in the 1980s, an anti-rejection drug that has made transplants much more of a routine operation. India and China have become international centers for organ transplants, because of the lack of the stringent rules on organ transplantation that exist in most other countries and the large number of desperately poor people who are prepared to part with their organs, especially a kidney, for cash.

In January 1995 a series of kidney scandals were uncovered in major Indian cities. In Delhi, hundreds of people had been persuaded to go abroad on "kidney tours," to have their kidneys removed and transplanted. In Bangalore, nearly 1,000 unsuspecting people who thought they were donating blood had had their kidneys removed. In Villivakkam, a village near Madras, people were openly offering their kidneys for sale to agents. An Indian health organization estimated that the number of people selling their organs had risen to 2,000 per year in the 1990s

compared to 500 in 1986 and only 50 in 1983. The Indian government tried to stop the growing trade by banning the sale of human organs, but there are fears that the legislation will simply drive the trade underground. Meanwhile, the demand for organs continues unabated.

For wealthy people who are desperately in need of a transplant, buying an organ is a way to bypass long waiting lists. For the donors, it can appear to be a simple and safe way to make money. However, this is often not the case. Donors can be cheated and their health can deteriorate if they are not given adequate follow-up care. One example is a Turkish man who sold a kidney to pay for urgent surgery for his four-year-old son. Promised $30,000, he only received $10,000. After the operation, the doctor vanished. The man was never well enough to work again and could not afford the surgery for his son.

Operation scars
An Indian kidney donor shows the enormous scars left after his operation to remove a kidney. Donating an organ is seen as an easy way of making money by the one-in-three Indians living in absolute poverty.

Corona Unita (*see p77*) and other organized crime groups are involved in overseeing the Italian leg of the journey.

Immigrants from Africa make the dangerous crossing of the Strait of Gibraltar to Spain from Morocco, often in small, unseaworthy craft. Hundreds are drowned each year. The trade is organized by Moroccan, Spanish and international gangs.

Trafficking in Human Organs

International organized crime gangs also exploit another desperate human condition – illness. Acting as middlemen for those who need organ transplants, they charge high prices to the patient needing an organ, and underpay or dupe the organ donor. The sale of human body parts is illegal in most countries, though in some, including Israel, Turkey, Russia, India, and China, organ sales are carried out fairly openly. Indeed, in Israel the national health service pays at least part of the costs involved in the transplanting of a "harvested kidney," as it is cheaper than the cost of dialysis. Both Islam and Shinto prohibit the mutilation of the body, so

Japan and the Gulf have a constant demand for organs, as does all the developed world, due to the shortage of voluntary donors.

Although hearts, livers, and lungs are sometimes sold, kidneys are the most popular organs for trafficking as there is a great demand for them, and they can be supplied by a live donor. Occasionally kidneys from cadavers are bought illegally (in China the organs of executed prisoners are sold), but survival rates for patients who receive a kidney from a live donor are far

better, so the market in human organs is a profitable one. Traffickers naturally prefer not to pay for the organs they sell. Interpol has repeatedly investigated cases of young people apparently killed for their organs, especially in Brazil.

Normally, the transplant operation is carried out in a country where hospitals do not ask too many questions, such as Turkey or the United States. Most of the fee goes to the medical staff. The broker's percentage varies, as does the sum paid to the donor.

Detecting illegal immigrants
An X-Ray of a truck containing illegal immigrants on the Mexico–U.S. border. Drive-through X-Ray machines at U.S. border posts can detect both human beings and contraband.

Supplying the Illicit

Modern, industrial organized crime came of age during the US Prohibition era in the 1920s. Meeting market needs by smuggling across international borders, exploiting differences in state legislatures, and developing underground distribution methods established a *modus operandum* which, when Prohibition was repealed, could be rapidly adapted to supplying other illicit or contraband products on a similar, transnational scale.

Rulers and governments have long sought to raise revenue by taxing merchants and the goods they supply, leading to the development of smuggling to avoid paying those taxes. The most popular smuggled goods worldwide include cigarettes, alcohol, and diamonds. Unauthorized trade in various other goods, such as narcotics, weapons, and exotic animals is prohibited internationally. They continue to be traded illegally because of high demand and the large profits that can be made.

Behind the supply of illicit goods and services is a web of international organized crime. Although a crime gang may specialize in one aspect of illegal trade, it is possible that they will be involved in others. For example, an arms trafficker's couriers will return paid in gems or drugs. These assets are in turn passed through the laundering process, emerging as untraceable funds deposited in a respectable bank. The interwoven strands of such diverse illegal activities make it almost impossible to separate one from another.

The International Narcotics Trade

The illicit trade in narcotics has the highest profile, and the biggest profits. Although narcotics are specifically opium and its derivatives (laudanum, morphine, and heroin), the term is often used to include other restricted drugs such as cocaine,

Chasing the dragon
A heroin user in Warsaw, Poland. North America is the biggest market for illegal drugs, but since the 1990s the trade in hard drugs has expanded rapidly in Eastern Europe.

marijuana, ecstasy, and LSD. People have used narcotics for medicinal, recreational, and religious purposes since prehistoric times. Scientific advances during the 19th century led to the refinement of morphine (1805) and then heroin (1874) from opium. In 1855 cocaine was produced from South American coca leaves. In turn, each of these new products was hailed as a "wonder drug" and prescribed for many ailments. The sale of narcotics was almost totally unregulated. Patent medicines, frequently containing up to 50 percent morphine or similar, were blamed for the estimated two million drug addicts in the United States at the beginning of the 20th century. In 1914, the Harrison Act criminalized the non-medical use of opium, morphine, and coca leaf derivatives. Criminals stepped in to supply the addicts

with what they required. A 1918 report by the U.S. Treasury commented that "the peddlers appeared to have established a national organization, smuggling drugs in through the Canadian and Mexican borders," a view that is not out of date some 80 years later. In Britain, the Dangerous Drugs Act of 1920 banned the use of cocaine, morphine, opium, codeine, hashish, and barbiturates for non-medical purposes. The British government criminalized the use of cannabis in 1928, and the United States enacted similar legislation in 1937.

In the 1960s, narcotics once again caught the public's attention. Glamorized by pop groups like the Beatles, the Grateful Dead, and the Rolling Stones, drugs such as the hallucinogenic Lysergic Acid Diethylamide (LSD) appeared alongside cannabis and antidepressants as recreational aids. Small laboratories sprung up to cater for the demand as it spread internationally. Cocaine and heroin re-emerged as fashionable drugs from the late 1970s. The rapid growth in the abuse of these narcotics led to the huge

Choosing his weapon
A man brandishes an AKS74 in a gun store in northern Pakistan. Small arms are the most popular items in the 21st century arms-trafficking business.

Drugs and Politics

So vast are the sums of money to be made from the drug trade that even the highest in the land may be tempted to profit from this trade in human misery. In December 1989, U.S. troops invaded Panama to bring the Panamanian dictator, Manuel Noriega, to court in the United States on drug-related charges.

Noriega's military and political career had advanced steadily between 1955 and 1983, when he was allegedly on the payroll of the Central Intelligence Agency (CIA). Noriega enjoyed U.S. support for his ruthless campaign against guerrillas in western Panama, and in turn channeled aid to pro-U.S. forces in Nicaragua and El Salvador. By 1983, Noriega's position as *de facto* ruler was so secure that he promoted himself to general and Commander of the Panamanian Defense Forces.

However, selling U.S. secrets to Cuba, the rigging of presidential elections, and Noriega's role in the killing of his leading critic, alienated U.S. support. In February 1988, the Drug Enforcement Agency (DEA)

indicted Noriega on federal charges. The following year, Noriega declared war on the United States. Panamanian forces were swiftly defeated and he was taken to the United States, where he stood trial in 1991.

The allegations against Noriega ranged from accepting bribes from Colombian drug cartels for allowing cocaine to be shipped through Panama to money laundering and racketeering. Noriega's personal pilot was shown to be the go-between used by the dictator and the Colombians. Noriega was found guilty of eight of the ten charges against him and he was sentenced to 40 years imprisonment, reduced on appeal to 30. The former ruler of Panama is now in a federal prison in Florida.

Fallen leader
The Panamanian dictator Manuel Noriega was convicted on several drugs charges in the United States after he fell out of favor with the U.S. government.

War on drugs
The Colombian authorities use a satellite imaging system to spot illicit crops in remote areas. Troops then move in to destroy the drug plantations and the processing facilities.

expansion and organization of drug production, distribution, and supply that are such generators of wealth for organized crime at the beginning of the 21st century.

Since the 1980s, the main producers of narcotics have been farmers in remote areas of Southeast and Central Asia and South America. Many are peasants controlled by guerrilla fighters, who trade the drugs to urban criminals in return for guns and equipment. One such example is the Islamic Movement of Uzbekistan (IMU), a group aiming to establish an Islamic state in Central Asia. The IMU is reported to control much of the opium from Afghanistan, the world's leading opium-producing country, on the first stage of its journey to Europe and the United States. Criminal groups in the Caucasus region pass the opium on to Turkish or Albanian organizations who refine the raw material into heroin.

Smugglers use an astonishingly ingenious variety of ways to import illegal drugs. Even endangered animal species have been used to smuggle drugs. In one case, in 1993, boa constrictors were

Selling opium
An opium trader displays his supply on the street, Afghanistan, 2000. In such a poor country as Afghanistan, the money to be made from growing opium poppies is hard for farmers to resist.

Organized crime and drug-trafficking

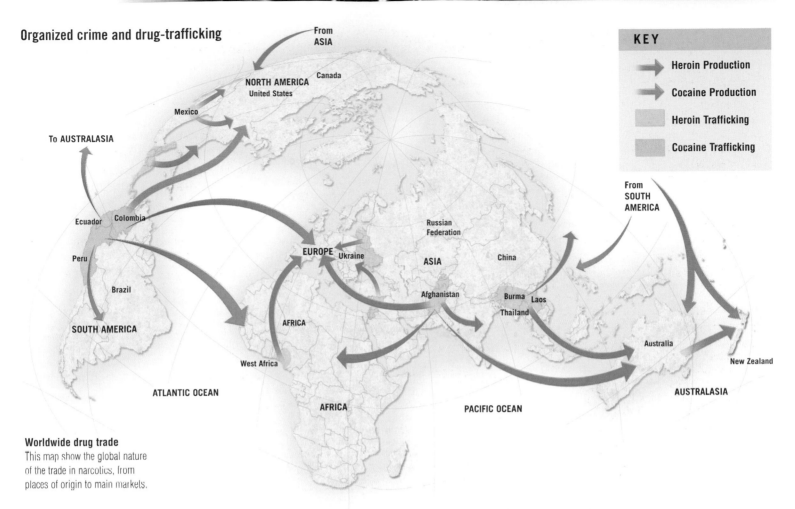

KEY

→ Heroin Production
→ Cocaine Production
▢ Heroin Trafficking
▢ Cocaine Trafficking

Worldwide drug trade
This map show the global nature of the trade in narcotics, from places of origin to main markets.

used. Heroin packed in condoms was inserted via the snakes' rectums into their guts. The rectums were then sewn up. The packages were found by alert customs officials.

The refinement of crack-cocaine has been a particularly dangerous development. The trade in this highly addictive drug has led to shootouts between rival drug pushers in cities across the United States and Europe.

that these products are not part of the essentials of life, and are a good way to raise revenue.Such was the reasoning in 1994 in Michigan, in the United States, when the state increased its tax on cigarettes by 200 percent. They did not succeed, however, because

cut taxes, halving the price of cigarettes. By doing so it ended its smuggling problem.

In January 2003, a leading multinational tobacco company was accused of exporting billions of cigarettes to places like Moldova, Andorra, and Kaliningrad, aware that the local markets could not absorb such quantities and that they would be illegally re-exported to Western Europe.

In 2000, it was estimated that

> "The methods by which underworld actors move drugs are the same routes that are used to move weapons and terrorists, and potentially, weapons of mass destruction."
> Former U.S. counternarcotics official

Tobacco Smuggling

Smugglers make a profit because some goods are markedly more expensive in one country than in another. This allows the criminal gangs to make their purchases cheaply in country A, sell the goods in country B at lower than the official price, and still cover their costs and profit margins. The differential is often due to tax. Governments tax tobacco and cigarettes, often heavily, taking the view

smokers simply crossed state borders to purchase cigarettes more cheaply, or bought from smugglers who had done so.

Similarly, Canada tripled its cigarette tax, put more manpower into enforcing its anti-smuggling laws, and increased the penalties for tobacco smuggling from five years in prison and a $25,000 fine to five years and a fine of $500,000. These measures had little effect, however, and in 1994 the government

Britain sustained tobacco tax losses in the region of £4 billion through smuggling and people buying cigarettes and tobacco in France. One in three packets of cigarettes smoked in Britain has been brought in from abroad, thus avoiding tax. Many of those convicted of tobacco smuggling have previous criminal records, including drug-related and violent crimes. The majority of cigarettes smuggled into Britain come from

CASE STUDY

Producing and Trafficking Cocaine

Cocaine is derived from the coca plant that grows mainly in Colombia, Bolivia, and Peru. Traditionally, the people of the Andes Mountains chewed coca leaves to counter the debilitating effects of high altitudes. They also used it in religious ceremonies because in South American folklore the coca plant was said to have come to Earth with the first man and woman.

Cocaine was first extracted from coca leaves in 1855, and for a while was regarded as another 19th-century "wonder drug" capable of curing a range of ailments. Even Pope Pius X endorsed it for its "life-giving properties." Small quantities of cocaine were even present in *Coca Cola*, which was originally sold in the 19th century as "a valuable brain tonic and cure for all nervous afflictions." However, in 1904, doctors warned of possible dependence among cocaine users and the drug was removed from the drink.

Three of the 250 varieties of coca plant are grown for the illegal market: Huancoca, produced in Bolivia and Peru; Colombian coca from Colombia; and Amazonian coca which is cultivated in the Amazon River Basin.

Coca is harvested up to eight times per year. Harvesting takes place more frequently when the plant is grown at low altitudes. The best quality product comes from more mature leaves. Coca harvesting is labor intensive; and time is often limited. The leaves must be dried or processed within three days of picking, otherwise they begin to rot. After being dried, the leaves are taken to a processing laboratory where they are turned into "base." The base is then shipped to another laboratory where chemicals are added to convert it into cocaine. Three metric tonnes of coca leaf convert into 8–15 lb (4–7 kg) of cocaine. The cocaine is then transported for sale. It is often smuggled to its final destination by couriers known as "mules" – people who risk imprisonment (or in some countries even death) should they be caught.

Drugs are smuggled in a variety of ways. A common method is for the mule to swallow condoms full of cocaine. On arrival at their destination the mules excrete the condoms. Up to 50 packages can be smuggled at a time in this way, but the mules risk death should one of the condoms burst while still inside their stomach.

In November 2002, a 59-year-old man was sentenced to 10 years for trying to smuggle £65,000 worth of cocaine into Britain in his false leg. He was arrested at Gatwick airport after a sniffer dog alerted customs officers.

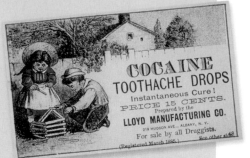

New wonder drug
In the 19th century, cocaine was used in a variety of patent medicines to cure everything from alcoholism to morphine addiction. It was also used as a local anaesthetic in dentistry and eye surgery.

Harvesting the profits
A young girl harvests coca leaves in Bolivia. Stemming the cocaine trade hits directly at the main source of income for local growers. U.S. attempts to restructure agricultural programs for the growers have been only partially successful.

outside the European Union. Seventy to 80 percent of illicit cigarettes are smuggled in with other goods. Penalties for tobacco smuggling include the seizure of the goods and the vehicles used, heavy fines, and up to seven years in jail.

The Illegal Trade in Arms

Arms trafficking has a long history, but during the last 20 years it has mushroomed into an international business on a huge scale, largely controlled by organized crime groups. Much of the illegal trade in arms stems from the collapse of law and order in many of the communist states of Europe and in particular Yugoslavia, Albania, and the Soviet Union. The opening of borders, the collapse of currencies, and the growth of terrorist groups with access to funds, have all played their part. With the breakup of the Soviet Union, former Soviet republics, such as Ukraine and Belarus, found themselves in possession of vast supplies of weapons. Ukraine was the major beneficiary of this windfall. Between 1992 and 1998, an estimated $32 billion worth of armaments, including helicopters, AK47

> ## "It is not difficult to get guns in the Balkans. You just need money."
> Comment from a member of the Kosovo Liberation Army

assault rifles, grenades, mortars, machine guns, and ammunition has disappeared from the former Soviet arsenals. Behind this business are two main dealers, a Ukrainian and a Tajikistan-born Russian – Leonid Minin and Victor Bout. The greater part of Bout and Minin's dealing were with sub-Saharan African countries such as Sierra Leone, Congo, Liberia, and the Ivory Coast. Bout started in business in 1992 using Antonov cargo planes to airfreight goods. The Antonov is a Russian aircraft designed to work from rudimentary "bush airfields," the perfect machine for illegal trading in the backwoods. Bout's airline moved from Russia to operate out of one of the Gulf states. The trade is highly lucrative. For example, an AK47 rifle bought for $20 can be sold for $300 with ammunition – an increase per bullet from 20 cents to 80. Payment is often made in cash or diamonds. Documentation intended to control the arms trade is known as the End User Certificate (EUC). This guarantees the destination of weapons. A certificate has to exist for every shipment, but they are easily obtained from corrupt regimes for a cut of the profit.

Avoiding Tobacco Tax

During an extensive surveillance operation in the year 2000, British customs officers seized more than 118 million cigarettes and £3 million in cash, with the help of law enforcement agencies in Italy, Greece, Germany, and France. Sixteen people were arrested, 13.8 tonnes of tobacco, and 26 trucks were also seized. Altogether, £16 million of tax was evaded.

One British gang caught in the operation purchased cigarettes in Greece and took them back to Britain by truck via France and Germany hidden among cargo such as fruit, vegetables, electrical goods, and drainage pipes. Loads were stored in commercial warehouses and eventually distributed. The gang then carried off the millions of pounds of profits in shoeboxes, bags, and holdalls to be counted and stored in a garden shed. The money was then smuggled out of the country, sometimes hidden in the spare tires of a variety of vehicles. Between them the gang of four people received a total of seven years in prison. The judge estimated that the duty evaded by this one group was between £5 and 10 million.

Seized contraband
A Belgian customs official inspects contraband cigarettes stored in a warehouse ready to be smuggled into Britain.

Selling Arms to Both Sides

Arms dealers are rarely concerned with the politics of the wars in which their weapons are used. Bout sold arms to the Rabbuni government in Afghanistan, and to the Taliban that opposed it. The complexity of bank arrangements that arms traffickers create to cover themselves and the lack of international law enforcement make it a highly profitable business.

However, in June 2001 Minin was arrested in Italy for arms dealing. He was charged with using fake EUCs to sell arms to Liberia and Sierra Leone, in particular two shipments, one of 113 tonnes to the Ivory Coast in July 2000 and one of 68 tonnes to Burkina Faso in March 1999. With Minin out of the picture, Bout now appears to be the major player. One commentator described him as "....the McDonalds of arms trafficking – he was the brand name."

Police raid
Armed members of Russia's customs police seize a truckload of illegally imported cigarettes in 1998. Tobacco smuggling will be attractive to criminals as long as taxes remain high.

"Loose Nukes"

In November 1993 a thief broke into the Sevmorput shipyard, near Murmansk, in northern Russia. He entered through a hole in the fence and easily hacked off the padlock on a storage facility. Inside was the fuel for nuclear submarines. Three containers were taken, each holding 10 lb (4.5 kg) of enriched uranium. The substance can be used to make nuclear weapons. Fortunately, the uranium was recovered. The report of the investigation into the theft remarked that: "Even potatoes are probably much better guarded today than radioactive materials."

Russia, Ukraine, Belarus, and Kazakhstan are the prime source of illegally obtained nuclear materials. The trade in "loose nukes," as such material is known, is potentially fatal for humanity. The production of a nuclear weapon takes remarkably little material: 6.6–55 lb (3–25 kg) of enriched uranium or 2.2–17.6 lb (1–8 kg) of plutonium. It takes 17.6 lb (8 kg) to make a bomb as powerful as that dropped on Hiroshima, Japan, in 1945.

In 1998, Russia's Federal Security Bureau (FSB) is believed to have broken up a crime ring, allegedly of staff members, who were plotting to steal 41 lb (18.5 kg) of weapons-grade material from the Chelyabinsk nuclear weapons plant. Dozens of suitcase-sized nuclear weapons are now believed to be missing from former Soviet facilities. It is possible that some of these have reached terrorist groups. The involvement of organized crime in this trade is difficult to assess. The small size of the materials involved and its highly specialized nature may encourage the foolhardy amateur but discourage the professional. However, that organized crime has not yet been involved in nuclear trafficking does not mean it will avoid this market in the future.

Weapon of choice
The availability of small arms – and willingness to use them – among even petty criminals has caused a radical reassessment of policing methods in most countries.

Diamonds, Gemstones, and Gold

Diamonds, gold, and platinum are high value, internationally acceptable mediums of exchange, second only to hard currency in terms of their convenience for illegal trading. Unlike weapons, diamonds require no end user certificate and are virtually untraceable. Angola, Sierra Leone, and Congo in Africa are particularly rich in diamonds, and are major sources for the world's illegal trade.

Many of the smuggled diamonds are used to fund the illegal importation of weapons. In Sierra Leone, weapons are bought from dealers like Viktor Bout and paid for in diamonds that are smuggled out via Liberia. The world's main importer of diamonds is Belgium, where the Diamond High Council reports that Liberia exports 6 million carats of diamonds, but produces only 150,000 carats. The balance must come from somewhere – almost certainly Sierra Leone. A former rebel officer in Sierra Leone is quoted as saying: "We were restricting it [diamond smuggling] because the leadership...believed... everybody would concentrate on

Vehicle Theft and Resale

The Ukrainian and Russian Mafiyas are now specialists in this business. Cars stolen in Western Europe are taken via Poland and Kaliningrad to Russia, Hungary, Romania, and North Africa using links with local criminal organizations along the way. During 1993 more than 250,000 European cars disappeared without trace.

According to police sources, the process often begins when a "customer" who wants a particular vehicle puts in an "order" with a criminal group to steal the car from a country from where it cannot be traced to the new customer.

The chosen vehicle will be driven into Poland and given a new identity. It is the luxury end of the market that is most targeted: Mercedes, Jaguar, Range Rover (a particular favorite of Russia's new rich), and BMW. SUVs (sports utility vehicles) are popular in countries with poor road conditions, such as the Middle East. To avoid damage the cars are put into sealed-container trucks, shrink wrapped, and taken to their destination. Cash is paid on delivery, the transaction usually taking place near a large city such as Moscow, where it can vanish into the traffic. Russian military planes and airfields are often used if a quick delivery is required.

Kaliningrad car market
Legitimate and stolen cars are sold side-by-side at very low prices in the automobile markets of the Russian enclave of Kaliningrad on the Baltic Sea.

Armageddon
U.S. representative Curt Weldon with a mock Soviet-era "suitcase" bomb. There is a possibility that organized crime groups, terrorists, or rogue states may have acquired some of these suitcase-sized nuclear weapons, one of which is capable of killing up to 100,000 people.

Smuggling diamonds is quite simple. Bags of uncut stones are flown from their place of origin, split into smaller packages and shipped to one of the major diamond markets, such as Bombay, Tel Aviv, or Antwerp. Russian Mafiya figures like Marat Balagula and Viktor Bout are believed to be heavily involved in diamond and gold smuggling. It is claimed that Osama bin Laden's al-Qaeda terrorist network converted $20 million into untraceable gemstones before the attacks on New York on September 11, 2001. In the words of a United Nations official: "There are no fingerprints on diamonds." In the 1990s, diamonds replaced gold and platinum as the most smuggled commodity because metals are difficult to refine and transport.

The Automobile Racket

There are two main types of car thieves. The first is the joyrider who looks for vehicles to steal as a form of temporary transportation, and who then abandon them. The second is the professional who steals specific vehicles to order, either to export or to sell on, having changed its identity, for example, the vehicle may be re-sprayed, modified, and resold with different registration plates and identification numbers.

The creation of the European Union, and the opening up of borders has made the work of the dealer in stolen cars much easier. Huge container trucks allow stolen vehicles to be moved around Europe easily and speedily. A stolen vehicle can be taken across several countries before the owner has realized it has been taken and informed the police. International vehicle crime is organized, complex, lucrative, and growing. Recent examples of the trade include: the discovery in Pakistan of a large number of Land Rovers which had been stolen from Britain; a number of stolen Ladas shipped

mining...not concentrate on war." The Congo is also divided between private armies who fund their military operations with smuggled diamonds and gold. The people subject to these warlords are forced to mine the commodities to perpetuate the fighting. Rebels in Angola are believed to smuggle $2 million worth of diamonds per week. It is estimated that there are 100,000 *garimpeiros* (freelance diamond hunters) in Angola.

Panning for diamonds
Men working a diamond mine in Sierra Leone in 1996. The country is a leading source of smuggled diamonds, which are used to pay for illegal weapons.

back to Russia and sold at prices lower than their market value; and the discovery in Malta of stolen BMWs and Mercedes en route to the Middle East. Heavy goods vehicles are also targets. Many construction sites in Eastern Europe boast such vehicles when there is no legitimate local dealer.

Smuggling Rare Animals

The illegal trade in animals is worth billions of dollars each year. It is said to be the third most lucrative form of global smuggling after drugs and arms. Most of the smuggled animals go to scientists or pet collectors, though there is an increasing trend for them to be sold for fur, potions, or

Endangered species for sale
A criminal dealer in Moscow shows the exotic animals he has for sale. The growing trade in rare and endangered animals is often linked to other illegal activities, such as drug trafficking.

ornaments. Most rare animals are sold to the U.S. market, though they are also popular with Europeans and the Japanese. Rare animals are usually caught by local poachers who are paid a trifling amount by dealers for their efforts. The dealers then find other people to smuggle the animals abroad. The animals often die on the journey, which is hardly surprising given that they are often stuffed into small bags or containers. Animals are also sent by mail, and sales may be arranged over the Internet.

The reason for the smuggling and sale of these animals is very simple: profit. Some breeds of rare macaws can sell for as much as $70,000; one trader was accused of smuggling a rare Komodo dragon and a plowshare tortoise, each of which would sell for $30,000. In Mexican markets green parrots and toucans are sold alongside brown snakes. In Brazil one can buy macaws and small jungle finches. Advice about how

Captured skins
Russian police in Siberia display captured tiger skins. A network of Chinese and Russian gangs cooperate to poach and sell Siberian tigers, which are prized for their fur and other body parts, which are used in traditional Chinese medicine.

to smuggle them home is often thrown in for free. Many of the animals come from the Amazon jungle, yet another blow to the rain forests that are also facing deforestation at an alarming rate. The variety of illegal animals available for purchase around the world is endless and continues to increase.

The Bush Meat Trade

During a check of the baggage on a flight from Nigeria to Britain in 2001, customs officers found several suitcases leaking blood. Inside they discovered 2.5 tonnes of meat in 56 bags. Bush rat, antelope, chicken, pork, bat, fish, live crabs and snails, goat carcasses, and "bush meat" are just some of the delicacies illegally imported into Britain.

The term "bush meat" is used to describe the flesh of animals which are killed illegally, notably endangered species such as gorillas and chimpanzees, which are being hunted to extinction. Meat smuggled into Britain via Heathrow and Gatwick airports can be found for sale as far away as Newcastle and Glasgow, and is regularly found openly for sale in markets in London. It is estimated that one million tonnes of illegal meat products are smuggled into Britain each year. There are obvious health risks to the final consumers in this trade. The meat is not transported in refrigerated trucks, and animals often carry infectious diseases, for example, monkeys and chimpanzees carry monkeypox and ebola fever, while other animals may carry tapeworms, giardia, and salmonella.

Throughout many areas of Africa, bush meat is important as a source of affordable food (for example, it is a quarter the price of domestic meat in Zimbabwe) and only secondly as an opportunity for trade. As the availability of bush meat declines, more species are hunted, and commercial trading is replacing local consumption. Buffalo used to be popular, but since numbers have declined hunters now go for animals that were at one time taboo, such as hippopotamus and zebra. In Central Africa international companies driving new roads into what had been inaccessible areas have opened up vast new hunting grounds. Indeed, it has been claimed that some companies not only make it possible for hunters to access new areas, but also supply transport, ammunition, and guns. A four-year-old chimpanzee was found so tightly chained to a wall that he was unable to lie down. He had been owned by a wealthy family, but was later passed on to a succession of owners and his life had become unending torture. Another captive chimpanzee was discovered in a park chained up as a tourist attraction. She was suffering from

Illegal poaching

A market trader (right) with a variety of wild animals in Uganda, Africa, and (below) a haul of illegally smuggled bush meat discovered in baggage by British customs officers at Heathrow airport.

malnutrition and had lost nearly all of her hair. The chimps were casualties of the bush meat trade, their parents having been shot illegally by hunters. Both chimps were rescued and taken to an animal sanctuary.

Ever Expanding Markets

Markets will always exist where products are illegal or where legal excise revenues make them appear unreasonably expensive to the consumer. In this way legislators and organized criminals exist in a symbiotic relationship. With each new piece of restrictive or prohibitive legislation, with each new attempt to levy higher taxes on products, the opportunities for organized criminals to adapt to new markets are extended.

Extortion and Protection

Amassing a regular revenue of money or goods from fellow citizens by ilicit means is a criminal activity which depends upon organization. The threat of violence, the provision of security, the coercion of the customer into an act of crime by purchasing illegal goods are primary activities of the gangster. The ways in which such techniques have been introduced into legitimate enterprises and labor unions have transformed this area of activity into a major income earner.

Both extortion and protection are crimes with long histories, provide the plots for many gangster movies, and are lucrative sources of revenue for organized criminals. Extortion is demanding money from an individual or a business, which, if not paid, will result in the individual or business being physically or financially harmed. Protection is money paid on a regular basis to an organized crime group to "protect" the individual or business from other criminals.

Extortion can range from the school bully demanding another student's lunch money to a mob such as New York's Black Hand Gang extracting payment from immigrants newly arrived in the United States (*see p122*). Protection can be the local store paying $50 a week to a gang of juveniles to protect their windows or a large employer paying millions to an organized mob to ensure harmonious labor relations.

Extortion in the United States

In the 19th century, an organization that helped newly arrived Italians in the United States to find homes and work was the *Unione Siciliana,* which had branches across the country. It was infiltrated by extortionists, the so-called "Black Hand Gang," the foremost of whom was Ignacio Saietta. By 1901 Saietta had become the national chairman of the *Unione Siciliana* and he filled its regional offices with many of his

Gangster territory
A view of North Clark Street, Chicago, in 1929, scene of the notorious St Valentine's Day Massacre (*see p*141). Turf wars often arose over areas of control for raising protection revenues.

criminal associates. Many new Italian immigrants, especially in New York, were leaned on to pay a percentage of their weekly wage to the extortionists, fearing violence and the loss of their jobs. Small businesses such as grocers, drug stores, and barbers also paid "protection."

However, the Mafia was not confined to New York. As early as the 1880s the Sicilian Matranga brothers had attempted to extort money from the Provenza family, who imported fruit from South America into New Orleans in Louisiana. The Matrangas wanted to make all importers and freighters pay a percentage to guarantee trouble-free loading and unloading of their goods. Violence and terror was the order of the day. One of the Provenzano men had his head pushed into a lighted stove and burned, to encourage compliance with the Matrangas' demands. This sort of violence characterized

the early days of the Italian Mafia in the United States, and the conflicts continued into the 1920s, when gangsters indulged in turf wars with their criminal rivals to keep control of the illicit businesses they had set up.

On the Waterfront

The New Orleans waterfront war of the 19th century showed just how profitable U.S. docks could be to organized crime. Whoever controlled the docks had the chance to steal at will. There was also money to be made from the companies that used the dock facilities. In the 1960s, containerization of imported goods altered working practices and, here again, organized crime moved in, as it did to U.S. airports as well.

In the 1990s, U.S. federal authorities began to investigate a number of irregularities on New York's waterfront. A United States attorney alleged that the Genovese crime family had won "extortionate control of the New York, New Jersey, and Miami piers."

New York docks
The Brooklyn Port Authority Pier 3 of New York docks in the 1960s. The waterfront of the city has always been a profitable feeding ground for organized crime.

The Laundry Wars

Any business can be the target of criminal extortion. From the mid-1920s, organized crime in the city of Chicago was controlled by Al Capone (*see p129*). Capone's associate, an intelligent young Welshman named Murray Llewellyn Humphreys, later a key figure in the Chicago Outfit, expanded the Capone organization's interests into a number of new fields. Humphreys' greatest coup was the takeover of the laundry business. He began by buying two legitimate laundries. These provided him with a legal source of income, and were used to recycle profits from extortion and bootlegging, hence the expression "money laundering." In Chicago, with its huge hotels, the laundry business was lucrative and competitive. During the "Laundry Wars," stores were bombed and trucks hijacked. "Legitimate" businessmen, such as Walter Crowley, head of the Master Cleaners and Dyers Association, attempted to control the Chicago market, driving his competitors out of business by bombing their premises and terrorizing their workers. His main target was Morris Becker, who ran 10 dry-cleaning facilities. Becker took Crowley to court, which acquitted Crowley despite the mass of evidence against him. Becker contacted Al Capone. This was the chance Humphreys was waiting for. A new corporation was set up, Sanitary Cleaning Shops, Inc. Capone sat on the board, and Humphreys was paid to arbitrate labor disputes. Humphreys then terrorized Crowley and took over the Master Cleaners and Dyers Association. In 1928 Capone's laundry racket took in $10 million, rising to $50 million by 1931.

CASE STUDY

Financial Fraud

In the legal context the term "fraud" has no precise definition and can include forgery, deception, pecuniary advantage, and false accounting. However, whatever guise fraud adopts it has three elements that are unchanging:

ELEMENT 1: Inducement
To interest a victim into parting with their money it is vital to provide an individual with some form of bait. This can take the form of cash prizes, sexual gratification or the opportunity to make an easy profit.

ELEMENT 2: Pretense
The fraud has to appear convincing to its victim. To encourage would-be victims organized criminals will go to remarkable lengths. Headed notepaper, advertising campaigns on the Internet, flyers dropped through mailboxes are all weapons in their arsenal, used to convince the gullible of the fraudsters' good standing.

ELEMENT 3: Result
What the fraudster generally gains in the short term is money. However, most valuable in the long term are credit card and banking details. More sinister is the theft of identity and the use of that identity to perpetrate further fraud. The sentences passed for fraud are much less than those handed down for drugs and arms dealing.

THE SET-UP: Inducements
Exploiting the gullibility of people is sometimes very simple even in countries that have a supposedly financially astute population. In countries where the people are less financially sophisticated apparently foolproof get-rich-quick schemes take them in very easily.

The advent of the Internet and e-mail has provided organized criminals with a prime opportunity to trawl the world for victims. The "419" Fraud, ironically named after the number of a Nigerian law forbidding the transfer of funds to a foreign bank, is ubiquitous on the Internet. Thousands of e-mails are sent out offering the recipient a share in money to be transferred to an overseas account from a bank in Nigeria. The sum is usually millions of dollars, and the percentage for "helping" is high. The targets are people in Europe and the United States where PCs and bank accounts are widespread.

On a different level, in poverty-stricken war-torn Kosovo in the Balkans in southern Europe in 2002, a series of TV advertisements showed happy lottery players telling how winning large amounts of money had transformed their lives. They had all bought a ticket in a private company lottery. Ticket sales for that particular lottery boomed. However, employees of the company were found to be withdrawing winning tickets before they went on sale.

THE STING: Pretense
In the 419 Fraud the initial contact with the victim can be very convincing, as the senders often pose as Nigerian government officials. If a victim agrees to help they are asked for an "advance fee" to cover legal and administrative costs. These fees can be upward of $250,000. When this money is transferred contact with the victim is broken off.

In the case of the Kosovan lottery tickets, who knows who wins anyway? A lottery ticket looks as convincing as the buyer wants it to.

THE RAKE-OFF: Results
Fraudulent lotteries yield an immediate cash payment and almost 100 percent profit if there are no winners. 419 victims will have provided, as well as the advance fee, details of themselves, including their name, address, and bank account number. This information is open to criminal use in order to fabricate false identities, and to create credit cards and passports, which are two vital tools for international criminal groups.

A Russian Mafiya group in London used a network of accomplices working as waiters and store assistants to secretly clone credit card transactions with special swipe machines. The police later seized equipment capable of forging Visa and Mastercard hologram security marks. The forged cards were either sold on or used by gang members themselves.

All these frauds rely on the willingness of members of the public to participate. Indeed, they play on people's greed and their hopes to "get rich quick." In all cases the old saying applies: "If it looks too good to be true, it probably is."

Golden opportunities
Organized crime has been quick to exploit the numerous opportunities for profit in credit card and identity fraud, as well as in lottery scams and Internet cons. The spread of electronic communications and online banking has meant that the world of finance is now at the criminal's fingertips.

Labor racketeer
Arnold Rothstein, big time gambler and financier, was responsible for the involvement of organized crime in the garment industry in New York City in the 1920s.

The New York Labor Rackets

In New York, Arnold Rothstein (see p148) was the first to see the possibilities of labor racketeering. The garment industry employed each new wave of immigrants — Irish, East European, and Italians — as cheap labor. As early as 1890 the "garment district" employed 83,000 people. As labor unions began to form, employers hired thugs to break their power before they grew too strong. Rothstein first supplied strikebreakers to the employers, then the same thugs to the unions, becoming the indispensable mediator between the two sides and profiting from both. After Rothstein's murder in 1928, Louis Buchalter and Jacob Shapiro took over the racket on behalf of the New York Syndicate. In a short time they controlled the entire business: truckers' unions, designer firms, and employer associations. After Buchalter was executed for murder in 1944 and Shapiro jailed for life, control passed to the Lucchese and Gambino families.

The key to control lay in the trucking business, which ferried the cut goods from the designer firms to the contractors that sewed the cloth together, then back for inspection and then to the retailers. Fashion depends on timing, so it was essential that deliveries were not interrupted by strikes. The New York families set up a trucking cartel, the Master Truckmen of America (MTA), controlled by the Colombo family, which prevented independent truckers from entering the market and charged inflated rates for transport. They also specialized in high-interest loans to designer firms. This web of interrelated interests generated enormous amounts of money. The costs were passed on to the consumer in the price of the finished garment.

The Big Four Unions

Four of the largest unions in the United States have traditionally been controlled by organized crime. The largest is the International Brotherhood of Teamsters. With almost two million members, from truck drivers to airline pilots, it wields immense political and economic power. Since the days of Jimmy Hoffa (see p166) its pension fund has been thought to finance organized crime activities of every sort. The Laborers' International (LIUNA) has half a million members in the construction and building trades. Leaders of the union have been repeatedly charged with price-fixing, bid rigging, and extortion. The Hotel Employees and Restaurant Employees' International (HERE), again with almost half a million workers, is said to be controlled by the Chicago mob. Its pension and welfare funds have been looted by the Outfit for years. The International Longshoremans' Association has 100,000 members. Union leaders are believed to get a rake-off from everything shipped through U.S. ports.

Labor Racketeering

The exploitation of labor has not been confined to the United States. During the 1990s Moscow, the Russian capital, underwent

Manhattan skyline
The Empire State Building dominates New York's garment district, seen here in the 1920s. The area of the city was home to the garment industry, one of the the first centers of U.S. labor racketeering.

Modern Piracy

Since the 1980s, there has been a resurgence in an age-old criminal activity – piracy on the high seas. Long thought to have been consigned to Hollywood movies, piracy created such a problem that, in 1992, the Piracy Reporting Center was established to collect and disseminate information. In 2002 the Indonesian, Bangladeshi, and Indian coastlines were ranked first, second, and third in the world for the numbers of recorded pirate attacks: 103, 32, and 18 respectively.

THE *ANNA SIERRA* HIJACK

On September 13, 1995 the freighter *Anna Sierra,* carrying a cargo of sugar, was boarded by more than 25 pirates while sailing off the coast of Thailand. Climbing aboard from a motorboat, the heavily armed pirates imprisoned the crew. In two days the criminal gang repainted the ship and renamed her *Arctic Sea.* Casting the crew adrift in life rafts, the pirates took the ship into the Chinese port of Beihai, and, presenting Chinese officials with false paperwork, the gang sold the cargo. The crew, who had survived, eventually reported the hijack to the *Anna Sierra*'s owners and the ship was located. A legal battle then ensued between the owners and a company in Hong Kong. The *Anna Sierra* was beached and left at Beihai. The pirates

Philippines pirate
A modern-day buccaneer displays his weapon aboard a fast pirate vessel. Piracy is far from being a thing of the past and is on the increase in many of the world's shipping lanes, especially those in poorly policed maritime regions such as the South China Sea

were released without charge. That the pirates released the crew of the *Anna Sierra* is remarkable; in most cases of hijacking they are usually thrown overboard and left to drown.

Off the coast of Somalia, Africa, the owners of vessels that slow down are forced to pay ransoms to pirates who climb aboard and hold both the ship and its crew to ransom until they are paid off.

Masked men
In Batam, Indonesia pirates operate out of Riau Islands. Piracy is a big problem in the South China Sea and has been furthered by corrupt officials. Here pirates rehearse boarding ships using a bamboo rod with a hook attached.

a remarkable transformation from the drab grey conformity of the communist era to a bright modern city. The speed and scale of the building works was in some instances a product of organized crime. With the collapse of communism, entrepreneurs took advantage of the opportunities presented. However, the contracts undertaken proved to be problematic for many of the building companies. The difficulty lay in obtaining a sufficiently skilled labor force. Employers turned to the republics of the former Soviet Union. Negotiating through middlemen, skilled workers were brought from Georgia and Azerbaijan to Moscow. However, the recruiting middlemen were part of organized crime syndicates and the workers little better than slaves. The men would pay a percentage of their wages as a joining fee and after deductions for travel, the men usually begin their contract in debt. When weather conditions were too bad for working the men were not paid. As a result, many found themselves carrying out illegal activities for the criminals who recruited them, such as stealing cars or providing the muscle for protection rackets.

Blackmail

Blackmail is a simple crime. One person threatens to expose another's guilty secret unless money is paid or favors are granted. The payment or favor can be a "one off," or demands may carry on for an indeterminate period. The blackmailer is in control once the victim has agreed to their terms.

The expression "blackmail" derives from the extortionist practice of threatening a victim by sending a letter with the imprint of a black hand on it. In the modern world, where politicians and public servants often lead lives under the continual gaze of a public fascinated by scandal, the least indiscretion, if disclosed, can lead to ruin. Therefore, organized criminal gangs exploit the weaknesses of those that can grease the wheels of their illicit activities. This is particularly true of countries where the salaries of officials are low and the rewards for cooperating with criminals high. The "gift" of a car or of a vacation in return for a small favor may lead to an increase in

In the bear pit
The trading floor of the Chicago Stock Exchange. The stock market is now a target for organized crime.

the favors demanded in return. Similarly, the "honey trap," where an apparently happily married official is lured into a sexually compromising situation and then threatened with public humiliation unless favors are granted, is a well-known ploy used by organized criminal syndicates.

Greenmail

Greenmail takes part of its name from the color of the U.S. dollar (green). It describes the practice of buying shares in a company that is the target of a hostile takeover bid, and threatening to support the predator unless a financial reward is received. The payoff can be in cash or the purchase of the shares at an inflated price. It is in fact corporate blackmail, but it is legal.

Although not new, greenmailing first came to prominence on Wall Street during the 1980s. Two major players in this ruthless world of corporate high finance were Michael Milken and Saul Steinberg. Milken's methods of financing share deals cheaply allegedly caused huge problems for some of America's biggest companies. In 1987 alone, he earned over $500 million. Finally in 1990, Milken was sentenced to 10 years in prison for racketeering and other financial crimes. He served just under two years of his sentence. Following the jailing of Milken in 1990, greenmailing

Million dollar fraudster
Junk bond king Michael Milken leaves a United States District Court in 1989 after pleading innocent to charges of insider trading in the America's most extensive criminal securities fraud probe.

subsided but did not die out completely.

Saul Steinberg, whose name will forever be remembered as the alleged greenmailer of the Walt Disney corporation and of Chemical Bank, saw his once mighty takeover vehicle Reliance crash in mid-2000. To pay off debts he was forced to sell his home on Park Avenue, New York, and his prized art collection.

Any connection between greenmail and organized crime has yet to be proved. However, given the huge amounts of money that Mafia organizations have at their disposal, and the fact that they need to launder those funds, it would not be surprising if in one of the less well-regulated financial markets of the world there are Mafia-backed corporate raiders who are manipulating their assets in just such a way. The essence of greenmail is that it is not technically illegal and it offers another point of entry for dirty money into a cleaner arena of operations.

The Future

Unlike many other areas of organized criminal activity, extortion, protection, kidnapping, and blackmail, seem easy to define, if not to bring to the courts. However, as new technologies emerge at a much faster rate than the legislation to contain and control them, again the openings for opportunist criminals seem endless.

Manipulating Money

As with legitimate business enterprises, the acquisition of money is the motivation for organized crime. For criminals, however, how they deal with accumulated wealth is a further challenge. Concealing funds, transforming "dirty" money into "clean" money, reinvestment, all these tax the ingenuity of organized criminals, but in a world where financial transactions are becoming increasingly complex, transnational and - through digital technology - virtual, new opportunities continually arise.

$500 billion is a conservative estimate for the amount of drug-generated revenue that is laundered on behalf of organized criminals annually across the globe. This figure is almost five percent of the world's gross domestic product. But drugs are only a part of the international business of organized crime, which generates more than a trillion dollars annually.

Money Laundering

The greatest problem facing organized criminal groups is how to legitimize their profits. In countries where the banking system is in its infancy, the simplest solution is to take over a bank. This is believed to be the case in Russia where, it is reported, various Mafiya groups have bought or coerced their way into small banks and bureaux de change, which they use as conduits through which to process their cash.

It is widely believed that the model on which modern-day launderers base their operations was developed during the years of Prohibition in the United States (1920–33). Providing illicit liquor earned large amounts of cash that needed to be "cleaned up." The cleaning or "laundering," as it became known, required that the money passed through some apparently cash rich legitimate business, such as a restaurant, taxi firm, charity, or bank itself. A Canadian supplier of alcohol to the gangs of Chicago and

Hotel Flamingo
Playground of the élite, the famed Hotel Flamingo in Las Vegas, Nevada, seen here in 1949. The Flamingo was the first Mafia-backed casino built in Las Vegas and was run by Benjamin "Bugsy" Siegel.

Detroit allegedly opened a bank account in a fictitious name and used it as a depository for the crime gangs' payments. These assets were then used to finance legitimate enterprises, protected by the bank's aura of respectability and its code of privacy.

During the later part of the 20th century money laundering became a more complex process, involving shell companies, tax havens, orders for non-existent products or services, corrupt or inept officials, bribery, and huge amounts of money moving in and out of bank accounts all over the world at mind-numbing speed.

Gambling, Casinos, and Bookmaking

Probably the place that first comes to mind in association with the topic of casinos and gambling is Las Vegas, that grew with Mafia money during the 1940s. The Hotel

Flamingo was opened in Las Vegas in 1947 by Benjamin "Bugsy" Siegel, friend of Meyer Lansky and Charles "Lucky" Luciano. Organized crime made a great deal of money skimming profits from the casinos for 40 years, until the laws regarding gaming were strengthened, and it became impossible for anyone with links to organized crime to openly operate in Las Vegas.

Today most casinos are owned by publicly owned companies that are responsible to shareholders. They have accountants, auditors, and all the other accoutrements associated with big business, and licensing is strictly regulated. This is not really an atmosphere conducive to crime of any kind, and certainly not organized crime.

While organized crime is not involved in legalized gambling, there are many other opportunities for becoming involved in the business of gambling which are either less well regulated, or indeed completely outside the law. It has been estimated that illegal

Bright lights of the city
The neon signs of Las Vegas, Nevada, are a distinctive feature of the gambling capital of the United States. For many years, the Mafia ran the city but now the casinos are all legitimate.

gambling in the United States makes profits in excess of $100 billion per year.

In this electronic age, the Internet is being widely used to make large profits from gambling. Bets can be taken and placed anywhere in the world. For example, a bet that is illegal in Canada can easily be placed with a bookmaker in London. The only way law enforcers can work out what is going on is by tracking the money; there is simply no way for them to track or stop the original bet from being made.

Most "virtual casinos" are based offshore and are therefore very difficult to regulate. Because the Internet can cross any national border, organized crime can exploit the opportunities for online gambling with some degree of safety. However, arrests have been made in the United States, and, from the investigation, it is understood that Russian organized criminals are also involved. The gambler, of course, has no way of knowing whether the roulette wheel has been "fixed," and it can only be considered extremely unwise to give credit card details to an organization that is almost certainly based on some offshore island.

Lotteries and the Numbers Racket

In the United States, many states have attempted to eradicate illegal gambling by instituting their own lotteries. For more than a century organized crime has run its own lottery: "the numbers racket."

The numbers racket, also known as the numbers game or the numbers pool, is a

---

The Three–Step Money Laundering Plan

The following describes the sophisticated modern money-laundering cycle, from the process known as "placement" – where criminal profits are placed into the legitimate banking system – through to integration, where the "dirty" money is finally integrated with the "clean".

PLACEMENT

Methods of placement are varied. One way is for numerous small deposits to be made with different banks by errand runners known as "Smurfs." None of the deposits are large enough to attract the bank's attention to them. The money can then be withdrawn at a later date with the proper paperwork to show where it came from. Another method is for a gang member to buy high-value goods in cash – items such as antiques or luxury cars. These can then be resold, the buyer paying by bank transfer into a legitimate account.

From the late 1940s until relatively recently, the casinos of Las Vegas provided an ideal "laundromat," through which to pass large sums of cash. The technique was simple. A gang runner would buy a large amount of gambling tokens or "chips," and would then proceed to gamble away a token amount, before cashing in the remainder.

LAYERING

Once in the legitimate financial system, the money from organized crime undergoes a series of complicated transactions to distance it from its illicit origins. Each transaction forms a layer of cover. "Shell" companies come into play at this point. A shell company is a registered company with an office somewhere such as the Dutch Antilles, Liberia or Nauru, which serves only as a name on a bank account. By passing through a series of such shells in different locations around the world, layers of legitimacy are built up and the origins of the money are obscured. Such offshore companies then invest in apartments in Florida or London and wait until such time as the criminals decide to realize their wealth.

INTEGRATION

The sale of the assets at the end of the paper trail completes the money-laundering cycle. Such a sophisticated process makes the task of detecting money launderers almost impossible.

At the root of the problem can be a simple factor, such as the rendering of a name from Arabic or Japanese into English. In the wake September 11, 2001, an investigation into 27 terror organizations led to the discovery of almost 2,000 suspect bank accounts. This provided a wakeup call, drawing the attention of governments globally to the scale on

which money laundering was being carried out. In the U.S. and Britain, legislation has been enacted to facilitate closer monitoring of national and international financial transactions. However, this has raised potential problems. One may be the over-reaction of workers in the financial industry. An over-zealous bank teller in Wyoming, passing on his suspicions to fraud investigators, may generate mountains of paperwork. Multiply this by the vast numbers of similar workers and the problem becomes huge. It therefore becomes clear that the monitoring of Internet banking and of electronic international money movement needs to be more efficient than the organized criminals that employ these methods, both now and in the future.

Laundry wars
In the 1920s, Al Capone's Chicago Outfit moved into the laundry business, taking protection money from rival laundry companies and raking in vast sums of cash.

Caribbean accounts
Dutch-style houses line St. Anne's Bay in Curacao in the Netherlands Antilles. Caribbean tax havens such as this are used by organized crime groups as a base for shell companies that enable them to launder their profits.

CASE STUDY

Rogue Trader

In 1995, the infamous financial trader Nick Leeson single-handedly brought down Britain's oldest merchant bank Barings, which finally crashed and was bought by the Dutch insurance group ING for £1. Leeson started life in Watford, England, leaving school with a minimum of qualifications, having failed an examination in mathematics. He was delighted to get a job as a clerk with Coutts, bankers to the British Royal Family. This was followed by a series of positions in various banks, and his career was crowned when, at Barings, he was promoted to work on the trading floor.

He was extremely successful at Barings and was made manager of the operation in futures markets on the SIMEX (Singapore Monetary Exchange). By 1993, he was making 10 percent of Baring's annual profits. His work involved buying and selling derivatives. However, in 1994 things began to go wrong. He had undisclosed losses of $512 million hidden in an account named Error Account 88888. He did his best to cover his losses, but by the time the market took a dive after the earthquake in Japan in January 1995 and did not recover, he had run up £800 million worth of liabilities – virtually the entire assets of the bank.

Leeson claimed that he was carrying out purchases for a client, so Barings was unaware of the losses to which it was exposed. His bosses were alerted to a possible problem when Leeson requested more money. An audit was carried out and the truth became clear. The bank crashed with losses of £850m. Investors lost all their savings and 1,000 of the bank's employees their jobs. When the losses were discovered, Leeson disappeared, but was soon arrested in Frankfurt, Germany, and extradited back to Singapore. In December 1995, he pleaded guilty to two counts of deceiving the bank's auditors and cheating the Singapore exchange. He was sentenced to six and a half years in jail. He was released in 1999.

The man who broke the bank
Nick Leeson under arrest at Frankfurt airport in 1995. Although Leeson probably operated alone, his activities indicate the vulnerabilty of international finance houses to scams.

popular form of gambling, and is especially so in low-income areas in cities. Usually it is run by organized crime families, who operate from anywhere that is convenient – parking lots, bars, vacant storefronts – and where there is passing trade.

This illegal form of betting has its attractions for the gamblers: typically the winnings are higher with the numbers than on state lotteries for the same stake; it is not difficult to avoid paying taxes on winnings; and some operators offer credit. The public is quite tolerant of this kind of crime, which is part of many peoples' lives. What many do not realize, however, is that the profits are used to finance other organized crime activities, like the trade in illicit narcotics.

In the 1930s, winning numbers could come from a combination of numbers from a horse race or from figures from the close of business on the New York Stock Exchange. More recently the rackets have used numbers taken from state lotteries.

In Ohio in August 2003, after the Internal Revenue Service (IRS) and the Federal Bureau of

Investigation (FBI) had spent six years investigating illegal lotteries in Cleveland, six people were charged with running an illegal gambling business and two with tax violations. It was claimed that they had accepted hundreds of bets a day and operated an illegal lottery based on the Ohio Lottery's daily Pick 3 game. The operation used the same winning numbers, but a bet of $1 could result is a win of $750, in contrast with the Pick 3 game, in which the corresponding prize was $500.

The IRS claimed that the group of six had several associates who

Playing the lottery
A lottery player punches in her number choices for the Ohio Super Lotto. Official lotteries compete with organized crime's numbers rackets for public participation.

The Benex Scandal

In 1996 large amounts of money were transferred from two Russian banks to accounts at the Bank of New York that had been opened in the name of Benex Worldwide. From there it was distributed through various shell company accounts in Europe. Two years later, in 1998, British authorities, who were investigating Russian Mafiya activities, informed the U.S. Federal Bureau of Investigation (FBI) of irregularities involved in the transfers of International Monetary Fund (IMF) dollars via the Bank of New York to the Russian capital, Moscow. The British investigators suspected collusion between a Russian company, YBM Magnex, believed to be a front for the alleged Russian Mafiya boss Semyon Mogilevich, and Benex in New York..

The owner of Benex, Peter Berlin, was married to a vice-president of the Bank of New York, Lucy Edwards. In late 1998, Berlin was arrested. It was reported that $4.2 billion had moved from Russia in more than 10,000 transactions between October 1998 and March 1999, many through Benex accounts at the Bank of New York. Money routed back to Europe passed through a British shell company and then on to Italy or France.

A two-year long police operation culminated in the arrest in June 2002 of more than 50 people. Two of these, Igor Berezovski and his twin Oleg, ran 10 shell companies from a one-roomed office in Paris that drew the authorities attention to them. Money transferred through Berezovski's labyrinth of financial accounts eventually made its way back to companies reportedly linked with the Ismolskaya and Soltsnevo criminal syndicates in Moscow.

The Italian authorities believe that as much as $9 billion of Russian Mafiya money was laundered between 1996 and 2002, the biggest international laundering operation ever uncovered.

Global finance
It was at the Bank of New York that accounts in the name of Benex Worldwide were used by Russian criminals to channel cash worldwide.

threats about what would happen to her and her family if she did not make the repayments, threats that continued until the communal suicide of a family that had given up all hope.

It is very easy for people on low budgets to become the victims of the loan shark. The loan may start small, but when the borrower cannot afford to pay the interest rate they are forced to borrow more until they rapidly get swallowed up in a spiral of debt.

Typically, loan sharks buy lists of names of individuals who have failed to keep up repayments on loans and "cold call," offering a further loan. Initially the lender is friendly, pleasant, and helpful, but will later employ threats to intimidate the customer who fails to keep up the extortionate repayments. Organized crime plays its part in this scam. The Japanese Yakuza is believed to be responsible for about 25 percent of the loan sharking that takes place within that country. In a nation where bankruptcies have risen dramatically between 2002–2003 because of a ten-year recession, loan sharks are circling ready to snap up their profit.

Counterfeiting and Forgery

The terms "forgery" and "counterfeit" are interchangeable. During the late 20th century, the problem of counterfeit goods grew rapidly for one simple reason: advances in technology. Currency counterfeiting used to be a very specialized "industry" but with the advent of computers, and laser printers and scanners, it is not difficult to make passable bank notes.

It has been estimated that around 5–7 percent of the entire trade throughout the world consists of counterfeit goods, and the list of items that are illegally copied is a lengthy one, including computer software, CDs, videos, perfume, cigarettes, alcohol, designer clothing and accessories, and pharmaceuticals. Counterfeiters will copy anything if they can make a profit from it, and while some goods do no physical damage to those who purchase and use them, others do. Counterfeit pharmaceuticals may not be quite what they seem, and there have been cases of counterfeit vodka containing methylated

accepted, collected, and hedged bets. An IRS agent said in his statement in court that records showed that employees of those charged received large volumes of telephone calls in the hour just before the regular daily lottery draw. Phone calls were so frequent, it was alleged, that one of the defendants had said he needed a computer to deal with the volume. On Sundays, however, when there was no draw, few phone calls were received.

Loan Sharking

The practice of loan sharking – the lending of money at very high rates of interest – affects people who are desperate for cash, and who cannot borrow from the normal sources such as banks. They need money straightaway and have nowhere else to turn. Consider the tale of a 69-year-old Japanese

woman who, already in debt, borrowed the equivalent of $150 to pay for rent and medical treatment for her husband and brother. Three months later she, her husband, and her brother were found dead – they had been killed on a railroad crossing by a train. It was no accident. The woman had borrowed the money from a loan shark. Initially the woman was told that, if she repaid the loan quickly enough, the interest would be in the region of 10 percent. However, less than four weeks after the loan was made, the debt had incurred "interest" at the rate of 500 percent. She had been to the police for advice in the matter (in Japan, there is a 29 percent limit on the amount of interest that can be charged). She was told to stop making payments. The loan shark who lent her the money made serious

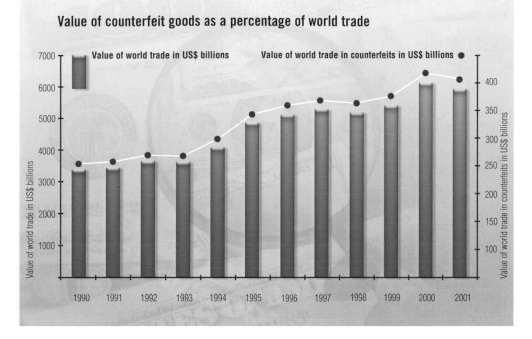

Value of counterfeit goods as a percentage of world trade

Value of world trade in US$ billions

Value of world trade in counterfeits in US$ billions

The value of counterfeit goods in world trade
Counterfeiting is a major global problem, and while accurate figures are hard to come by, estimates put it at 6 percent of world trade. The chart compares the cost of pirated goods to legitimate products.

spirits. Even when the counterfeit products do no actual harm to the purchaser, the practice does have other harmful effects, including loss of profits for the company that researched, made, and marketed the original goods, and loss of tax revenue.

When the criminal gang has identified the product it is going to copy and gathered the necessary materials, production takes place in rather different circumstances to those that saw the creation of the original product. For example, there will not be the same control of quality and finish, and workers will not be treated as well. There is also a link with the world of smuggling, as the goods have to be transported and distributed without attracting attention.

Counterfeiting is a natural environment for organized crime, and in many ways is a safer and easier way of generating money than many other activities: it has been said that organized crime can make more money out of a kilo of CDs than the same weight of cannabis – and the penalties for doing so are not so high. Counterfeiting is frequently a crime that is condoned by consumers, who want to purchase designer goods more cheaply.

Cyber Crime 700

Cyber crime is one of the most rapidly growing criminal activities in the world today. Organized criminals exploit the systems to make a great deal of money. One estimate suggests that the financial cost throughout the world might be in excess of $40 billion a year. According to the FBI, in 2002 Internet fraud cost its victims $52 million, a steep rise from 2001, when they say victims lost a mere $16 million. It has been estimated that half of the total fraud in the United States is perpetrated electronically. While many people work from home, using a computer, it is just as easy and convenient for the criminal to do likewise. Indeed, it would be somewhat surprising if crime, whether "organized" or not, did not rise to the opportunities that the electronic age can offer.

The list of felonies that can be embraced by the term "cyber crime" is seemingly endless. Organized criminals are now able to carry out "protection rackets" without

Copying for profit
A selection of the consumer goods that are now being copied by organized crime groups. Fake designer clothes and pirated computer software products are always popular.

moving from their desks. In what is termed a "network-based denial of service," a firm may find that its website has become unavailable to customers for a time. In fact, it had been made unavailable by criminals who then, posing as an Internet security consultancy, swoop. They claim that they can prevent such attacks in future, in return for a substantial payment for their services. Like the thugs who arrive at a store demanding "insurance" against "accidents" such as arson, this kind of criminal is offering to protect the business from himself – for a fee.

Another type of cyber crime is the establishment of false companies on the Internet. Orders are taken, and personal details and credit card numbers are obtained from customers, who are tempted by bargain prices. However, the goods never arrive, and the criminals have valuable information for future use. The foundations are laid for the crime of identity theft, which does not necessarily require such a sophisticated method of collecting information. Criminals can very easily find personal information about individuals such as social security numbers, dates of birth, and addresses, and then use the information to apply for credit cards with which they can go on a spending spree. Today everyone is aware of the term "hacking," used to describe the computer geek who gets satisfaction out of the challenge of electronically "breaking into" the computer systems of big companies and governments, on occasions wreaking havoc. The hacker who is also criminally minded can download a lot of information that can have many uses, including blackmail.

A very common kind of computer fraud is to create a fake bank website (as similar as possible to a genuine one) and then to

> ## "Modern technologies such as the Internet offer up huge legitimate benefits, but also powerful opportunities for criminals, from those involved in financial fraud to the unlawful activities of paedophiles."
>
> Jack Straw, British Home Secretary

Citibank, New York City
In 1994, Citibank was the victim of a sophisticated computer hacking operation that resulted in the loss of $11 million.

The Internet and Organized Crime

In May 2003, two suspected members of a U.S. Mafia group were arrested and appeared in court for allegedly perpetrating a $230 million Internet fraud scheme begun in the late 1990s in New York City. It is believed that this is the largest such scheme ever prosecuted.

The investigation was launched in response to a flood of customer complaints to credit card companies. The Federal Trade Commission responded by starting an enquiry into a number of websites. In this scam, the criminals launched several pornography sites using images from a selection of "specialist" magazines. Visitors to the sites were asked for credit card details as a method of proof of age. In return they would get a "free" tour of the site. Customers were assured that their credit cards would not be billed; the tour was free.

The reality was very different. Across the United States, Asia, and Europe customers' cards were charged on a monthly basis, repeatedly, for the sum of $90. The money was then laundered via a circuitous route and eventually reached the two alleged perpetrators of the crime. The earnings from this racket were spent on multi-million dollar homes, visits to ultra-expensive hotels, and many other luxuries.

The case illustrates the shift in the types of activities in which organized crime has been involved over the last half-century. Until the 1940s and 1950s organized crime, in the main, did not include drug running in its activities because it was considered morally unacceptable. However,

from the 1960s, organized crime became very much involved in the trade in illicit narcotics. Similarly, until relatively recently, many of the organized crime bosses refused to get involved in the trade in pornography. This situation is now changing, as they begin to see the massive profits that such operations can realize.

Gotti junior
In 1998, John A. Gotti, son of the crime boss (*see* p170), was charged with telecommunication fraud and extortion.

Window on the world
The Internet has opened up a multitude of new opportunities for organized crime in fraud and extortion scams.

e-mail customers stating that it is necessary to re-confirm their passwords. Targets are then directed to the fake website where they are invited to fill out their details. Armed with this information, the fraudsters can then transfer money from the individuals' accounts. In 2003, exactly this kind of fraud was committed in Britain. Customers of many of the main British banks were targeted and substantial sums were stolen.

Other crimes perpetrated with the help of computers include the theft of industrial trade secrets and credit card numbers, bogus auctions, dubious work-at-home schemes, money laundering, virus attacks, fraud, industrial espionage, organized property theft, tax evasion, and more simply the invasion of a person's privacy.

Cyber crime is an international problem that is unaffected by national boundaries. Consequently, it is now being taken

seriously at an international level. Following the electronic trail of cyber crime may take investigators on a rollercoaster ride through a number of far-flung countries, and detection of the criminal is impossible if there is not a high level of international cooperation from law enforcement agencies.

One problem that law enforcers frequently encounter is the reluctance of many companies to report that a crime has taken place, for fear that their reputations will be sullied. In 1994, Citibank (New York) became the victim of a hacker who removed, electronically, $11 million. As a result of the negative publicity, many of the bank's customers moved their accounts elsewhere. In a growing trend, instead of contacting the police after the event, who may or may not be able to gather evidence and prosecute the offenders, many companies now prefer to employ a cyber crime consultant to prevent

their most sensitive systems from being infiltrated in the first place.

The seam between legitimate business and organized crime is maybe at its thinnest in the area of financial dealing. There are plenty of examples. To what extent "God's Banker" Roberto Calvi and the Vatican's Banca Ambrosiana were involved with the Sicilian Mafia will probably never become clear. Similarly, exploiting an apparently legitimate loophole in California's waste reycling compensation scheme, saw a group of Mexican businessmen importing trash from south of the border to claim $5 million in state compensation. In Europe, at the time of writing, the Italian judiciary are reopening of investigations into Silvio Berlusconi's business practises, which may provide a more chilling reminder of the scale and depth of venality which money, and its manipulation, can create.

Aliases: Monty Trent, David Gill, Tren
Monterey Johnson, Trent Smith, Morg
Lloyd Trevar, Gill Trent, Trent McKnigh
Rodney Gaab, Avery Trevell, Avery Mc
"Z-Day", "T-Bone"

Photographs taken 5/2/80

ORGANIZED CRIME GROUPS

A survey of the main geographical and cultural organized
crime groups, their evolution, traditions,
and areas of operation around the world.

SPIRACY TO DISTRIBUTE COCAINE

TED BY FBI

984 9

MONTEREY TREVELL III

Date of Birth: September 24, 1959
Place of Birth: Los Angeles, California
Height: 6'
Weight: 180 pounds
Build: Medium
Hair: Brown

Eyes: Blue
Complexion: Pale
Sex: Male
Race: White
Nationality: American

Scars and Marks: Tattoo of dollar sign ($) on left shoulder.
Remarks: Trevell is heavily involved in narcotics trafficking in association with the CRIPS stre
Lloyd has at least two California driver's licenses issued in the name Monty Trent McKnight
name of Trent Trevell.

Social Security Numbers Used: 566-190-0805; 566-190-1805; 553-970-8747; 555-970-8747

SICILY

THE ORIGIN OF THE TERM "MAFIA"

The origin of the term "Mafia" is obscure. Some suggest that it derives from Arabic words such as *mahfaz* (protection) or *mahfil* (a gathering.) Others claim it is an acronym, for example *Mazzini Autorizza Furti, Incendi, Avvelenamenti* (Mazzini authorizes robberies, arson, poisoning). This is an attempt to link the Mafia with the 19th-century nationalist movement led by Giuseppe Mazzini. Most definitions seek to give the Mafia an ancient origin.

TERRITORY

The Sicilian Mafia has traditionally been based in the west of the island around Palermo and Trapani, but after World War II, it expanded to the eastern cities. The Mafia is now active across Italy, and has worldwide contacts, with especially strong links to the U.S. Mafia which date back to the late 19th century.

● **PALERMO (SICILIAN CAPITAL)**
The home of leading Mafia families.

● **TRAPANI**
Traditional Mafia town and region.

● **CATANIA**
The biggest Mafia base in eastern Sicily.

● **MESSINA**
An important port and Mafia stronghold.

● **CORLEONE**
Gives its name to the Mafia don in *The Godfather*.

In 2000, the Italian authorities estimated that the Mafia's annual turnover had risen to about $133 billion, the equivalent of 15 percent of Italy's GNP. Although it is impossible to be accurate, some rough figures regarding the Mafia's finances and where that money has been invested are as follows:

Combined capital	$800 billion
Real estate	$11 billion
Financial investment	$11 billion
Black market profits	$15.5 billion

The Sicilian Mafia

> " The Mafia finds its strength in *omertà* and in the sacred and impregnable structure of the family, the only secure place. Only blood does not betray. "

SALVATORE ACCARDO, PARISH PRIEST OF CAMPOREALE, 1995

The word "*mafioso*" (in Sicilian *mafiusi*) first appeared in print in 1863 in the title of a popular melodrama by Giuseppe Rizzotto (*I mafiusi di la Vicaria*) about a prison gang in Palermo. The word "Mafia" appeared in a dictionary in 1868, defined as "the actions, deeds, and words of someone who tries to act like a wiseguy." A useful definition occurs in old editions of the *Oxford Dictionary of Current English*. "Hostility to law and its ministers among Sicilian population, often shown in crimes; those who share in this."

Sicily has been governed by non-Sicilians through history: Greeks, Carthaginians, Romans, Vandals, Byzantines, Arabs, Normans, Bourbons, and northern Italians. The characteristic of "hostility to law and its ministers" can be traced to the fact that this law was usually imposed by conquerors.

From Norman times, the political system in Sicily was feudal. Foreign rulers controlled the island by cultivating the local aristocracy, who obtained concessions in return. The law was whatever the rulers made it. There was no concept of common justice and the peasants were excluded from the political process. They lived desperate lives on the margin of survival. It was from this social milieux that the Mafia eventually arose, not

Mafia target

Policemen inspect the wreckage of a car after a bomb attack by the Mafia in Sicily in 1984. In the 1970s, the Mafia began a campaign of terror against intrusive state institutions, targeting judges, politicians, and other public figures.

as liberators of the oppressed, but as able individuals intent on obtaining their share of wealth and privilege however they could. Traditional Sicilian suspicion of state institutions created the conditions in which the Mafia could develop.

Ties of Blood

In a world where power was arbitrary, safety lay in the family. The larger and more extended the kinship group, the more protected the individual, especially in a social system of vendettas, where honor demanded that no offense should be

Of the people?

A Sicilian peasant family in the early 20th century. The Mafia extorted money from both landlords and peasants, and connived with the authorities to crush socialist reform movements in Sicily.

allowed to pass unavenged. An army of brothers and cousins was the best protection in an unjust world. Nothing is as important to a Sicilian as the ties of blood.

Feudalism was abolished in Sicily in 1812. The ruler at the time was King Ferdinand, whose kingdom consisted of Naples and Sicily (The Kingdom of the Two Sicilies). He fled Naples to escape Napoleon's invading armies. The Sicilian barons agreed to shelter him in return for reforms, including a constitution and the

THE SICILIAN MAFIA

The supergrass Tommaso Buscetta described in 1984 how a Mafia family is organized. It is a hierarchic organization, with the *capofamiglia* elected by the family. He in turn appoints his *sotto capo* and one or two *consiglieri*. Below the "men of honor" are aspiring members, who run errands and so forth, hoping that they might one day become "men of honor" themselves.

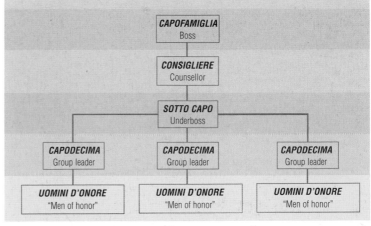

Vito Cascio Ferro (Don Vito)

Vito Cascio Ferro, known as Don Vito, was a boss of the Sicilian Mafia for many years. His advice on protection rackets was: "Don't ruin people with absurd demands for money. Offer your protection instead. Help them prosper in business and they'll not only be happy to pay the *pizzu* (protection money) but they'll kiss your hand in gratitude."

Cascio Ferro was born in Palermo in 1862 on the estates of Baron Inglese. He became a *gabellotto* (revenue collector) for the baron and for a rich politician and businessman, Domenico De Michele Ferrantelli.

Cascio Ferro was already a respected *mafioso* by the time he went to New York in 1901, where he instructed the Black Handers (*see* p125) in the finer points of the protection racket, laying the foundations for

the U.S. Mafia. In 1903 he was arrested by New York police officer Joe Petrosino on suspicion of murder. Although not convicted, he returned to Sicily. In 1909, Petrosino was murdered in Palermo while in Sicily on U.S. police business. Cascio Ferro was arrested, but released on the strength of an alibi given by Ferrantelli.

Cascio Ferro claimed to be Petrosino's murderer, which gave him great prestige, and allowed him to assume the leadership of the Palermo Mafia. Although arrested 69 times, he was always acquitted. He became a highly respected member of Palermo society.

In 1927, Cascio Ferro was finally convicted by Mussolini's anti-Mafia prefect Cesare Mori and sentenced to 50 years. He died in prison in Palermo during Allied bombing in 1943.

Dates 1862–1943
Details Cascio Ferro was the first *capo de tutti capi* (boss of bosses) of the Sicilian Mafia. He is also credited with laying the foundations for the growth of the U.S. Mafia.

abolition of feudalism. The feudal estates were transformed into private property, and divided up among the barons.

The landowners rented the administration of their estates to *gabellotti* or tax-collectors, in return for a percentage of the harvest. The *gabellotti* in turn divided the land into smallholdings and rented them out to tenant farmers, in return for a percentage of the harvest. They kept the peasants in line, made sure crops were harvested, settled disputes, and generally acted as the agents of absentee landowners who lived in the cities. The *gabellotti* were the mediators between landowner and peasant, the urban and the rural worlds, and they used their position to exploit both groups. They fenced off common grazing lands, usurped water rights, and organized gangs of cattle rustlers, selling the stolen animals in Palermo. Because they controlled the urban food supply, they were ideally placed for extortion, and soon they and their confederates controlled the markets in the major cities. The Mafia was born, forming a sort of rural bourgeoisie in collusion with absentee landlords and urban merchants.

The *gabellotti* were the forerunners of the modern Sicilian Mafia and their *modus operandi* was followed with equal success a century later in the United States, where the Mafia became the interface between capital and labor, impartially exploiting both.

Triumph and Disillusionment

When Garibaldi and his one thousand red-shirted troops landed in Sicily in 1860, they were rapturously welcomed, and men flocked to join them. Two thousand brigands formed squadrons known as *squadri della mafia*. Sicilians voted in a 1861 plebiscite overwhelmingly for union with

Invading Sicily
Garibaldi and his Redshirts in the Battle of Calatafimi, Sicily, May 15, 1860. Garibaldi's opening campaigns relied on squadrons of Sicilian brigands.

the mainland. Ever since then, Italian governments have counted on the Sicilian vote, delivered by the Mafia in return for generous concessions.

Although the Sicilian people initially welcomed unification, they rapidly became disenchanted. The new Italian government was based in Turin, and the officials who were sent to govern the island were almost all northerners. Soon Sicilians began to consider the new government no more than yet another form of alien rule. Young men called up for military service escaped to join brigand bands in the hills. Poverty levels increased and such public order as there was collapsed. The government responded by increasingly draconian measures. Sicilian nationalism intensified as a result, as did adherence to the tradition of *omertà* (see box below) and the power of the Mafia, which many saw as their only protection from the government. Rich and poor united in opposition to the central government and its efforts to "modernize" Sicily. The Mafia gained in strength, its members including brutal rural brigands and urban

Messina earthquake
A street in Messina, Sicily, showing the damage caused by the 1908 earthquake. The government helped many of the survivors to emigrate to the United States.

aristocrats, until it almost constituted a state within a state, or even an antistate, with its own rules, laws, and economy.

The crime rate in Sicily rose 87 per cent between 1863 and 1870. It rose dramatically throughout Italy after unification, so the rise may reflect better keeping of statistics, but in Sicily serious crimes were still much higher than anywhere else. In Lombardy, there was one murder for every 44,673 inhabitants in 1873. In Sicily there was one for every 3,194.

The island was so crime-ridden that in 1874 the conservative Italian government declared an emergency and sent a military force to police the island. The resulting controversy brought down the government, and Italy's first left-wing government to power. Most of the 48 Sicilian deputies of the new government were *mafiosi*.

The Sicilian Mafia, now organized, offered to police the island and save the government the embarrassment of sending in troops. The government agreed, and some of the more prominent non-Mafia affiliated bandits were arrested or killed. Once again, the Mafia had positioned itself between two opposing groups and profited from its relationship with both.

Failure to Progress

In 1887, one of the first movements for workers' rights in Italy, the *Fasci*, began in Sicily. The barons and the Mafia were horrified at this attack on their power and the lack of respect it showed. The movement was harshly suppressed. The repercussions of the failure of this early progressive movement echo today. Sicily has never lacked social reformers, but almost all attempts at progress have been repressed.

The effect on the United States was even more dramatic. Many thousands of Sicilians emigrated, hoping for a better life. Between 1900 and 1913, of the 1,092,527 emigrants who left Sicily, 797,191 went to the United States. Those were the official statistics. Many more entered the United States clandestinely, aided by gangs specializing in illegal immigration. Sicily lost a quarter of its population – an entire generation.

INSIDE STORY

OMERTÀ

Omertà, meaning "manliness" in Sicilian, is a code of behavior that extends far beyond the traditional wall of silence with which Mafia members, their victims, and witnesses of their crimes meet the enquiries of the agents of law and order. The marks of the true *mafioso* are that he speaks little, makes each word count, and maintains a grave and dignified presence at all times, even under extreme provocation. Indeed, this is a pan-Mediterranean ideal of manhood, going back to the Stoic tradition of ancient Greece and Rome. *Omertà* is bound up with the larger category of *onore* (honor), the code that rules not just the Mafia, but also other traditional societies across the Mediterranean. This code demands that slights to a person or his family and friends, however small, be avenged. A man's status is dependent upon his readiness to use violence to defend his honor. The man who defends his honor in this way accumulates that precious commodity, respect. Respect creates authority, and authority is power.

With power comes obligation, and the true *mafioso* looks after his crime family like a father, often serving as godfather to the children of his underlings, attending their weddings and funerals, and holding frequent, almost ritual, banquets, where the seating arrangement reflects each person's status in the family. The Sicilian Mafia refers to itself as the *Onorata Società* (the Honored Society) and to its members as "men of honor."

Sign of respect
The funeral of the leading Mafia godfather, Don Calogero Vizzini, in Palermo in 1954. At Vizzini's funeral many hundreds of floral wreaths were given anonymously as a sign of respect to a "man of honor."

Calogero Vizzini (Don Calo)

Calogero Vizzini, called Don Calo, was born a peasant in 1877 in Villalba in the province of Caltanissetta. As a young man, he acted as a middleman, transporting grain from farms in the region to be milled in Villalba. The region was full of bandits, so Vizzini teamed up with the most ferocious of them, Paolo Varsalone, to ensure safe passage for his grain. He became Varsalone's friend and through him made another powerful friend, Baron Giuseppe Rizzo di Camamarata. Vizzini and the baron were indicted for consorting with bandits, but later acquitted.

In World War I Vizzini was a war profiteer, selling stolen horses and cattle to the army. He and other Mafia leaders bought up feudal lands, displacing the local aristocracy. Vizzini invested much of his profits in mining and,

in 1922, attended an international mining conference in London. He had made the transition from peasant to broker capitalist in a remarkably short time. He also created a network of powerful friends, many of them Freemasons, in business, the army, and politics. This network stretched to the government in Rome and across the Atlantic to the Unione Siciliana in New York.

Vizzini, an anti-fascist, survived the Mori purges of the 1920s, although he was made an internal exile and lost some power and privileges. In World War II, he collaborated with the Allies and was made an honorary colonel in the U.S. Army. His postwar aim of uniting Sicily with the United States never came to pass. Vizzini died of natural causes on July 10, 1954, in Villalba.

Dates 1877–1954
Details Calogero Vizzini rose to become the most respected Mafia don in Sicily after the death of Don Vito Cascio Ferro in 1943. His funeral was one of the largest ever held in Sicily.

The Sicilian immigrants were catapulted from a traditional agrarian society into New York, a teeming industrial city. They came with strong ties to their traditional past, family loyalty, and contempt for any but their own law. These traditions stood those who chose a life of crime in good stead.

The period after World War I was bitter for Sicily. Poverty was worse than ever, prices were rising and demobbed troops found that landowners, war profiteers, and black marketeers had grown rich while they had been fighting. In 1919 there was a general strike against the high cost of living. Proportional representation was introduced, which began to break the power of the Mafia and their political

cronies who had controlled Sicily since unification. Returning soldiers had lost the traditional deference to their patrons that lay at the root of Mafia control. The Italian government tried to defuse the situation by sowing division in what was increasingly a mass movement for change

sweeping across the country. Land grants were made to ex-soldiers, which alienated non-soldiers from the reform movement. In Sicily, the Mafia infiltrated the movement to destroy it from within by violence and corruption. Many leaders were simply killed. Once again a progressive, anti-Mafia movement was subverted and destroyed.

Mori's Mafia Purge

When Benito Mussolini came to power in Italy in 1922, he was determined to destroy the Mafia. He assigned Cesare Mori to the task, appointing him prefect of Palermo in 1924, and granting him extraordinary powers. For four years this astute and indefatigable "prefect of iron" waged war against the Mafia. He arrested suspected members in their thousands. Mass trials were held, with the defendants held in huge iron cages. Almost all were found guilty and sent to penal colonies. Those convicted were

The Allies arrive
U.S. Army vehicles arrive in Pollina, Sicily, in 1943. The Mafia collaborated with the Allies and many of them were given positions of responsibility in the Allied civil administration.

CASE STUDY

Salvatore Giuliano: a Sicilian Bandit

For seven years, from 1943 to 1950, Salvatore Giuliano was the most famous bandit in Sicily. This was three times the typical bandit's active life. He lasted so long because he was protected by the Mafia and the political class – the two great powers in postwar Sicily. When he was no longer useful to them, he was killed.

Salvatore Giuliano was born in 1922 into a peasant family in Montelepre. During World War II he traded on the black market. In 1943 he became an outlaw after killing a policeman when he was stopped at a checkpoint with a load of contraband grain. Four months later, he killed another policeman. In January 1944 Giuliano raided the local jail and released all the prisoners. Several of the freed men took to the hills with him and formed a bandit gang.

Giuliano showed a flair for press manipulation. He wrote letters to the newspapers and granted interviews to journalists. He was young and photogenic. His celebrity

spread throughout Italy and the rest of the world. Beloved of the peasants, their self-appointed protector was staunchly anti-communist at a time when both the ruling Christian Democrats and the U.S. government feared the increasing power of the left wing, both in Sicily and mainland Italy.

Giuliano joined a separatist group with strong links to the Mafia, carrying out attacks on the government and police in its name. He was made a colonel in the Volunteer Army for an Independent Sicily.

In April 1947, the left wing won a majority in the elections to the Sicilian parliament. There was a mass meeting to celebrate at Portella dell Ginestra near Montelepre. As 3,000 peasants began the celebrations, Giuliano's men opened fire from the hills. Eleven people were killed, including children, and 65 wounded.

Support for Giuliano gradually began to fade. On July 4, 1950, the press reported that Giuliano had been killed in a gunfight with the newly formed

Banditry Suppression Taskforce Command. In fact he had been shot while asleep by his cousin, Gaspare Pisciotta. His body had then been moved to a courtyard in Castelvetrano and riddled with machine-gun fire by the police.

Pisciotta was arrested and charged with the murder. He admitted that he had killed Giuliano, but said he had done so on the orders of Mario Scelba, then the minister of the interior. Pisciotta requested that he be allowed to reveal the links between Giuliano's band and a number of powerful politicians who were behind the May Day massacre at Portella della Ginestra, but the court ruled that such matters should be left to a later trial.

Pisciotta was returned to prison in Palermo, where he was immediately poisoned by strychnine in his coffee. The same day, January 8, 1954, Mario Scelba became the new prime minister of Italy.

Violent folk hero
Salvatore Giuliano in the 1940s. Despite his violent actions – he was believed to have killed as many as 100 people – he post-humously achieved heroic status. Several successful films and novels have been based on his life.

Staged death
Salvatore Guiliano's body, with his carbine and automatic pistol beside him, lies in a courtyard in Castelvetrano where the police claimed to have killed him in a gunfight. In fact Guiliano had been shot dead earlier by his cousin.

Politician accused
Italian Premier Mario Scelba at a meeting in Rome in June 1955. Guiliano's murderer, Gaspare Pisciotta, claimed he had acted on Scelba's orders. Scelba, a member of the Christian Democratic Party, was minister of the Interior at the time of Guiliano's death.

---

overwhelmingly from the lowest levels of the Mafia, although they included the most powerful Mafia boss, Vito Cascio Ferro (*see p56*).

Mori was recalled in 1929, probably because he insisted on investigating the Mafia links of the minister of war, General Di Giorgio. Mori's legacy was ambivalent. While very effective, his methods were extra-legal, and included torture. Cascio Ferro, indubitably guilty of multiple murder and extortion, was convicted on a trumped-up charge. *Mafiosi* fleeing arrest went to the United States, where they swelled the ranks of the U.S. Mafia. Prisoners convicted under fascism were seen as heroes after the war. Some were appointed to high positions in the Allied civil administration.

By 1943, mid-way through World War II, it was clear that the fascist regime in Italy was collapsing and a postwar socialist or

communist government seemed inevitable. Mafia leaders Calogero Vizzini (*see box p58*) and Andrea Finocchiaro Aprile met Count Lucio Tasca, a landowner, in Rome. They formed a committee and announced the National Renaissance of Sicily. They were now in a position to present themselves to the new conquerors as victims of fascism, but at the same time enemies of communism. Vizzini even envisioned Sicily becoming part of the United States.

Hand in hand with the Allies

When the Allies landed in Sicily in 1943, the ground had already been prepared. The U.S. Mafia boss "Lucky" Luciano had been secretly asked to help win support for the invasion from the Sicilian Mafia (*see pp154–157*). Leading *mafiosi* such as Calogero Vizzini were happy to help. The Allies were welcomed as liberators and in

return released all the prisoners convicted by Mori. Finocchiaro Aprile emerged as the leader of the Sicilian anti-fascists, founding the separatist Movement for an Independent Sicily. Charles Poletti, the Allied military governor of Sicily and later Italy, always denied that the Mafia was involved in the conquest and occupation of Sicily, adding, surprisingly, that he had never even heard of the Mafia, despite the fact that he was a former mayor of New York, and his adviser and translator was Vito Genovese (*see p156*).

The postwar history of Italy was determined by the relationship forged between the Mafia and the Allied occupiers of Sicily in 1943. After the war, the Mafia ensured for almost 50 years that Sicily voted for the Christian Democratic Party, keeping the communists and the socialists out of the government and, in exchange, obtaining a free hand in Sicily.

In 1944, supporters of Calogero Vizzini (*see* p58), the Mafia mayor of Villalba, shot and seriously wounded the communist leader Girolamo Li Causi as he addressed a meeting. Over the next decade, 43 left-wing leaders were murdered, and the Mafia's systematic elimination of left-wing politicians continued until the mid-1960s. In the 1947 regional assembly elections, however, left-wing parties polled 30 percent of the vote in Sicily, while the Christian Democrats polled only 21 percent. The 1948 national elections threatened to bring in a left-wing government, possibly even one dominated by communists. Britain and the United States watched the elections with great concern. The Cold War had begun, and Sicily's two million votes could decide not only the fate of Italy but that of the postwar balance of power in Europe.

Captured bandits
Seven bandits, including a young boy, captured near Palermo in January 1950. These rural criminals were soon to be surpassed by the more dangerous and powerful urban Mafia.

The Christian Democratic Party won a resounding victory in the 1948 elections. In Mafia-controlled areas its votes increased by more than 50 percent from 1947. Once in power, the Christian Democrats banned the Communist Party from ever holding office. The stage was set for the Mafia to become a powerful presence not just in Sicily, but in the whole country.

Land reform
A Sicilian peasant holds a communist flag as he leads his companions to claim land near Palermo after World War II. The Allies' fear of communism led them to allow the Mafia to retain control in Sicily after the war.

The new urban Mafia was born and set to work in the lucrative postwar black market. In 1943, the Allies granted the trucking concession in the Palermo area to Michele Navarra, a doctor, director of a hospital, head of the local landowners' association, and leader of the Corleone Mafia *cosca* (clan) The concession gave the Corleone clan access to Palermo's flourishing black market. Between 1944 and 1948 the Corleonese killed 153 men. Many of them were murdered by Luciano Leggio, an ambitious young *cosca* member. Leggio became a *gabellotto* by shooting another *gabellotto* in the back and taking over his position. He then bought an estate where he slaughtered stolen cattle, taking the meat to Palermo in Navarra's trucks. A ravine on the property served to dispose of his victims' bodies.

The Urban/Rural Power Struggle
By 1958, Navarra had had enough of his brutal subordinate and sent 15 gunmen to Leggio's estate to kill him. Leggio managed to escape and went to

Michele Greco

BIOGRAPHY

Michele Greco was born in Palermo on May 12, 1924, into a family with strong Mafia connections. His power base was Ciaculli, a coastal town west of Palermo. His brother, Salvatore "Little Bird" Greco, was the first head of the Cupola, a position Michele himself assumed in 1978. His prominent Mafia role was unknown until 1982, when the testimony of the *pentito* Salvatore Contorno revealed Greco's true power, shown by his nickname, *Il Papa* ("The Pope").

Beginning as a *gabellotto*, Greco became a wealthy landowner, and entertained powerful politicians and businessmen at his villa. The grounds contained hideouts for *mafiosi* on the run and a heroin refinery. Greco controlled a third of Palermo's water supply,

and was awarded government grants to drill wells on his own land. He then sold the water back to the city, raising the price during shortages, which were often engineered by Greco himself. He was also involved in scams involving European Community agricultural subsidies.

Greco was controlled by the Corleone clan, and carried out their bidding during the great Mafia war of the early 1980s. He went into hiding in 1982, but was discovered and arrested in 1986. During the maxi-trials of 1986, he was convicted of involvement in 38 murders. Although released in 1991 by Judge Corrado Carnevale, he was almost immediately re-arrested by Judge Giovanni Falcone and sent back to prison.

Dates 1924–
Details Michele Greco's power as a Mafia boss was a well-kept secret for many years. He was the tool of the Corleonese clan as head of the Cupola, the Sicilian Mafia commission.

---

war with Navarra. Salvatore "Totò" Riina and Bernardo Provenzano, two of Leggio's most effective gunmen, killed Navarra by machine-gunning his car as he was driving home. Leggio then hunted down and killed Navarra's supporters in the streets of Corleone. The Navarra faction lost 29 men in this war and the Leggio faction 13.

This was a conflict between two opposed world views, that of the traditional agrarian Mafia concerned with relationships, power, and respect, and the new postwar Mafia in

> ## "How gracious life can be when one has friends in the right places."
> Giuseppe Bonanno, Italian-American *mafioso*

which money ruled. Lucciano Leggio became the first boss of the new Mafia, adopting the methods of U.S. gangsters such as Capone. The world that had produced men like Vito Cascio Ferro, Calogero Vizzini, and Michele Navarra was vanishing, as the huge estates were divided up among the peasants, giving them an independence that made their traditional protectors and exploiters an anachronism. The old rural Mafia became a victim of modernity, and men like Leggio were both its product and its executioners.

Sicily became an autonomous region of Italy in 1947. Palermo boomed as peasants flocked to the city and by the early 1950s, the population had reached one million. The city was divided up among 39 Mafia families, who fought each other for control of the food markets and the booming construction industry and its suppliers. They collected protection money from every business in their territory. In 1955, Leggio moved on Palermo, and began ruthlessly extending his control.

Into Narcotics

On October 12, 1957, the new generation of Sicilian Mafia bosses met their U.S. counterparts at the Grand Hotel des Palmes in Palermo. The meeting was proposed by "Lucky" Luciano (*see p157*), who had been exiled to Italy from the United States in 1946. The U.S. delegation was headed by Giuseppe "Joe" Bonanno and Francesco Garofalo. The Sicilians were led by Genco Russo, who had succeeded Calogero Vizzini as head of the Sicilian Mafia families.

The main business of the meeting was to organize the international narcotics trade, particularly heroin. This was a growing market, with the United States by far the largest consumer. Luciano had been

Mafia town
The town of Corleone, Sicily, whose Mafia connections were made famous by Mario Puzo's book *The Godfather*. In recent years it has tried to change its name to avoid such notoriety.

CASE STUDY

The "Sack of Palermo"

Before World War II, Palermo was one of the most charming cities in Europe. The old Arab quarter, La Kalsa, was particularly noted for its fine architecture and evocative atmosphere. Arab writers described Sicily as a garden of Eden and called Palermo the most beautiful city in the world.

Little trace of the glorious past remains. The postwar period saw the building boom known as the "Sack of Palermo," in which fine old palaces were leveled and cheaply built concrete buildings were thrown up to house peasants flocking to the city in the 1950s seeking work. Public parks, once the delight of Palermo, were concreted over and the city expanded into the belt of orange groves that surrounded it. The old city was purposely allowed to fall into ruin, and denied essential services like water and electricity. Families were forced to move to jerry-built suburbs. Real estate developers, contractors, and speculators made a fortune.

Sicily received government funding to stimulate development. Much of this money was siphoned off by the Palermo Mafia clans and their political protectors. For example, the mayor Salvatore Lima and the assessor of public works Vito Ciancimino — both connected to the Corleone clan — issued 2,500 building permits to just three people, all fronts for Cosa Nostra groups. Ever since, property development, construction, and cement production have been prime Mafia activities in Sicily and Calabria.

An elegant capital
A view of Sicily's capital, Palermo, in 1925 before Allied bombing and the postwar building boom destroyed much of the historic old city and lined the pockets of Mafia-connected construction companies and local politicians.

organizing the heroin trade in the United States via Havana since 1946, but Cuba was on the brink of revolution so new distribution networks were needed. The National Commission that handled matters of policy for the U.S. Mafia still formally opposed narcotics trafficking, but profits were so large that there was no way to stop it. At Luciano's suggestion, the Sicilian families formed their own governing commission to regulate the affairs of the more than 150 Sicilian clans. Known as the Cupola, it was headed by Salvatore "Little Bird" Greco and had 12 members, each representing three Palermo families. Under the aegis of Palermo, provincial commissions were also formed. It was a horizontal federation: each family kept its own structure and territory and the bosses were more or less equal. All were supposed to obey the Cupola's rulings. The U.S. National Commission could now deal directly with the Cupola and together they could control the import of heroin to the United States.

In the 1950s, the main narcotics suppliers were Corsicans in the south of France, where they refined morphine base brought from Turkey and the Lebanon. With their U.S. connection, the Sicilian Mafia became the Corsicans' best customers. Heroin was sent to Sicily then to the United States, usually

The Grand Hotel des Palmes, Palermo
The location of a historic meeting between the U.S. Mafia and Sicilian Mafia in October 1957. At the meeting the two groups agreed to work together to control the lucrative international heroin trade.

packed in shipments of Italian specialties, such as oranges, cheese, and olive oil.

In 1962, war broke out among Palermo's Mafia families, and the peace imposed by the Cupola was shattered. Although the immediate cause was a drug deal that went wrong, at a deeper level the conflict was between the old urban Palermo mafias, represented by the La Barbera clan, and the new arrivals from the provinces, Lucciano Leggio and the Greco clan. On January 17, 1963, Salvatore Greco kidnapped and killed his rival, Salvatore La Barbera. Exactly one month later, a car blew up outside Greco's house in Ciaculli. Greco survived. The violence between the two sides littered the streets of Palermo with bodies at the rate of one a day. The Cupola, designed to prevent exactly this sort of violence, proved to be powerless to stop it and was discredited.

The Police Crack Down

Another car bomb exploded in Ciaculli on June 30, 1963, killing seven policemen. This time the Italian government reacted. Police cordoned off Palermo street by street, confiscating weapons and arresting 1,900 men. Some 250 Mafia leaders were brought to trial and many sent to jail. Some were

The Corleonese clan in court
Sicilian *mafioso* Luciano Leggio (seated) talks with his lawyer during the trial of 60 members of the Corleone clan in February 1969. Leggio was cleared of all charges against him.

sent into exile to the north of Italy, allowing the Mafia to gain a foothold there. Most escaped, some into hiding, others to the Americas, setting up a global network.

As a result of the Ciaculli bombing, the Italian government passed new anti-Mafia laws and established a reformed and invigorated Anti-Mafia Commission. The Cupola was disbanded for the moment. However, the trials were disappointing.

Leggio, for example, arrested in May 1964, was given an amnesty in 1965. Tried again, he was once more absolved in 1969. Finally sentenced in 1970, he escaped, and was only recaptured in 1974.

A new Cupola was constituted in 1975. This time it included Stefano Bontate, Pippo Calderone, Rosario Di Maggio, Salvatore Scaglione, Giuseppe Calò, Rosario Riccobono, Filippo Giacalone, Nené Geraci,

and Leggio. Since Leggio was in prison, he appointed Totò "The Beast" Riina as his representative.

The Mafia's structure began to change, becoming more hierarchical, probably in response to the increasing complexity of its operations in drugs and arms trafficking and urban infrastructure racketeering. Centralization was the only way to control what had become a complex multinational. It took place under Leggio's representatives, Provenzano and Riina. Their method for transforming the "federation of Mafias" into the virtual dictatorship called "La Cosa Nostra" was simple : murder.

The Turkish Connection

In 1975, a Turkish crime group led by Abuzer Ugurlu became the Sicilian Mafia's main supplier of morphine base. Ugurlu exported arms on behalf of the Bulgarian government to the Middle East in exchange for morphine base which was shipped to Bulgaria and then re-exported to western Europe. European demand was still low, and Ugurlu wanted to break into the U.S market

Salvatore Lima

Salvatore "Salvo" Lima was the politician to whom Cosa Nostra turned most often to resolve problems whose solution lay in Rome, according to Tommaso Buscetta.

Lima was for many years the key Christian Democratic Party politician in Palermo, and later served in government positions under Giulio Andreotti and for a time as a member of the European Parliament. He was assistant mayor of Palermo from 1956 to 1958 and mayor from 1958 to 1963 and again from 1965 to 1968. He then held a number of posts in the national government.

His father Vicenzo had been a "man of honor" in the Palermo-Centro *cosca* of Angelo and Salvatore La Barbera. Vicenzo Lima recommended his son to them, which was the beginning of a long and fruitful relationship. Salvatore Lima was a friend of Tommaso Buscetta, whose testimony during the maxi-trials clarified Lima's role as the "Mafia ambassador" to Rome. Lima

supported the Stefano Bontate faction in the Mafia wars of the 1980s.

Even while out of office, Salvatore Lima was the most powerful politician in Palermo, presiding over the "sack" of the city, awarding lucrative public-works contracts to Mafia-connected firms, giving cronies and clients jobs in the public administration, and above all, bringing in the vote for the Christian Democratic Party. Originally a supporter of the Armintore Fanfani faction within the Christian Democratic Party, he switched his allegiance and block of captive votes to Andreotti in 1964.

On March 12, 1992, Lima was shot and killed in Mondello, the seaside resort near Palermo where he lived. He had been killed because of his inability to "fix" the maxi-trials that unravelled at last the intricate web of relationships that linked Cosa Nostra to the upper reaches of the Christian Democratic Party.

Dates 1920–1992
Details Salvatore Lima was the leading Christian Democratic Party politician in Palermo and was the "Mafia ambassador" to the Italian government, according to the testimony of supergrass Tommaso Buscetta. He was assassinated when he could no longer be of any use to the Mafia.

Mafiosi in exile
Some of the 17 Mafia leaders exiled to the remote island of Linosa off Sicily in May 1971. They are from left to right: Rosario Mancino of Palermo, Salvatore Sanfilippo of Agrigento, Calogero Migliore of Agrigento, Giuseppe Sirchia of Palermo, Rosario Riccobono of Palermo and Vincenzo Parlapiano of Agrigento.

Vito Ciancimino

Vito Ciancimino was born in 1924 in Corleone, where his father was a barber. He was assessor of public works in Palermo from 1959 to 1964. He was elected mayor in 1970, but was forced to resign after only two months because of persistent rumors of his connections with the Corleonese faction of Cosa Nostra. The rumors were confirmed in 1984 by the Mafia informer Tommaso Buscetta, who said that: "Ciancimino is in the hands of the Corleonese."

Ciancimino and Salvatore Lima presided over the "sack of Palermo" after World War II, funneling public works contracts to firms connected to Cosa Nostra. Both Ciancimino and Lima were originally supporters of the Arimintore Fanfani faction of the Christian Democratic Party, but later switched to Giulio Andreotti's center-right coalition.

Ciancimino was responsible for the "development" of Palermo's historic center, which led to the destruction of many fine old buildings. At the time of his arrest in 1984, it is estimated that he was receiving $250,000 a month in kickbacks from municipal contracts. He was the first Italian politician to be condemned for "Mafia associations," receiving a 10-year sentence, reduced to eight on appeal in 1993. He later received further sentences for corruption and was fined 150 million Euros by the Commune of Palermo. When notified of the fine, he said, 'Would they like it in cash?' Ciancimino died in Rome while under house arrest in 2002.

Dates 1924–2002
Details Vito Ciancimino was responsible for the "sack of Palermo" and the first politician to be imprisoned for his Mafia associations. He himself claimed that "the Mafia died in 1958 with Michele Navarra."

The Sicilians joined forces with the Neapolitan Camorra, which had a pan-Mediterranean tobacco smuggling network that could be adapted to handle morphine base. The Mafia set up drug refineries in eastern Sicily. For the first time cities such as Catania and Messina became Mafia bases.

The drug trade involved thousands of non-Mafia associates, who could not be directly controlled through the traditional mechanisms of loyalty and fear. The Mafia network was thus vulnerable, but the profits were so great that they overrode caution. These profits, estimated to be equivalent to 12 percent of Italian GNP, also posed a problem. The Mafia needed to launder the money through the banking system without disclosing its origins. A leading Sicilian

financier, Michele Sindona, was able to help them (*see box below*.)

In 1981, Riina moved against his fellow Cupola members, Stefano Bontate and Salvatore Inzerillo. The conflict is known as the Second Mafia War, but it was not so much a war as a campaign of carefully targeted assassinations. The Corleone clan suffered no casualties. Their enemies lost between 500 and 1,000 men.

Enterprise Versus Power

Bontate and Inzerillo represented the old Palermo families. They had long-standing political connections, and they organized the distribution of heroin to the United States, administering the profits and paying out dividends to investors in the trade. The Corleone clan naturally invested in Cosa Nostra heroin deals, but did not have Bontate and Inzerillo's U.S. connections.

Bontate and Inzerillo and their allies were the entrepreneurs, an enterprise syndicate, while the Corleone clan was the military arm of Cosa Nostra, a power syndicate. Leggio and Riina were determined to synthesize the two and take sole control of Cosa Nostra.

CASE STUDY

Propaganda 2

In 1971, the Bank of Italy began to investigate Sicilian banker Michele Sindona, a financial adviser to the Vatican and one of the leading financiers in Europe. Sindona was a member of Propaganda 2 (P2), a powerful and secretive Masonic lodge run by financier Licio Gelli in Arezzo, Italy. Sindona handled P2's finances as well as those of Cosa Nostra and the Vatican. It was discovered that the Italian political, industrial, and Mafia establishments laundered their money through Sindona. However, he was so well-connected that no charges were brought against him.

Sindona went to the United States in 1972, but his wild speculations on the stock markets led to the crash of the Franklin Bank in October 1974, the largest bank failure in U.S. history; Sindona's Banca Privata Italiana followed suit. So much money was

Masonic Lodge leader

Leader of the powerful P2 lodge, Licio Gelli, poses at his home in Arezzo in Tuscany. Police later found 150 gold bars, worth nearly $2 million, in terracotta pots on the terrace of the house. Gelli was a key player in the fraudulent collapse of Italy's largest private bank

lost that the Italian state was almost bankrupted. So was the Vatican, P2, and even more importantly for Sindona's personal health, Cosa Nostra.

In 1979, Sindona was charged in New York on 99 counts of misappropriation of funds, fraud, and perjury. The receiver investigating his financial affairs, Giorgio Ambrosoli, was shot dead in Milan. Sindona was spirited out of New York by the old Mafia trick of a faked kidnapping. He was brought to Palermo and, in consultation with Stefano Bontate and Salvatore Inzerillo (who wanted their money back), he tried to blackmail his powerful associates by threatening to reveal the names and financial details on his list of 500 leading clients as well as the funds he had made available to political parties and politicians. The blackmail attempt went disastrously wrong.

Sindona was sentenced to 25 years in the United States, then extradited to face trial in Italy. In 1986, he was given a life sentence for the murder of Giorgio Ambrosoli. Two days later, Sindona was brought a cup of coffee laced with cyanide and died immediately.

Fraudulent dealings
International financier Michele Sindona laundered money for the Mafia and engaged in large-scale fraudulent financial deals. He was given a life sentence for the murder of Giorgio Ambrosoli, who had been assigned to investigate his dealings.

The roots of the conflict between these two groups were social as well as economic. The Palermo clans regarded the Corleonese with a mixture of fear and contempt, as peasant upstarts attempting to move into their territory. They saw themselves as guarding the traditions of the "true" Mafia.

Leggio and Riina had been planning to take control of the Cupola and thus Cosa Nostra for years. They were able to do deals and form partnerships with "men of honor" from other families without their bosses' permission because narcotics were not seen as a traditional Mafia trade.

In 1972, and again in 1975, Riina undermined the authority of Bontate and Inzerillo by two kidnappings that struck directly at their political connections, and showed that they did not have the authority to protect their allies. Then, in 1978, Riina had Gaetano Badalamenti dismissed as head of the Cupola, and ejected from the Mafia, a very rare example of this punishment, made all the more puzzling because Badalamenti

Mafia arrests
Italian police escort young Mafia suspects. In the early 1980s a vicious war broke out between rival Palermo Mafia clans.

Politician under pressure
Flaminio Piccoli, secretary of the Christian Democratic Party, answering questions during a news conference in Rome in June 1981. Most questions concerned the Masonic lodge P2 directed by Licio Gelli.

was allowed to live. Riina's position was strengthened as a result. The new head of the Cupola was Michele "The Pope" Greco (see p61), who was a puppet in the hands of the Corleone clan.

Riina ordered the deaths of Bontate and Inzerillo after hearing that they were considering his assassination, and that they had been skimming the proceeds of heroin sales. Bontate was shot with a Kalashnikov on April 23, 1981. The same gun was used to kill Inzerillo three weeks later. The purge went on for two years. The immediate and Mafia families of both men and anyone suspected of being loyal to them were murdered. The Bontate family, which had 120 members at the start of 1981, was virtually exterminated.

Riina's Rise to Power

Riina's Cosa Nostra was a dictatorship, with power centralized in the Cupola, still headed by Greco but now made up of Riina's allies. Riina dealt directly with the political world, receiving Italian prime minister Giuliano Andreotti on a visit to Palermo like a head of state. The "Mafia kiss" they exchanged on this occasion returned to haunt Andreotti later (see p72). Riina had destroyed the Mafia clans' independence along with their

traditions and values. Powerless to take revenge as their code demanded, "men of honor" for the first time began to break the code of *omertà* and speak to the authorities. The first and most important of these men, known as *pentiti* (penitents), was Tommaso Buscetta, one of the highest-ranking "men of honor" left alive after the 1981–83 Mafia war. His confessor was assistant prosecutor Giovanni Falcone.

Mafia Initiation Rites

Buscetta described Mafia initiation rites, remarkably similar to 19th-century descriptions and to those described by Joe Valacchi (*see p163*). Initiation consisted of a blood oath and an oath of obedience. The aspiring member had to be presented for initiation by at least three "men of honor" from the family. Blood was drawn from the initiate's finger and sprinkled on the picture of a saint, which was set on fire and passed from hand to hand while the initiate swore to keep the code of Cosa Nostra, which he was bound to for life. His *cosca* was his new family, and he could not switch allegiance.

Membership was only open to Sicilian men. Anyone related to someone in law enforcement or whose father had been killed by a "man of honor" was barred. The initiate had to have killed a man. A high standard of sexual morality was demanded, as the Mafia believed in the sanctity of the family (although a discreet mistress was tolerated). Adultery with fellow member's wife was punishable by death. Women and children were not to be killed. (This rule did

CASE STUDY

Sicilian Supergrasses

Tommaso Buscetta was the first high-ranking *mafioso* to become a *pentito* (penitent) or turn state's evidence. His testimony in U.S. and Italian courts led to the convictions of hundreds of mafiosi and revealed the command structure of Cosa Nostra. Until then, the authorities had denied the existence of a Mafia organization, preferring a model of many unrelated groups, incapable of organizing themselves.

Buscetta, a native of Palermo, killed for the La Barbera brothers. After being convicted of a double murder in 1963, he fled abroad and lived in the United States and Brazil. Anti-Mafia judge Giovanni Falcone flew to Brazil to interview Buscetta, who had lost two sons and other relatives in the Mafia war of 1981–83. Surprisingly, Buscetta agreed to talk, largely because of the rapport he struck up with Falcone. His testimony led to the arrest of 464 "men of honor," most of whom were convicted in the first maxi-trial.

Buscetta only testified against the allies of his enemies, the Corleonese. Other enemies of the Corleonese who became important *pentiti* included Salvatore Contorno, a soldier in the Bontate family, who began to talk when he learned that Buscetta had broken the vow of *omertà*. His testimony led to 120 arrests. Francesco Marino Mannoia was the first *pentito* from the Corleonese side. He became a *pentito* after Riina killed his brother, a leading hitman for the Corleonese. The floodgates opened after Falcone and Borsellino died, with more than 600 *pentiti* coming forward. Remarkably, one of the most recent "men of honor" to turn state's evidence is Antonino Giuffrè, head of the Cupola.

Compromising positions
Italian prime minister Giulio Andreotti on a television show, with screens showing the supergrass Tommaso Buscetta in court behind him. Andreotti was later accused of having Mafia connections.

not last; the Corleonese frequently punished their enemies by wiping out their families.)

Strict rules applied to Mafia killings: they had to be cleared by the *capofamiglia* and carried out on the *cosca*'s territory, and only for certain specified reasons. Although the Mafia code forbade the

killing of non-Mafia members, this rule was clearly never taken very seriously.

"Distinguished Corpses"

Leggio's drive for absolute power over Cosa Nostra went in tandem with a campaign of terror against the state. The series of murders of politicians, judges, prosecutors, and journalists between 1979 and 1992 proclaimed the power of Cosa Nostra and showed how powerless the Italian state was to protect its servants. Both strategies were ultimately counterproductive, however. The

Death on the street
A victim of the Mafia shot dead in his car. Until the mid-1980s it was almost impossible for the police to prosecute Mafia crimes because Sicilians stuck to the code of *omertà*, which prevented them revealing any information to the authorities.

murderous rise of the Corleonese produced the *pentiti* whose confessions led to the maxi-trials of 1986 (*see below*). The *pentiti* were almost all men whose families had been killed by the Corleonese. The attacks on politicians and prosecutors led to the military occupation of Sicily, the fall of Andreotti, and in 1993, the dissolution of the Christian Democratic Party.

The first person to be killed was Michele Reina, president of the Christian Democrats in Palermo province. Next were Boris Giuliano, deputy police chief of Palermo, and Judge Cesare Terranova, who had presided over the Mafia maxi-trial of 1963. There followed a long list of *cadaveri eccellenti* ("distinguished corpses") that included both brave and resolute men who were killed for opposing the power of the Mafia and those like Salvatore Lima (*see p63*) for whom La Cosa Nostra no longer had a use. During 1981, the Corleonese were occupied with the elimination of the Bontate and Inzerillo families and their supporters, but the litany of distinguished corpses began again in 1982, with the assassination of Pio La Torre, head of the Italian Communist Party in Sicily and an anti-Mafia commission member. General Alberto Della Chiesa, who had arrested Lucciano Leggio while still a lieutenant in 1964, and who had since risen to become prefect of Palermo, was killed in September, along with his wife and driver.

CASE STUDY

The 1986 Palermo Maxi-trials

In June 1984, Falcone extradited Tommaso Buscetta from Brazil and issued 366 arrest warrants on the basis of his testimony. In December the Naples–Milan train was blown up, killing 16 people – a clear message from the Mafia warning the state to back off. Then *mafioso* Salvatore Contorno decided to cooperate with the authorities leading to further arrest warrants. Since many of the accused were fugitives, a special police squad was detailed to hunt them down. Headed by Giuseppe Montana, the squad captured eight fugitives before Montana was killed. Within a few weeks, Antonio Cassarà, the deputy chief of the Palermo investigative squad, was shot dead. Falcone and Borsellino were quickly spirited away to the island of Asinara to protect them while they prepared the indictments for the largest Mafia trial in history.

CAGED DEFENDANTS

The Palermo maxi-trials began on February 10, 1986. There were 475 defendants, 117 of whom were fugitives. The defendants were held in 30 high-security cages along the walls of the bunker courtroom. The trial lasted 22 months, and took place amid growing public support for the prosecutors and constant attempts to undermine their authority from the media and politicians. There were even pro-Mafia demonstrations and attacks on the proceedings by the archbishop of Palermo. Michele "The Pope" Greco, head of the Cupola, was charged with 78 murders. Lucciano Leggio was absolved, his counsel arguing that since he had been in Ucciardone Prison since 1974, he could not be held responsible for murders committed after that date. Greco and 343 other defendants were convicted.

One of the great achievements of the maxi-trials was to affirm the rule of law in a democracy. The defendants' rights and legal processes were scrupulously respected. The other great achievement was the discovery of the existence and structure of Cosa Nostra and the proof that it was highly organized. The testimony of more than 1,000 witnesses revealed a worldwide network of arms and drugs trafficking. The anti-Mafia pool began gathering evidence for the next maxi-trial, to be devoted to the Mafia in Palermo province. Eighty defendants were indicted.

Yet the pool's work was systematically undone. In 1991, Italian Supreme Court judge Corrado Carnevale, known as *l'ammazza sentenze* ("the sentence killer"), began to throw out the convictions. He overturned Greco's life sentence and released Antonio Salamone, a Cupola member who had been instrumental in setting up cocaine trafficking in South America, on grounds of his age and ill health. Salamone left immediately for Brazil.

By the time Carnevale was done, only 60 of the original 344 convictions were still in force. Policemen who had worked with Falcone and Borsellino were transferred from their posts and documents were mysteriously mislaid. As it became evident that official support was being withdrawn from the investigations, colleagues ceased to cooperate.

Gradually, Falcone and Borsellino found themselves isolated and under attack. A mixture of bureaucratic inertia, professional envy, inefficiency and political obstruction made their positions increasingly untenable. "I am a dead man," Falcone told a group of fellow magistrates.

In the 1987 elections, Cosa Nostra notified the Christian Democrats of its displeasure for having allowed the maxi-trial to take place by switching its captive Sicilian votes to the Socialist and Radical parties. In return, these parties opposed Falcone's investigations, forcing a national referendum to reduce the powers of the judiciary. All of the major political parties, in the name of supporting defendants' rights, colluded in this move.

Caged criminals
The 1986 Mafia maxi-trials were held in a specially constructed high-security bunker next to Ucciardone Prison in Palermo. Mafia suspects were held in cages, as they had been during Mussolini's Mafia purges of the 1920s.

Buscetta arrested
Mafioso Tommaso Buscetta arrives in Rome in December 1972 to face a 14-year jail term. His testimony against other Mafia members led to the maxi-trials of 1986.

had divulged little on the relationships between Cosa Nostra and politics).

Falcone now had the chance to penetrate the heart of Cosa Nostra's power. Acting on Calderone's testimony, he issued 160 arrest warrants. Then the Italian supreme court, under Corrado Carnevale, ruled that the individual cases should be prosecuted in 12 different provincial jurisdictions, because there was no evidence of a controlling Cosa Nostra commission. In other words, the supreme court rejected the findings of the anti-Mafia pool, and the testimony of the witnesses in the first maxi-trial. All but 11 of those arrested were released. Carnevale was later given a six-year jail sentence for colluding with the Mafia in 2001 but, on appeal, the conviction was overturned.

The Italian parliament then promulgated a reformed penal code that made it more difficult for judges to order arrests and hold prisoners in jail pending trial. Even more ominously, the new code contained a provision under which prosecutors could be held liable for errors, opening a whole new field for defense lawyers to have convictions delayed or overturned. Correctly gauging the state's weakness and its lack of support for the anti-Mafia pool, Cosa Nostra began adding to the list of "distinguished corpses" beginning on January 12 with Giuseppe Insalco, a former mayor of Palermo who had revealed links between the government and Cosa Nostra. In September 1988 they killed three more prominent anti-Mafia figures. In November the Italian Supreme

Capture of "The Beast"
Totò "The Beast" Riina after his arrest in Palermo on January 15, 1993. He had been a fugitive for more than 20 years before being arrested six months after the murder of the anti-Mafia judge, Giovanni Falcone. Riina had ordered the assassination.

In July 1983, chief prosecutor Rocco Chinnici issued a warrant for Michele Greco's arrest for Della Chiesa's murder. He was blown up by a car bomb 22 days later. His replacement, Antonino Caponetto, formed an anti-Mafia pool in November of which Giovanni Falcone and Paolo Borsellino were members. Their courageous work led to the maxi-trials of 1986 (see p69). When Camponetto retired, the post went to the inexperienced Antonino Meli, who severely hampered the pool's work. Although discouraged, Falcone and Borsellino continued their investigations. A new *pentito*, Antonino Calderone began to divulge important information about the provincial Mafia and its political links. His most startling information had to do with Cosa Nostra's links to Salvatore Lima (Buscetta

CASE STUDY

The Murder of Giovanni Falcone

A courageous judge
Giovanni Falcone, a native of Palermo, and his wife, also a judge, knew the huge risks involved in prosecuting the Mafia. A previous attempt to kill him in 1987 had failed.

The murder of Giovanni Falcone shocked Italy. He had become a symbol of hope and the possibility of reform. The public regarded him as a martyr, and many suspected government complicity in his murder. A strike was called in Sicily. The Italian parliament declared a day of mourning and suspended its sessions until after the funeral. Mafia prisoners in Ucciardone Prison rejoiced, but for almost the first time Palermo citizens openly displayed their grief and anger.

On May 23, 1992, Falcone and his wife, Francesca Morvillo, flew to Palermo from Rome on a government plane. They had been scheduled to leave a day earlier, but changed their departure date at the last minute. They were met at Palermo Airport by three police cars and seven bodyguards. The added protection of helicopter surveillance, formerly standard practice, had recently been withdrawn to cut costs. Falcone decided to drive his own car, his wife beside him, while his driver took the back seat. When the convoy reached

Capaci, a large charge of plastic explosive placed under the highway was detonated by remote control. The three policemen in the lead car were instantly killed. Falcone and his wife were seriously injured, and both died later that day. Their driver and the occupants of the rear escort car survived.

The murders of Falcone and his friend and colleague in the battle against organized crime, Paolo Borsellino, led to the formation of the Italian equivalent of the FBI, the *Direzione Investigativa Anti-Mafia* (DIA) and the passage of a witness protection law. Superlative police work, helped by increasing numbers of *pentiti*, identified the killers. In total, 18 "men of honor" were involved in the murder, which was ordered by Totò Riina. He was finally arrested six months later.

Murder location
The remains of Falcone's car after the assassination on the main road near the town of Capaci.

Court under Carnevale overturned most of the 1986 maxi-trial convictions. Italian organized crime was extending into new areas. Not just Cosa Nostra, but also other crime organizations – the Camorra, the 'Ndrangheta, the Stidda, and the Sacra Corona Unita – were expanding their operations. Arrests for serious crimes fell, while the crime rate rose more than 50 percent. Cosa Nostra was now firmly ensconced in cities such as Milan and Bologna, buying construction companies and banks with profits from the drugs trade and then bidding for lucrative public works contracts in Sicily through legitimate businesses. All over Sicily, judges presiding over regional Mafia trials were intimidated or bribed. *Pentiti*, realizing that the state would not protect them, retracted their testimony and potential informers

hesitated. Buscetta and Contorno's information was by now out of date, and no new informants were forthcoming.

The fall of the Berlin Wall in 1989 had seismic effects on Italy. For almost 50 years, the Christian Democratic Party had justified its grip on power by the danger of the Communist menace. The break up of the

> ## "There was no Mafia war in Palermo. There was a massacre."
>
> Gaspare Mutolo, Mafia informer

Soviet Union removed this threat. Cosa Nostra realized that its traditional service to the state, the delivery of the Sicilian vote, was no longer required. Moreover, the collapse of communism coincided with growing public indignation at government corruption in Italy. Magistrates in Milan

Public anger

A demonstration against the Mafia in Sicily in 1986, the year of the maxi-trials in Palermo resulting from the work of the anti-Mafia judges Giovanni Falcone and Paolo Borsellino. The public were increasingly concerned about the Mafia's power.

were beginning to investigate the culture of bribery and corruption that for so long had been tacitly accepted but was now without any justification.

In 1991, Judge Carnevale ordered the release of Michele Greco and 41 other defendants convicted in the first maxi-trial. The new justice minister Claudio Martelli quickly passed a decree ordering their re-arrest and on January 31, 1992, the Supreme Court, no longer under Carnevale, confirmed the original sentences. This decision, justifying all Falcone and Borsellino's work, was a direct blow to Riina's authority. His supporters could no

Giulio Andreotti

Giulio Andreotti dominated Italian politics for 50 years. Seven times prime minister, he held many other ministerial posts and was a member of parliament continuously after 1945. In 1991, he was made senator for life. Born in Rome in 1919, by age 28 he gained his first important public office, under-secretary to De Gasperi, the first postwar prime minister. Italy's proportional representation system lent itself to the exchange of patronage for votes. Andreotti, whose faction in the Christian Democratic Party was supported largely by the Sicilian vote, was accused of colluding with the Mafia.

Andreotti became prime minister in 1972. His was the shortest government in Italian history, lasting only nine days. His second term coincided with the worst crises in postwar Italy, the collapse of the economy and the rise of the Red Brigades, a left wing terrorist group.

Andreotti's last term as prime minister began in 1991, coinciding with the *mani puliti* ("Clean Hands") trials. This reform movement led to the incrimination of many politicians, but not Andreotti. However, in 1995, he was tried in Palermo for collusion with the Mafia. The *pentito* Balduccio Di Maggio testified that Andreotti had exchanged a Mafia kiss indicating mutual respect with Totò Riina, head of the Cupola and a fugitive from justice. In 1999, Andreotti was absolved, then tried again and finally absolved in November 2003.

Dates 1919–
Details Giulio Andreotti led a powerful faction of the Christian Democratic Party for many years. He has been accused several times of Mafia associations, but they have never been proved in court.

destabilize the institutional political structure and give the *coup de grace* to a dying political class, creating a favorable climate for the emergence of a new political group more inclined to dialogue with Cosa Nostra."

On January 15, 1993, Riina was finally arrested in Palermo. He had been a fugitive for 20 years, most of them spent in hiding in Palermo. He was betrayed by Balduccio Di Maggio, who had been until then his most loyal follower. His place at the head of the Cupola was taken by Giovanni Brusca.

Riina's arrest took place against the background of a movement for political reform, driven by an increasingly angry public and carried out by magistrates following in the footsteps of Falcone and

longer count on his political connections to keep them out of jail or have their sentences reduced. To demonstrate his power to punish political "traitors," Riina struck at the key figures in Cosa Nostra's criminal–political nexus. On March 16, 1992, his gunmen killed Salvatore Lima, Cosa Nostra's link to the Christian Democratic Party. Cosa Nostra's conduit to Lima, Ignazio Salvo, was killed on September 8.

Shortly after Lima's murder, on May 23, Giovanni Falcone, his wife Francesca Morvillo, and three police agents were blown up at Carpaci as they drove into Palermo. On July 19, Falcone's colleague, Borsellino, and five bodyguards were blown up by a car bomb placed outside his mother's house in Palermo.

Four days after the death of Borsellino, Prime Minister Giuliano Amato sent 7,000 troops to Sicily, in effect proclaiming martial law. He immediately authorized the witness protection program that Falcone and Borsellino had been urging for years. The result was an astonishing wave of more than 600 *pentiti*. One of these new informers, Maurizio Avola, explained Cosa Nostra's aims: "To hold the state to ransom in order to force it to revoke the laws allowing the testimony of *pentiti* and top security prison for the bosses, and at the same time

Head of the Cupola arrested
The arrest of Mafia boss Giovanni Brusca on May 2, 1996. Nicknamed *u Verru*, (the Pig) he was notorious for killing an 11-year-old boy after holding him prisoner for two years, and then dissolving the body in acid.

Borsellino. It began in Milan, in early 1992, when a prominent Socialist politician was arrested for bribery. This was the beginning of *Operazione Mani Puliti*, (Operation Clean Hands), a drive against the culture of bribery and political corruption, led by the magistrate Antonio di Pietro. It snowballed into a massive investigation into corruption at every level of Italian society, involving not only politicians but state and private industries. The Socialist foreign minister was indicted for bribery then, on February 11, 1993, Bettino Craxi, former prime minister and head of the Socialist Party, was indicted on the same charges and forced to resign. On March 27, Giulio Andreotti was indicted for "Mafia associations" and later faced trial for complicity in the murder of the journalist Mino Pecorelli. A referendum was held in April which abolished the system of proportional representation that had engendered so many abuses over the years, in favor of a simple majority system.

Desperate Strategy

Cosa Nostra's response to these dramatic events was a terrorist attack on the state. On May 27, 1993, a car packed with explosive was detonated by remote control in front of the Uffizi Gallery in Florence, killing five bystanders, destroying the Torre del Pulci, and damaging art works in the gallery. Another bomb planted in the Boboli Gardens failed to go off. The same day two more bombs exploded in Rome, damaging two churches. Cosa Nostra was seeking to dominate rather than coexist with the state; clearly a strategy born of desperation.

In July, the Christian Democratic Party formally disbanded, regrouping as the Popular Party. But the new political forces in the country were represented by Silvio Berlusconi and his Forza Italia party and the small but significant Lombard League. The political landscape of Italy had changed out of recognition. The task facing Cosa Nostra was how to survive having lost its political protection and traditional code of behavior.

That the code had truly ceased to be relevant is shown by the behavior of Giovanni Brusca, who was arrested on May 20, 1996. Brusca commanded the military wing of the Corleonese. He detonated the explosion that killed Falcone and orchestrated the bomb attacks on Florence and Rome. When he appeared before the judges, he turned state's evidence and revealed the location of Pietro Aglieri, his successor at the head of the Cupola. That a "man of honor" who had been head of the Cupola should become a *pentito* shows how the culture of *omertà* had ceased to exist.

Aglieri was arrested on June 6, 1997, in Bagheria, near Palermo. Among other crimes, he had killed Bontate for Lucciano Leggio

Invisible *mafioso*
The only known picture of the head of the Sicilian Mafia, Bernardo Provenzano, who has been in hiding for several decades.

and taken part in the killings of Lima, Falcone, and Borsellino. He had planned to abandon all political connections, and concentrate on purely criminal activities, such as extortion and drug dealing, forging stronger links with other crime groups. He clearly no longer trusted politicians.

The current head of the Sicilian Mafia is Bernardo Provenzano, whose whereabouts are unknown. He has been a fugitive for almost 30 years.

Cultural vandals
The devastation caused by the detonation of a car bomb at the Uffizi Gallery in Florence in May 1993, which killed five people and damaged the famous art gallery.

ITALY

ITALIAN CRIME GROUP NAMES

The most likely derivation of "Camorra" is from *morra*, a gambling game. The game is moderated by a *capo*, hence "Camorra" from *capo morra*. The word first appears in a document dated 1735, referring to gambling dens in Naples. "'Ndrangheta" is said to be derived from a Greek word meaning "heroism." The name "Sacra Corona Unita" (United Sacred Crown) has a religious symbolism, referring to the rosary (*corona*). "Stidda" is Sicilian dialect for "star." The name comes from the star tattooed on the right hand, used by members as a sign of recognition.

TERRITORY

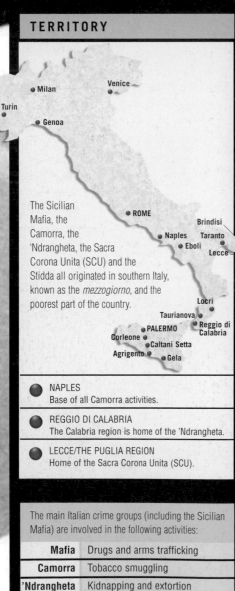

The Sicilian Mafia, the Camorra, the 'Ndrangheta, the Sacra Corona Unita (SCU) and the Stidda all originated in southern Italy, known as the *mezzogiorno*, and the poorest part of the country.

- **NAPLES**
  Base of all Camorra activities.

- **REGGIO DI CALABRIA**
  The Calabria region is home of the 'Ndrangheta.

- **LECCE/THE PUGLIA REGION**
  Home of the Sacra Corona Unita (SCU).

The main Italian crime groups (including the Sicilian Mafia) are involved in the following activities:

Mafia	Drugs and arms trafficking
Camorra	Tobacco smuggling
'Ndrangheta	Kidnapping and extortion
SCU	Drugs and people trafficking
Stidda	Drugs smuggling and prostitution

Other Italian Groups

" The Camorra is cynically and opportunistically present wherever there is something useful to obtain, a service to ensure, or a profitable business to do. It is an army that lives off society, works against society and interacts with it. "

CARLO ALFIERO, CARABINIERI BRIGADIER GENERAL

The Camorra is a crime group based in Naples. Evidence that it is highly structured dates back to 1820, when police found documents on its policies and initiation rites. The Camorra originally controlled the city's prisons, collecting a tax from prisoners as well as a fee from the authorities for keeping order. They also organized gambling and theft in Naples and took a 10 percent cut on all cargo arriving at the docks.

The Camorra played a prominent role in controlling Naples during the campaign for Italian unification in 1860: one member was even made chief of police. However, within a few years, the government had arrested many *camorristi* (Camorra members). By the late 19th century, the Camorra was involved in politics by guaranteeing votes for the Liberal Party. Some *camorristi* emigrated, founding a Camorra branch in Brooklyn, New York.

Postwar Revival

The Camorra almost died out during the fascist era of Benito Mussolini (1922–43), but revived after World War II. The presence of Vito Genovese and "Lucky" Luciano made Naples a magnet for Sicilian criminals, and the city became the smuggling capital of Italy. Smuggling was controlled by the

Naples wharf
A late 19th-century view of Naples, the intellectual and cultural center of southern Italy. The Camorra later turned Naples into the smuggling capital of Italy.

Shoot-out in the street
Family members grieve over the body of Salvatore Valente, the alleged leader of the 'Ndrangheta, the Calabrian-based crime group, lying in a street in Strongoli, Italy, in February, 2000.

Sicilians, but much of the street-level work was carried out by Neapolitans, who became the nucleus of the postwar Camorra. Rural Camorra groups controlled the food supply entering the city, extorting money from both farmers and buyers, and intimidating those who refused to pay up. This was a small-scale racket compared with the activities of the Mafia. However, the tobacco smuggling business transformed the Camorra into an urban organized crime group. The profits from tobacco smuggling were enormous. In 1959, a case of cigarettes

bought in Tangier, Morocco, for $23 could be sold in Europe for $170. Originally a monopoly of Corsican gangs, the network was taken over by the Italians in the 1960s, who drove the last of the Corsicans from Naples in the early 1970s. Today, a network of Camorra groups, each with 30–40 members, controls its own territory. Together they form a kind of parallel government and are intricately interwoven with regional politics

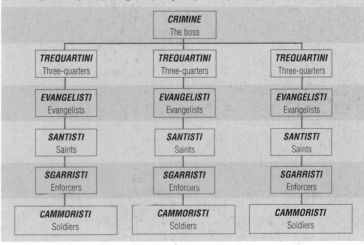

THE SACRA CORONA UNITA

The Sacra Corona Unita, an Italian crime group based in the Puglia region, borrowed elements of its structure from both the Camorra and the 'Ndrangheta. At the top of the Sacra Corona Unita is the boss, the *crimine*. The lowest ranks are composed of *cammoristi* (soldiers), then *sgarristi* (enforcers), *santisti* (saints), *evangelisti* (evangelists) and *trequartini* ("three-quarters").

CRIMINE — The boss		
TREQUARTINI Three-quarters	**TREQUARTINI** Three-quarters	**TREQUARTINI** Three-quarters
EVANGELISTI Evangelists	**EVANGELISTI** Evangelists	**EVANGELISTI** Evangelists
SANTISTI Saints	**SANTISTI** Saints	**SANTISTI** Saints
SGARRISTI Enforcers	**SGARRISTI** Enforcers	**SGARRISTI** Enforcers
CAMMORISTI Soldiers	**CAMMORISTI** Soldiers	**CAMMORISTI** Soldiers

Breakaway Group

In 1970, Raffaele Cutolo founded the New Organized Camorra (NCO) to resist Sicilian Mafia encroachments on Naples and Campania. The NCO was motivated by regional patriotism as well as by profit. Cutolo revived the rules that had governed the Camorra in the 19th century. His organization was hierarchical, centralized, and violent. The NCO specialized in extortion and to a lesser extent cocaine, whereas the Naples Camorra specialized in tobacco and heroin and was moving into construction and real estate. In 1979, Cutolo forced leading tobacco smuggler Michael Zaza to pay him a large sum to be allowed to continue smuggling. The next year, Camorra

groups in Naples united against the NCO, forming the Nuova Famiglia. The two groups fought partly over control of central government funds pouring in for the reconstruction of Campania following the devastating earthquake of November 1980. Over the next two years, the war claimed 500 lives.

In 1983, the police and carabinieri launched a combined operation leading to the arrest of 800 men, 300 of whom were convicted. The power of the NCO was broken, although not the power of the Camorra.

Stolen funds
An earthquake struck Campania in November 1980. The Camorra siphoned off much of the reconstruction funding.

and business. The money stolen from the government's reconstruction funds after the 1980 earthquake – one of the 20th century's great financial scandals – plus profits from the drugs trade were invested in legitimate businesses in Italy, France, and Germany.

'Ndrangheta

The 'Ndrangheta is based in Calabria, the poorest, most crime-ridden region of Italy. Like Sicily, the region has suffered for centuries from a backward economy and government neglect. The Calabrians are suspicious of authority and fiercely loyal to both their extended families and to the code of honor and vendetta.

Mountain hideout
Paramilitary police at the entrance to a tunnel discovered in Plati, near Reggio di Calabria, in July 2002. It led to a complex of tunnels, probably used by the 'Ndrangheta in the Aspromonte Mountains of Calabria.

The 'Ndrangheta originated in the late 19th century. Its precursor was Calabrian banditry. When the railroad between Reggio di Calabria and Eboli was built in the 1880s, the government waged a major offensive against the bandits in the Aspromonte Mountains. The criminals were displaced to the towns and cities. By 1900, family-based criminal gangs were active in many

Calabrian towns. They were the nuclei of the 'Ndrangheta, now the largest and most violent of Italian criminal associations. The group is omnipresent in Calabria, with 4,000 to 6,000 active members.

'Ndrangheta Activities

The basic unit of the 'Ndrangheta is the *'ndrina*, the extended family or clan, which controls a specific quarter of a town or city. The core of the *'ndrina* is composed of blood relatives. The *capobastone* is the head of the family, and commands around 30 members. The *capobastoni* meet once a year at the village of San Luca, in the foothills of the Aspromonte Mountains, or at Locri.

The Sicilian Mafia used the 'Ndrangheta to sell contraband tobacco in the 1960s, but during the 1970s the 'Ndrangheta became powerful enough to shake off its Sicilian connections and develop its own criminal economy, specializing in kidnapping and siphoning off money from state-funded construction projects. The 'Ndrangheta is now heavily into narcotics and tobacco smuggling, arms dealing, and extortion.

The scale of the problem was brought home to the public by a horrifying incident in Taurianova, a town near Reggio di Calabria. The local *'ndrina* beheaded a town councillor, then used his severed head for target practice in the town square. It was the 32nd murder in the small town in two years. A later investigation found that the town had been controlled by the 'Ndrangheta for the Christian Democrats for years. The posts

The fight against smuggling
Customs officers remove contraband cigarettes from a confiscated boat in southern Italy. Smuggling is the main activity of the Sacra Corona Unita crime group based in Puglia.

of mayor and party president had become hereditary in one family, which had grown wealthy by defrauding the health service and taking kickbacks on construction projects.

Sacra Corona Unita

The Sacra Corona Unita (SCU), or United Sacred Crown, was founded in Bari Prison in May 1983 by Giuseppe Rogoli to resist the attempt by a new crime group, Raffaele Cutolo's New Organized Camorra, to move into the region of Puglia. In the late 1970s, the police confiscated the Camorra's fleet and the Tyrrhenian Sea was effectively closed to smugglers. Cutolo turned to the Adriatic, and allied with Puglian crime bosses to form the New Camorra of Puglia.

The 'Ndrangheta and Cosa Nostra were also trying to move into Puglia in the late 1970s. The SCU was determined to protect its territory, especially the Salento Peninsula, from encroachment by other criminal groups. Puglia was divided into territories, corresponding to its major regions: Lecce, Brindisi, and Taranto. The regional bosses quickly became autonomous and in the

1980s were often at war with each other, but they still united against external threats. Today the SCU has about 1,000 members. After the group blew up the law courts in Lecce in 1990, it was officially recognized as a Mafia-type organization. It is dedicated to drug and tobacco smuggling, extortion, arms dealing, gambling, and people trafficking. The Salento Peninsula's strategic position became more important in the 1990s, when the wars in the Balkans closed the overland heroin route to Europe. By 2000, the Salento Peninsula, controlled by the SCU, was the major entry point into Europe for smuggled drugs, arms, and people.

Sicilian Stidda

The Stidda is the most recent and fastest-growing organized crime group in Italy, born in Sicily in the early 1980s and now entrenched in Sicilian cities and northern Italy. The Stidda was formed as a result of leading *mafiosi* Totò Riina's vicious war on the other Mafia families (*see p66*). Soldiers from the losing families, and even disaffected "men of honor" from his own clan, took

refuge in southern Sicily, particularly in the towns of Caltanisetta, Agrigento, and Gela. Here they formed new gangs, gradually coalescing under the leadership of Giuseppe Croce Benvenuto and Salvatore Calafato. Rejecting charismatic leaders and a hierarchical structure, the Stidda offers members quick promotion and a flexible, democratic organization. It may well evolve into the Cosa Nostra of the 21st century.

Female fighters
A woman lies dead after a shoot-out in Naples in May 2002 between women of rival Camorra families, the Cavas and the Grazianos. Three Cava women died.

BRITAIN

THE ORIGIN OF BRITISH GANG NAMES
Often British gangs took their names from their leaders, but some derived from the area where the gang flourished, such as The Dover Road Gang, named for a street in London. However, there have been a number of anomalies: The Brummagem Boys were based in London rather than in Birmingham; and The Forty Thieves took their name from the book *Tales from the Arabian Nights*.

TERRITORY

Organized crime groups are based in most of Britain's major towns and cities. Recently there has been a steady rise in gang-related gun crime. Britain is also used as a base by many international gangs.

- **LONDON:** Leading center of all organized crime activity in Britain, and arrival point for most drugs.
- **GLASGOW:** Central distribution center for drugs in Scotland. Long history of gang warfare.
- **MANCHESTER:** High incidence of gun crime related to the increased heroin supply in the 1980s.
- **BIRMINGHAM:** Leading gangs include the Burger Bar Boys and the Johnson Crew. It is also the base for many Jamaican Yardie gangs.

Gun crime is usually gang-related. Below are the serious crimes involving guns committed in Greater Manchester from April 2001 to March 2002.

Murder	11
Serious woundings	84
Violent incidents	639
Armed robberies	785
Burglaries	50

Organized Crime in Britain

" So that big, wide, handsome, and oh, so highly profitable black market walked into our ever open arms. "

BILLY HILL, BRITISH GANGSTER

Organized crime in Britain evolved slowly throughout the 20th century. Unlike Prohibition in the United States, there was no piece of major social engineering that transformed it into an industry until World War II (1939–45) provided the greatest single opportunity – the black market – for the underworld to both expand their existing markets and create new ones. Just as middle-class Americans would not have thought of consorting with criminals until Prohibition, the war narrowed the class boundaries. With dozens of prohibitive rules being made by the British government, here were opportunities beyond the underworld's wildest dreams.

The Sabini Brothers

From 1918 until the outbreak of World War II in 1939, the development of organized crime in London was largely in the hands of the Sabini brothers. The Sabinis were half Scottish and half Italian, and came from the Saffron Hill area near Holborn. Led by Charles Ullano Sabini, known as "Darby," the five brothers controlled several racing tracks, in theory protecting bookmakers, but in practice extorting money from them.

Soho scene
A Soho street in 1966 with an adult book shop and live sex shows, evidence of the postwar pornography industry in which London's gangsters were heavily involved.

The streets of London
A group of Italian men on Saffron Hill Street in the 1930s. This was the neighborhood of London run by the Sabini crime family.

Throughout the 1920s, the Sabinis fought a rival gang leader, Fred Kimber and his Brummagem Boys, for control of the lucrative racing tracks. They eventually reached an agreement that gave the Sabinis control of the southern racing tracks. The Sabinis then expanded their empire to the nightclubs and gambling dens of London, along with the occasional robbery, such as the theft of gold bullion from Croydon Airport in March 1936.

During the late 1920s and early 1930s, Darby Sabini gradually lost control of these ventures as rival factions began to gain power. A series of pitched street battles followed, culminating in the celebrated 1936 Battle of Lewes (recalled in Graham Greene's novel *Brighton Rock*), after which another division of territory was agreed.

The arrangement lasted until the Sabinis were interned under wartime regulations in 1940, when Italy joined the conflict on the side of Germany.

The Forty Thieves

Women played a supporting role in what passed as organized crime in Britain in the 1920s and 1930s. They provided alibis, negotiated bail, and sheltered wanted men or even escaped prisoners, but generally they did not take an active part in crime. One of the longest-running British organized gangs, the "Forty Thieves," was an exception.

From the 1890s until the 1960s, the Forty Thieves, a relatively structured female gang of shoplifters based in South London, flourished. In pairs and groups, the women would raid London stores. Women aspiring to join the gang would have to wait for vacancies arising from marriage or death. New recruits were then trained and served an "apprenticeship." The leader of the gang was known as the "Queen." Leadership changed hands with the imprisonment of members. Two famously long-running Queens were Alice Diamond and Maggie Hill, the sister of the gangster Billy Hill, who was a major crime boss in the London underworld of the 1950s.

Drug dealing in Britain at this time was largely run by Chinese criminal gangs and was relatively low-key. Prostitution – never of great interest to British criminals – was in the hands of French gangs until shortly before World War II, when it was taken over by the Maltese-born Messina brothers. These activities were the street-level end of organized crime. There were also many fraud operations in this period, but there is no real evidence of widespread cooperation between individual operators.

Organized Crime in World War II

Shortages and the rationing of essential goods in World War II provided an opening for British organized crime to supply items illegally. The war saw the expansion of the black market, bringing more people into contact with criminals, as otherwise law-abiding citizens were prepared to deal with blackmarketeers to obtain extra food, clothes, cigarettes, and gasoline coupons. Government offices were raided for ration books.

Billy Hill

BIOGRAPHY

Billy Hill was born in 1911 into a London family of criminals and began his career as a housebreaker in the late 1920s, moving on to "smash-and grab" raids on jewellers and furriers in the 1930s. At the outbreak of World War II in 1939, he entered the black market, supplying rationed foods and gasoline. He also provided forged documents for deserting servicemen.

After the war, he was charged with warehouse-breaking and fled to South Africa. Involved in a fight for control of the Johannesburg clubs, he was charged with assault and returned to Britain once more, where he served time in prison.

On his release, he opened a series of clubs with fellow crime boss Jack Spot. He also executed two spectacular robberies. The first, of a post office van in 1952, cleared more than £250,000. The second, two years later, £40,000. In addition, Hill organized the smuggling of cigarettes into Britain from Tangier, Morocco, where his girlfriend Gypsy ran a nightclub.

After a series of feuds in the 1950s with Spot, and the subsequent court cases, Hill more or less retired and contented himself with financing the illegal operations of other gangland figures. He did, however, run a club in the fashionable Sunningdale area of Surrey in the 1970s. A very wealthy man, he died of natural causes in early 1984. He was, perhaps, the nearest Britain has ever had to a criminal mastermind.

Dates 1911–1984
Details British gangster Billy Hill was a major figure in the London underworld, and was responsible for organizing criminal gangs during World War II and in the postwar period.

Crime opportunity
A poster urges British men to join the ARP (Air Raid Precautions) service during World War II. The unit was used as a cover by criminal gangs.

German bombing provided an opportunity for looting and thieves dressed as air raid wardens were often inadvertently assisted by members of the general public to clear stock from damaged stores.

Seeing the opportunities, people who would not normally commit crime helped

Wartime London
The back streets of London during World War II were the preserve of blackmarketeers, where anything could be obtained for the right price.

CASE STUDY

Brothers in Crime

Two families dominated crime in London in the 1960s. The Richardsons, brothers Charles and Eddie, led a South London gang that had pretensions to legitimacy. The Krays, Ronnie and Reggie, controlled a far less sophisticated operation, first in the East End and then in Soho.

THE RICHARDSONS

Eddie Richardson was born in 1932 and Charles two years later. Their first crimes as children were so-called "jump-ups" (stealing goods from the backs of trucks). Even at this stage Charlie Richardson was seen as an organizer and businessman. At the age of 19, he heard of a scrapyard for sale in Peckham and he and Eddie went into business. Shortly afterward he was convicted of receiving stolen metal, given two years' probation, and sent into the army. He returned to Peckham after World War II, and by 1956 owned five scrapyards. He also began to open drinking clubs. In May 1960, he was charged with receiving stolen metal and fled to Canada, where he built up another successful business. He sold it and returned to England, where he was acquitted of the receiving charge. Now was the time to restructure his empire. One of his drinking clubs burned down but with the insurance money it was reopened. Richardson then found he was being cheated by a series of conmen.

As retribution, he and his brother, along with "Mad" Frankie Fraser, held "kangaroo courts," where punishment was meted out. By this time the gang's scams included gaming machines, diamond smuggling, and a ticket swindle at the car park at Heathrow airport.

Fatally, Fraser and Eddie Richardson were invited to protect Mr Smith's, a club in Catford, and on March 9, 1966, a fight broke out there with rival South London interests. Dickie Hart, a Kray associate, was killed. Fraser was charged with murder. Now the men who claimed they had been tortured during the mock-trials approached the police. Charlie Richardson and almost all the members of his gang were arrested on July 30, 1966. In the subsequent trial he received 25 years. Eddie Richardson and Frankie Fraser, who had been acquitted of murder, received shorter sentences. Eddie Richardson was released in 1976. In 1990, he received a further 25 years after being convicted of drug smuggling. Charlie Richardson was released in 1984 and resumed his legitimate interests.

THE KRAYS

The Kray twins, Ronnie and Reggie were born in the East End of London in October 1933. Both of them boxed professionally and were used by Jack Spot as bodyguards. Then they acquired a series of clubs. By 1959, when Ronnie was released from a three-year sentence for causing grievous bodily harm, "the Firm," as their gang was known, was taking shape. Protection money was taken from drinking clubs and nightclubs in the West End. Later the Krays forcibly took over fashionable Esmeralda's Barn in Knightsbridge. By 1965, they were taking protection money from between a half and a third of all illegal gaming clubs in London.

For a time their organization was run on the lines of a company, with board meetings in which club managers handed over profits. However, 1964 saw their empire threatened. The brothers failed to keep a low profile and began to mix with celebrities. Ronnie Kray was photographed with influential British politician Lord Boothby. Although the photo remained unpublished, a newspaper, *The Sunday Mirror,* called it "the picture we dare not print," intimating an unhealthy relationship between the two men. The paper had to pay £40,000 to Boothby and apologized to Kray.

The following year the Kray's relations with the Richardsons came under increasing strain. The Krays had been dealing in stolen bonds and were fearful the Richardsons would try to move in on their position. There was also trouble over profit-sharing from a pornographic film racket. On a personal level, small time criminal George Cornell insulted Ronnie Kray in a nightclub. On March 9, 1965, Cornell was shot point blank by Ronnie Kray in the Blind Beggar public house.

In December 1965, the Krays organized the escape of Frank Mitchell, known as the Mad Axeman, from Dartmoor Prison in something of a publicity stunt, but when he later refused to surrender to the police, they had him killed. The twins had by now become increasingly erratic and had fallen out with their financial adviser Leslie Payne, paying a fringe member of the Firm, Jack "The Hat" McVitie, to kill him. He failed, but kept the money and boasted of his prowess. In turn he was stabbed to death by Reggie Kray on October 28, 1967. The following year a major police investigation turned Leslie Payne into an informer and arrests followed. Witnesses came forward to give evidence about the Cornell killing. The Krays were convicted of his murder and that of McVitie. On March 8, 1969, they were jailed for life. They were never released, both dying in prison.

> # "I have never felt a moment's regret."
> Reggie Kray

Crime celebrity
"Mad" Frankie Fraser was an enforcer for the Richardson gang. He now makes a comfortable pension from "true crime" memoirs and personal appearances.

Ronnie and Reggie
The Krays in 1965. They were the most notorious British gangsters of their generation, wielding enormous power in the London underworld.

The Krays on film
A still from the 1990 British film *The Krays,* which starred the real-life twins, Martin (left) and Gary Kemp. The film stressed the Krays' claim that they "kept the peace" in East London and that violence was restricted to "their own kind."

themselves. In 1943, thefts from railroad stations exceeded £1 million (£40 million today), and in 1944, the figure doubled. A new generation of criminals was born.

Criminal Cooperation

During the war, there was more cooperation among criminals throughout the country. Hill's later associate, the Jewish gangster Jack Spot, went north to Manchester and Leeds to advise and assist local criminals. Any city with docks was a particular target for thieves and blackmarketeers. Theft from military stores took place throughout the war, and whole consignments of razor blades and cigarettes simply disappeared.

The arrival of troops from overseas provided more work for prostitutes and those in the vice rackets. In turn, the ranks of professional criminals swelled with deserters from the armed forces, all of whom had to exist without a proper job. They needed false identity cards to survive and so, in addition to forged ration books, a market developed in counterfeit papers. British organized crime came into its own.

At the end of the 1940s, Billy Hill and Jack Spot transformed the structure of the London gangs.

The development of crime in postwar Britain has been described as an explosion. Hill realized that an association with senior police officers was essential to a successful criminal career. Hill and Spot controlled British horseracing courses and illegal gambling and drinking clubs in Soho in an increasingly uneasy partnership for the next 10 years. The Hill–Spot association deteriorated after a knife fight in Soho in

> # "All that 'King of the Underworld' thing. That was my mistake... publicity."
> Jack Spot

August 1955 between Spot and Hill's right hand man, Albert Dimes. Spot then lost control of his racecourse pitches to rival gangs. Now a spent force, Hill retired a rich man, and control of Soho passed to the Nash brothers of North London.

The Expansion of Organized Crime

In the postwar years, police took action against the prostitution empire controlled by the Maltese-born Messina brothers,

who were imprisoned and then deported. Control of prostitution in London passed to other Maltese immigrants, who first ran girls in the East End before moving on to Soho. The passing of the Street Offenses Act in 1957 cleared prostitutes from the streets. From then on, they were forced to work from apartments rented to them at exorbitant rates by criminal gangs . London's pornography business also began to grow and develop in the Soho district. During the 1960s, the British motorway network was developed, which enabled criminals to move about the country with speed. Changes in the law allowed gaming clubs to be set up. With them came links to U.S. organized crime. Albert Dimes, for example, became the British representative of Angelo Bruno's Philadelphia Mafia family. The British police acted and several suspects, including the U.S. movie star George Raft, then fronting the Colony Club in London's Mayfair, were expelled. The 1960s also saw the rise and fall of Britain's two most notorious crime families: the Richardsons and the Krays (*see box, p83*).

Scottish Gangsters

Crime in Glasgow, Scotland, followed the same pattern as that in London, with the exception that there were many more protection gangs based on Catholic and Protestant factions. Loan-sharking was always a traditional feature of Glasgow, and safebreaking was a speciality of Scottish criminals, based on experience with explosives in Scottish coalmines.

In the 1950s and 1960s, Glasgow was originally controlled by Mendl Morris, who owned a string of public houses and clubs. His mantle passed to his protégé Arthur Thompson, a safebreaker who built a crime empire. He is also said to have been an agent of British Intelligence (MI5), and therefore to an extent protected against the law. More recently, with the impact of drugs, Scottish criminals have established bases and homes in Spain, and are now linking up with European criminals to import illicit narcotics.

"The Great Train Robbery"
Ronald Biggs (left with police) was one of the British gang who stole £2.5 million from a mail train in 1963 in what was known as "The Great Train Robbery." Most of the gang were caught and jailed.

Media frenzy
The Great Train Robbery fascinated the British public. Some of the gang members became media celebrities.

CASE STUDY

The Jamaican Yardies and Asian Gangs in Britain

The Yardies came to Britain from Jamaica in the 1980s (*see pp*180–181). These criminal gangs originated in the impoverished back streets of Kingston, Jamaica. A base was established in Brixton, London, running prostitution, illegal drinking clubs, gambling, and drugs (mainly marijuana). By the mid-1980s they had made substantial inroads into the booming cocaine and crack market, and in 1987 the first so-called Yardie killing took place. Since that time, Yardie violence has escalated. It has been estimated that there are up to 300,000 illegal weapons in circulation in Britain, many in the hands of Yardies. The Metropolitan Police has been reluctant to use the term "Yardie" but set up Operation Trident to specialize in gang-related gun crime in 1998.

In 2003, Jamaican and British-born Caribbean criminals belonged to a hard core of around 200 crack-cocaine dealers split into 20 gangs. Because of increased security, drugs are rarely smuggled into British airports directly from Jamaica, but are moved from the Caribbean into mainland Europe. Yardie crime has now infiltrated almost every major English city but has yet to make any substantial inroads into Scottish ones because of the smaller immigrant population there.

Yardie shooting
Quincey Thwaites was jailed for gun crimes in Britain in March 2002, and was given a 14-year prison sentence.

WEST LONDON GANGS

A recent development in Britain has been the growth of Asian crime, based on traditional family loyalties. Original gangs from West London included the Tooti Nung and the Holy Smokes. For a time their activities were confined mainly to gang fights and car theft, but they have gradually expanded to include credit card fraud, immigrant smuggling, and drug dealing. In 2003, gang members from Southall in West London, known as the Fiat Bravo Boys, were jailed for 20 years. They had earned £6 million in three years of heroin trafficking, protecting their empire by shootings and, on one occasion, planting a nail bomb in a local public house. There has also been a rise in Asian-controlled prostitution in Britain.

Yardie drug dealing
Tools of the trade (left): an Uzi submachine gun and bags of crack cocaine. Drug-trafficking is now a major problem in Britain.

Tobacco smuggling has now become an industry and in 2003 a member of the powerful Daniel clan, regarded as Scotland's richest crime family, received four years for his part in a scam that evaded £4 million tax on smuggled consignments. In many cases, money has been laundered through mini-cab businesses and, more recently, body-tanning studios.

International Gangs

There has long been a Chinese criminal presence in Britain. In the early 20th century, much of the drug trade was run by Chinese gangs. The trade slowed after the deportation in 1924 of the London kingpin, Brilliant Chang. Triad gangs (*see pp*106–117) have long-established bases in the major British cities.

From the 1990s, there was a rise in both Triad and Snakehead (human trafficker) operations involved in smuggling people into Britain for an extortionate fee and then frequently keeping them in a state of virtual slavery, forcing them into prostitution or sweated labor to pay off their "debt." In June 2000, 58 illegal Chinese immigrants, who had paid deposits of £800 against a final fee of £18,000, suffocated in a closed container as they were being smuggled into Dover. There has also been a rise in incidents where the immigrants are kidnapped to extort money from their relatives in China.

Death trap
The container that carried 58 Chinese asylum seekers into Dover docks in June 2000. All 58 were found dead. Ying Guo, of South Woodford, Essex, was found guilty of consipiring to smuggle illegal immigrants.

Since the 1990s, Eastern European crime gangs have gained a presence in Britain, and are especially active in prostitution. Turkish gangs control most of the heroin market, and the Italian Mafia has established itself in white-collar crime. In addition, Yakuza gangs are now stealing top-quality cars and shipping them to Japan by way of Dubai.

RUSSIA

THE MEANING OF "MAFIYA"

The term "Mafiya" (the Russian phonetic transliteration of "Mafia") is used across the Russian Federation today not only to describe organized criminal activity but for almost any semi-legal or dubious deal, be it a storekeeper overcharging for a bottle of vodka or a corrupt bureaucrat demanding a bribe from a member of the public to carry out a simple function.

TERRITORY

St. Petersburg
MOSCOW
Yekaterinburg
Krasnoyarsk
Vladivostok

The map shows the main bases of organized crime activity in Russia. Below is a list of the most well known gangs in each city. These gangs are believed to have worldwide contacts and to be linked to other major crime organizations, such as the Colombian drug cartels and the Italian Mafia.

● ST. PETERSBURG
Main organizations: Tambov, Kazan, Malyshev.

● MOSCOW
Main organizations: Solntsevo, Izmaylovo, 21st Century, Luchanskiy, Podolsk, Kurgan.

● YEKATERINBURG
Main organizations: Uralmash, Central, Blues.

● KRASNOYARSK
Main organization: Bykov.

● VLADIVOSTOK
Main organizations: Mikho, Kostenaya.

By 2000, there were an estimated 60,000 members in Russian organized crime gangs. The leading Moscow organization, the Solntsevo, had a membership of approximately 4,000, while the second biggest gang, the Izmaylovo, had an estimated 1,000 members. The table below shows the huge growth in the number of organized crime gangs during the turbulent years since the end of Soviet rule in Russia in 1991:

Gorbachev era (1985–91)	790
1994	5,700
1997	8,200
2000	60,000

The Russian Mafiya

> " They write I am the Mafiya's godfather. It was
> Vladimir Lenin who was the real organizer
> of the Mafiya and set up the criminal state. "

OTARI KVANTRISHVILI, GEORGIAN GANGSTER

Russia has one of the highest crime rates in the developed world. Since the breakup of the Soviet Union in 1991, organized crime has taken advantage of the weakening of the rule of law to flourish. Organized crime in Russia has its roots in the Soviet system, where a black market developed in basic goods and services that the state was unable to provide. The black market also supplied luxury goods that became scarce after the communist revolution in 1917. For example, in March 1926 Mikhail Florinsky, a leading official in the Soviet ministry of foreign affairs, was arrested at what the police called "a house used by a gang to hoard stolen property," where he had gone to buy a camera. Florinsky was arrested in a raid by agents of the UGROZ (the Soviet department for criminal investigations), and he was only released from custody after the intervention of the head of the OGPU (the Soviet political police).

During the early Soviet period in the 1920s and 1930s, the Khotrovo Market in the capital city, Moscow, was a well-known source of luxury goods that were otherwise totally unobtainable. This thieves' market was tolerated by the authorities, although it was periodically closed down for the sake

Back street criminals
Black market traders conduct business in a back street of Moscow in 1917. The long existence of a black market – persisting through the communist era – has allowed criminal activity to develop very rapidly in Russia since *perestroika*.

of appearances. Such markets existed across the Soviet Union throughout the seven decades of communist rule. Whenever the state was unable to provide what the people wanted or needed, then other forces were on hand to satisfy demand – for a price.

Criminal Informers
During the Stalinist era (1924–53), the Soviet secret police often enlisted members of the criminal fraternity as informers. They were tasked with seeking out those who dared to voice any opposition to Josef Stalin, the Soviet communist dictator. The Soviet authorities regarded

common crime as less dangerous than political crime. In prisons, common criminals colluded with the authorities to make the condition of "politicals" even worse than it was by bullying and informing on them. The rewards for the criminals were less work and more tobacco and alcohol. The extended punishment for "politicals" resulted in longer working hours, beatings, and shorter rations. The Soviet labor camps, known as *gulags*, are often cited as being the birthplace

Police check at gunpoint
Russian anti-Mafia police doing a routine ID check of men near one of Moscow's many street markets. Markets in Russia are often controlled by organized crime gangs.

THE MAFIYA ORGANIZATION

At the summit of the organized crime hierarchy in Russia is believed to be the *bratski krug* (circle of brothers), an elite group of policymakers whose power is limited only by the thieves' code. The actual extent of their control or whether they even exist is unknown. Many Russian gangs are loosely organized, but some are highly structured. In one of these a typical boss controls four specialized cells known as brigades, each led by a brigadier who in turn leads groups of *boyeviky* (soldiers). There are restrictions placed on the membership of gangs, based on ethnicity, kinship, and criminal record (supported by tattoos). An applicant must be sponsored by a member and often have proved his worth by killing somebody.

PAKHAN/KRESTNII OTETS
Godfather/boss

BRIGADIER	BRIGADIER	BRIGADIER	BRIGADIER
Boyeviky Soldiers	*Boyeviky* Soldiers	*Boyeviky* Soldiers	*Boyeviky* Soldiers

of Russian organized crime, the cradle of the Mafiya. For although the criminals worked the system, they did not work for it.

A criminal honor code developed among the prison population, which had a number of strict rules. Those who followed the code had to swear, among other things: never to work legitimately; to support other criminals; and to have nothing to do with the state. These men were known in Russian criminal circles as *vory v zakone*, which translates roughly as "thieves in law," implying that thieves are bound to and united by a code of practice. They formed a kind of criminal aristocracy and are often found leading organized crime gangs today.

Crime and Punishment

Stalin's progress to complete control of the Soviet Union was accomplished between 1928 and 1938. It was accompanied by bloodshed and suffering on a colossal scale. Famine in the Ukraine, mass arrests, denunciation of friends, family, and rivals, and purges of the Communist Party and the armed forces all contributed to Soviet citizens' sense of insecurity and mistrust of government. Vast economic programs, called

INSIDE STORY
MAFIYA SLANG

Akademiya Literally "academy" but referring to prison as a place of furthering a thief's criminal education.
Bandity A militia term for criminals.
Dan Extortion money collected by gangs.
Krestnii otets Godfather or crime boss.
Krysha Literally "roof," in this context the paying of protection money to provide security.
Mafiya A catchall term which may include members of crime syndicates or simply a greedy storekeeper.
Nayekhat To collect, usually violently, *dan* or extortion money.
Pakhan Gang leader.
Panama A dummy company.
Skhodka Gang assembly.
Suka A snitch or traitor, someone who collaborates with the authorities; literally, "bitch."
Torpedo Contract killer.
Tsekhovik Illegal employer or underground entrepreneur during the Soviet period.
Vor v zakonye A "thief in law", a criminal who follows the thieves' honor code; a leader of an old Russian gang.
Vorovskoi obschak Communal fund to be drawn on by gang members in times of hardship.

Five Year Plans, expanded the Soviet Union's economic and manufacturing capacity, but at the same time institutionalized corruption, as factory managers had to

overcome shortages of essential supplies to meet strict production targets. Pilfering from state concerns was regarded as a perk but was carried out to an extent more akin to the looting of a captured city. Tools, fuel, and raw materials were all prey to criminal organizations that paid the bureaucrats responsible for their "disappearance." Those who carried out such activities, defined as "sabotage" or "counter-revolutionary activity" by the Soviet press, were called *bandity* (bandits).

Evolution of the Modern Mafiya

At the end of World War II, although victorious, the Soviet Union found itself with a shattered infrastructure, 20 million dead, millions of displaced persons, and areas of the country where *bandity* activity and the black market flourished in the absence of enforceable authority.

Large areas of the western Soviet Union were effectively controlled by criminals armed from the stocks of weaponry abandoned by the retreating German troops. These gangs were often deserters from the Soviet Union's Red Army, who brooked no opposition and respected only the authority of superior firepower.

The curious relationship between the criminal class and the Soviet state took another twist in the postwar years. When criminals who had served in the Red Army during the war tried to rejoin the underworld, they fell foul of the more traditional criminals, who considered them to be traitors for their alliance with the state. The resulting "war on traitors" fought in prisons in the late 1940s and early 1950s ended with the defeat of the traditionalists. A new oath was added to the thieves' code that permitted collaboration with the state. The criminal world and the Soviet

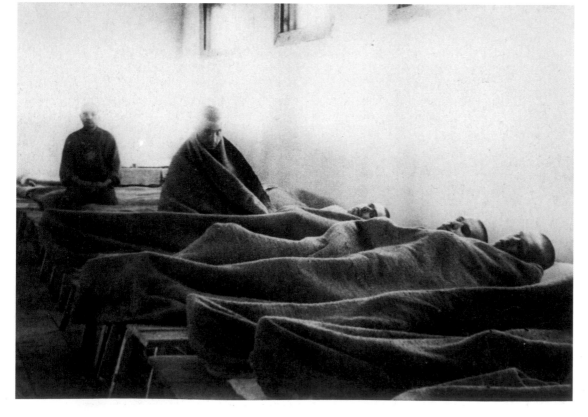

The Soviet gulag
A remote *gulag* in Vorkuta, Russia, in 1945. The prison honor code and roots of the modern Mafiya emerged from the labor camps during the Soviet era.

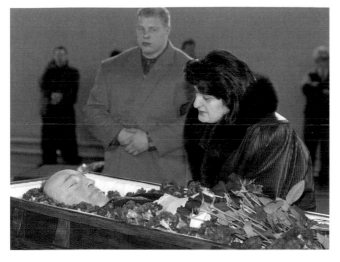

Funeral rites
Eliso Kvantrishvili sits by the coffin of her husband, Otari Kvantrishvili, rumored to be a leading crime boss. He was gunned down outside a bathhouse in Moscow in 1994.

Stalin's death in March 1953, and the accession of Nikita Khrushchev to power, led to the expansion of organized crime within the state economic system. It was during the Khrushchev years that *tsekhoviki* (groups of illegal employers or underground entrepreneurs) began to grow in power and influence within state-owned enterprises. By the late 1970s, crime and corruption were widespread.

authorities seemed to have discovered areas of common ground.

Meanwhile, outside the penal institutions by the late 1940s, the reimposition of legitimate authority, reconstruction, and resettlement had been achieved and for the great majority of Soviet citizens life returned to normal. Many members of criminal gangs were rounded up and imprisoned, but the more cunning among them managed to go underground.

Black market
Unlicensed traders sell watches and medals in the Arbat, Moscow, in 1992.

"They will shoot you just to see if the gun works."
New York policeman commenting on the Russian Mafiya

The term "Mafiya" was first used by the former Soviet defense attorney Konstantin Simis in the 1970s. Simis was reporting on the levels of corruption in various sectors of the Communist Party that involved party officials taking bribes to overlook or falsify records of the transactions of factories and other businesses. An example

of the "Mafiya mentality" cited by Simis involved three brothers who operated a business within and under the cover of a state-owned factory. The managers would, for a percentage, order more raw materials than necessary, then "lose" them to wastage. The materials would be used to produce black market goods. The authorities were bribed when necessary and the end product was sold in the flourishing underground economy. This form of business was common and accepted as the only means by which the moribund Soviet economy could satisfy consumer demand. What struck Simis was the way the 28 codefendants in the case behaved. Even those who pleaded guilty provided little or no evidence to indict the others. The simple fact was that the brothers were paying all the defense costs and supporting the families of their "employees" as long as they did not betray others and were not "overly frank" with the justice system. A code of honor appeared to be operating, involving mutual support and the giving of cash or favors to protect the criminals. It had similarities to the prison code of honor.

In 1985, Mikhail Gorbachev became president. He realized that if the Soviet Union was to survive, its

Fighting the gangs
A raid by Russian police on a Mafiya warehouse near Moscow on June 1, 1998, is followed by arrests and the seizure of illegal vodka.

ruling elite had to accept far-reaching changes. *Glasnost* (openness) and *perestroika* (restructuring) were the cornerstones of his new direction for Russia. Two major pieces of legislation significantly affected the underground economy, the law on Individual Labor Activity (1987) and the Law on Cooperatives (1988). With some restrictions, these laws legalized private business. As a result, almost at the stroke of a pen, illegal enterprises became legal. However, bureaucratic suspicion of buying and selling for profit brought a raft of

legislation on pricing, taxation, and licensing that drove many businesses back to the paying of bribes in order to carry on trading. At the same time the protection of small traders from Mafiya operatives broke down. In 1990–91 it was estimated that 90 percent of businesses in St. Petersburg and 75 percent in Moscow were paying protection money.

By the end of 1991, following a failed communist coup in Moscow, Gorbachev had resigned and the Soviet Union had been dissolved. Boris Yeltsin took the reins of power in Russia. Yeltsin soon conceded that the Mafiya was destroying the Russian economy and destabilizing the political structure. He declared "crime has become problem number one for Russians."

In 1994, the FBI opened an office in Moscow to cooperate with the FSB, its Russian counterpart, and other law enforcement agencies. They went into action with Operation Hurricane, ordered by Yeltsin. More than 2,000 Mafiya members were imprisoned but the operation was little more than a public relations exercise. Surveys of the Russian public on law and order

Street dealing

An old woman peddles drugs on the streets of Moscow. The economic and social collapse of the Soviet system in the 1990s drove many desperate people into crime just to survive.

issues brought these responses: "One cannot deal with taxation inspection without a bribe." "Legal and illegal methods [of doing business] are interlocked." "Mafiyosi can be found among members of the boards of banks." The police are demoralized and lack the equipment and resources to tackle the problem effectively. Their low salaries of around $200 a month make them vulnerable to bribery, and even when they catch gang members, Russia has few laws under which to prosecute them.

Decapitations and Amputations

The Mafiya's approach is characterized by extreme violence. Enforcers, often trained by former Russian Special Forces, many veterans of the wars in Afghanistan and Chechnya, mete out punishment to those who dare to interfere with Mafiya business. Victims may be tortured, stabbed, and mutilated. Decapitation and amputation are common methods of concealing the identity of a victim and also provide a message to others: "This will be your punishment."

The killing of those who stand in the way of profit and business is almost a daily occurrence. A kiosk owner reluctant to pay for protection will find his kiosk blown up and count himself lucky if that was merely a warning. A militia station that has carelessly imprisoned a Mafiya member will find itself under siege or ram-raided by a organized

INSIDE STORY

PRISON TATTOOS

The prison cult of tattooing first came to the attention of the authorities during the 1920s. Prison tattoos had a symbolic meaning and were often a method of displaying the criminal activities of the wearer as well as contempt for authority. Today the designs are similar in style and content, and continue to reflect the tradition of contempt for the law. A tattoo can only be applied after a crime has been committed; and the wearing of an incorrect or unauthorized tattoo is punished. Tattoos are created in prison using needles and electric razors. Urine, soot, and shampoo or urine and burnt shoe-leather are the ink ingredients. Unsurprisingly, infections and sometimes death result from these methods.
Each design has a specific meaning:
A skull on the finger: a murderer
Barbed wire across the forehead: a life sentence
A spider's web: the wearer is a drug addict

The head of a tomcat: a good luck charm
SS runes: the wearer is no stool pigeon

Sex offenders are often forcibly tattooed with a dagger running through the neck from shoulder to shoulder.

Prison artwork

A prisoner in Norilsk, Siberia, displays his tattoos. The six-point star on each shoulder indicates the length of his sentence — one point for each year.

Vyacheslav Ivankov (Yaponchik)

Vyacheslav Ivankov, nicknamed "Yaponchik" (meaning "little Japanese"), was born in the former Soviet Republic of Georgia but moved to Moscow to pursue his criminal career. His activities in Moscow included fraud, robbery, and extortion.

By the 1980s, his interests had expanded into drug dealing, but in 1982 he was sentenced to 14 years' hard labor in Siberia. In prison Ivankov acquired a tattoo of an eight-pointed star (one point for every year of his sentence) on each shoulder to denote his high criminal status as one of the *vory v zakone,* or "thieves in law." Ivankov was released early in 1991, allegedly thanks to the influence of a powerful politician and the bribery of a Russian high court judge.

In 1993, Ivankov emigrated to Brighton Beach, New York, where he was trumpeted by a local Russian language newspaper as the "red Godfather." From this base Ivankov is suspected of having expanded his criminal operations from the Russian enclaves into New Jersey and Philadelphia. The extent of Ivankov's activities is a matter of controversy, but he is alleged to have been involved in illegal gambling, drug smuggling, and money laundering, as well as extortion. In 1995, Ivankov was arrested for extortion and in 1997 given a nine-year sentence.

Dates 1940–
Details Ivankov is believed to be the highest ranking member of the Russian Mafiya to be convicted in the United States.

crime unit armed with equal if not superior firepower. In the early 1990s, more than 100 senior bank executives were killed in Moscow alone, usually for not showing a sufficiently "cooperative" attitude toward some of their clients.

The Russian government attempted to put a stop to large-scale money laundering by the Mafiya in 1991. It suddenly withdrew all 50 and 100 rouble notes from circulation to halt the illegal export and exchange of Russian roubles into hard currency. The Mafiya held vast stocks of these rouble notes, which, at the time, were the highest denominations available. The organized crime bosses moved swiftly. Untold millions in rouble notes were laundered through "supportive" state banks, factories, and stores. Some 25 percent of the proceeds were estimated to have been used as bribes to smooth the passage of these transactions.

By the year 2000, an estimated $200 billion had been taken out of Russia illegally. Money laundering for foreign criminal organizations such as the Colombian drug cartels through Russian businesses and banks provides a lucrative source of income for organized crime. Furthermore, such international contacts have led to the provision of alternative drug and arms supply routes across the porous borders of former Soviet republics. Indeed, one suspected leading crime boss bought a bankrupt airline in a former Central Asian Soviet republic reportedly to fly heroin out of the Golden Triangle heroin-producing area in Southeast Asia. Another Russian gangster based in Florida sold MM18 helicopters to Colombian drug cartels in 1993, and promised to supply them with a Russian submarine. He was arrested and deported before the deal was completed.

The Russian Interior Ministry believes that Russian crime gangs are operational in 26 countries, but the U.S. Federal Bureau of Investigation (FBI) estimates it to be closer to 50 or more. The Russian Mafiya is most active in the United States, Germany, Switzerland, Israel, Turkey, and Holland. There is evidence that Russian gangs are working not only with the Colombian drug cartels but the Italian Mafia as well.

The Mafiya Invasion of the United States

In the United States, members of organized crime groups have targeted Brighton Beach, New York, where many immigrants from Russia have settled. They are also active in other cities, notably San Francisco, Los Angeles, Chicago, and New York. Miami is believed to be the main base for Russian organized crime activity in the Caribbean. The Russian Mafiya are suspected of taking advantage of many Caribbean countries' complex and lightly regulated tax systems, setting up businesses and buying property to conceal their financial transactions.

There appears to be no common thread in the way that the Russian Mafiya works other than its desire to generate wealth and power. From art theft to contract killing via drugs, prostitution, and arms dealing, its activities know few limits.

Death in Siberia
Police in the Irkutsk region of Siberia investigate the scene of a murder. A man was beaten and then apparently left to freeze to death. His prison tattoos suggest that the victim was probably involved in organized crime activity.

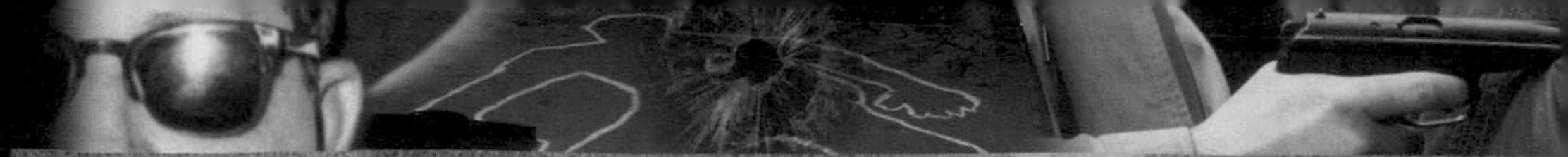

ALBANIA

Albania is a small mountainous country in southeast Europe. A proud people, the Albanians regained their independence from the Turkish Ottoman Empire in 1913. In 1945, the country became a closed communist state. In 1991, following the demise of communism, the country descended into anarchy. The Albanian Mafia then began to spread across Europe and North America. In Italy and the United States, Albanians worked for the Italian Mafia and became its trusted "soldiers." The experience helped them to become independent when the time was ripe.

TERRITORY

The map shows the main organized crime strongholds in Albania, although the crime network also has bases in neighboring Kosovo and Macedonia. Albanian organized crime has now spread across Europe and to the United States. The major Albanian towns and the types of organized crimes they are associated with are listed below:

Bajram Cum
Kukës
Durrës
TIRANA
Korça
Vlora
Saranda

- **TIRANA**
  Money laundering; political corruption.

- **SARANDA**
  Human trafficking to Italy; drug smuggling.

- **VLORA**
  Heroin refinement; people and drug smuggling.

- **BAJRAM CURRI**
  Human trafficking, arms, and drug smuggling.

- **KUKËS**
  Fuel, drug, and cigarette smuggling.

The chart shows the estimated percentage of the heroin trade controlled by the Albanian Mafia in 1999:

85%	Greece
80%	Sweden
78%	Norway
75%	Germany
72%	Austria

Organized Crime in Albania

" ...under the pressures of war, sanctions, and economic collapse, southeastern Europe has become one vast factory of criminality..."

MISHA GLENNY, BBC NEWS, APRIL 2001

Albania emerged from more than 40 years' isolation under a repressive communist regime in 1991, only to descend into social and political chaos soon afterward. Many Albanians, including criminals, left the country and settled abroad. Having gained experience of organized crime by working with other groups, an independent Albanian criminal network emerged a few years later.

Albanian communities, especially those in neighboring Kosovo and Macedonia, have a long tradition of suspicion of the state. The collapse of law and order in northern Albania in 1991 led to the revival of traditional medieval laws known as the *Kanun*. The *Kanun* stresses close family ties, honor, revenge, blood feuds, and is strongly patriarchal: a father has the right to beat,

Out on the street
Albanian prostitutes huddle in a doorway in the Czech capital, Prague. Over recent years, Albanian criminal gangs have moved into the vice trade in many European cities.

imprison, or even kill his son or daughter. The *Kanun* also allows a man to kidnap a woman he wishes to marry, and in general considers a woman to be the property of a man. The modern distortion of this law allows women to be kidnapped and sold into prostitution.

The Exploitation of Women

An example of how Albanian women have been exploited by criminals is the case of three sisters: Marjana, Klodeta, and Marta. Their story begins at Christmas in 1998, in northern Albania. Marjana, a 15-year-old student, had fallen in love with a man a few years older than herself. Her boyfriend wanted to marry her and they emigrated to Italy, where they planned a new and prosperous life together. Marjana did not want to leave Albania but her boyfriend and his older brother persuaded her and a friend to elope with them. One night they crossed the Adriatic Sea in a speedboat to land in Italy, which offered the promise of a golden future. However, their dreams were soon to be shattered. Both girls found that their "fiancés" were no more than pimps and that they were now to be prostitutes.

Back in their home village, Marjana's father faced another loss. Klodeta, aged 19, was kidnapped by neighbors and spirited away to be a prostitute in Belgium. The oldest sister, Marta, 35, reported Klodeta's abductors to the police. The kidnap gang sent a message to Marta via her 12-year-old disabled brother to drop the matter. One day at the end of May 2000, the girls' father returned to find his home covered with blood and no sign of his daughter. The following day, Marta's dismembered body was dredged out of a nearby river. Although the human traffickers were arrested soon afterward, the girls' father said, " I fear these wealthy men will get off. There is a lot of pressure and money to set them free."

Of Klodeta there is no word. Marjana is now living in Italy, sheltered by a religious order, too afraid to return home to Albania.

The "Balkan Route"

With the outbreak of war in neighboring Yugoslavia in 1991, Turkish heroin gangs needed alternative routes by which to smuggle their product to European markets. Albanian gangs stepped in to provide the missing link in the so-called "Balkan Route," along which passed some 60 percent of Europe's heroin. This lucrative trade is controlled by the "Fifteen Families," the major group of Albanian crimials, who operate from secret bases in the inaccessible mountainous country in the north.

Global Connections

Italian organized crime groups such as the Sacra Corona Unita (*see p77*) cooperate with Albanian groups, particularly in the human trafficking business, exploiting the length of Italy's coastline and the narrowness of the Adriatic Sea. In parts of Italy the prostitution, marijuana, and illegal immigration businesses are controlled by Albanians, who may pay a percentage to the local Mafia for the privilege.

Hidden arms cache
Police with an arms cache found in the southern town of Vlora, Albania, in 1997. The number of weapons in the Balkans soared in the 1990s.

During the 1990s, Albanian street-level heroin dealers in a number of European cities began to oust the Turkish "guest workers" who had once monopolized the trade. In 1996, more than 800 ethnic Albanians were imprisoned in Germany on narcotics charges. Inevitably there have been violent clashes with local drug sellers. In 1999, 10 people connected to Albanian gangs were gunned down in Brussels, and in the same year nine people were killed by Albanian dealers in Milan during a two-week heroin turf war.

Albanian criminals have forged links with South American gangs, who have begun to route cocaine shipments to Europe through Albania, and Belarussian criminals, who channel human traffic through Albanian networks. Cash is also passed though Albanian middlemen and laundered in respectable financial institutions in the West.

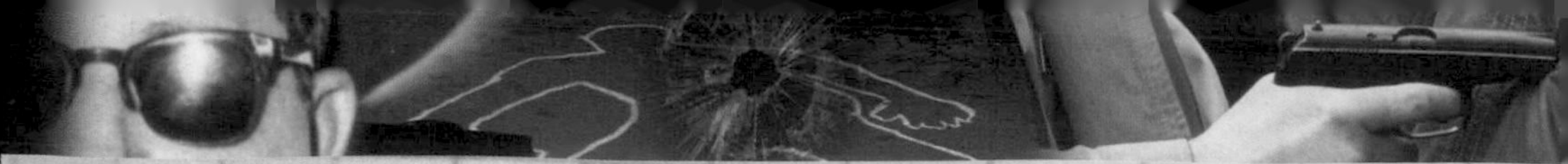

JAPAN

THE ORIGIN OF "YAKUZA"

According to Japanese tradition, the term "Yakuza" is derived from a losing score in a game called *oicho-kabu*, which is a version of the card game Black Jack. The phonetic sound of an 8-9-3 sequence of numbers – a losing combination – is *ya-ku-za*. Thus the word "Yakuza" is used to denote a person who is not valued by society, a misfit, loser, or outcast. The Yakuza tradionally liked to project the image of being underdogs or rejects.

TERRITORY

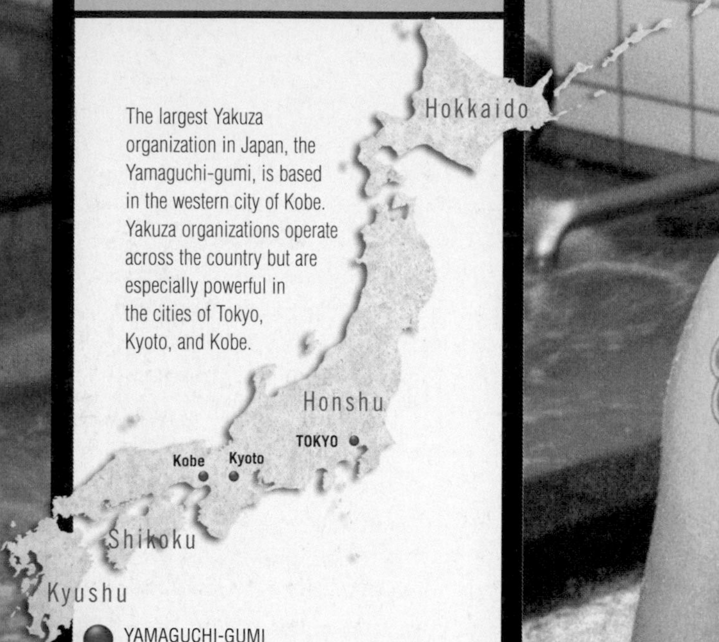

The largest Yakuza organization in Japan, the Yamaguchi-gumi, is based in the western city of Kobe. Yakuza organizations operate across the country but are especially powerful in the cities of Tokyo, Kyoto, and Kobe.

Hokkaido

Honshu

TOKYO

Kobe Kyoto

Shikoku

Kyushu

● YAMAGUCHI-GUMI
17,500 members; 750 clans.

● INAGAWA KAI
7,000 members; 300 clans.

● SUMIYOSHI RENGO KAI
7,000 members; 170 clans.

● KYOKUTO KAI
1,700 members.

It is impossible to find accurate statistics on the overall activities of the Yakuza. However, according to figures from the National Police Agency in Japan, 9,893 gang members were arrested in 2001. The number of people arrested on criminal charges connected to Yakuza's major sources of income can be broken down as follows:

Drugs	1,949
Extortion	1,398
Gambling	118
Racketeering	107

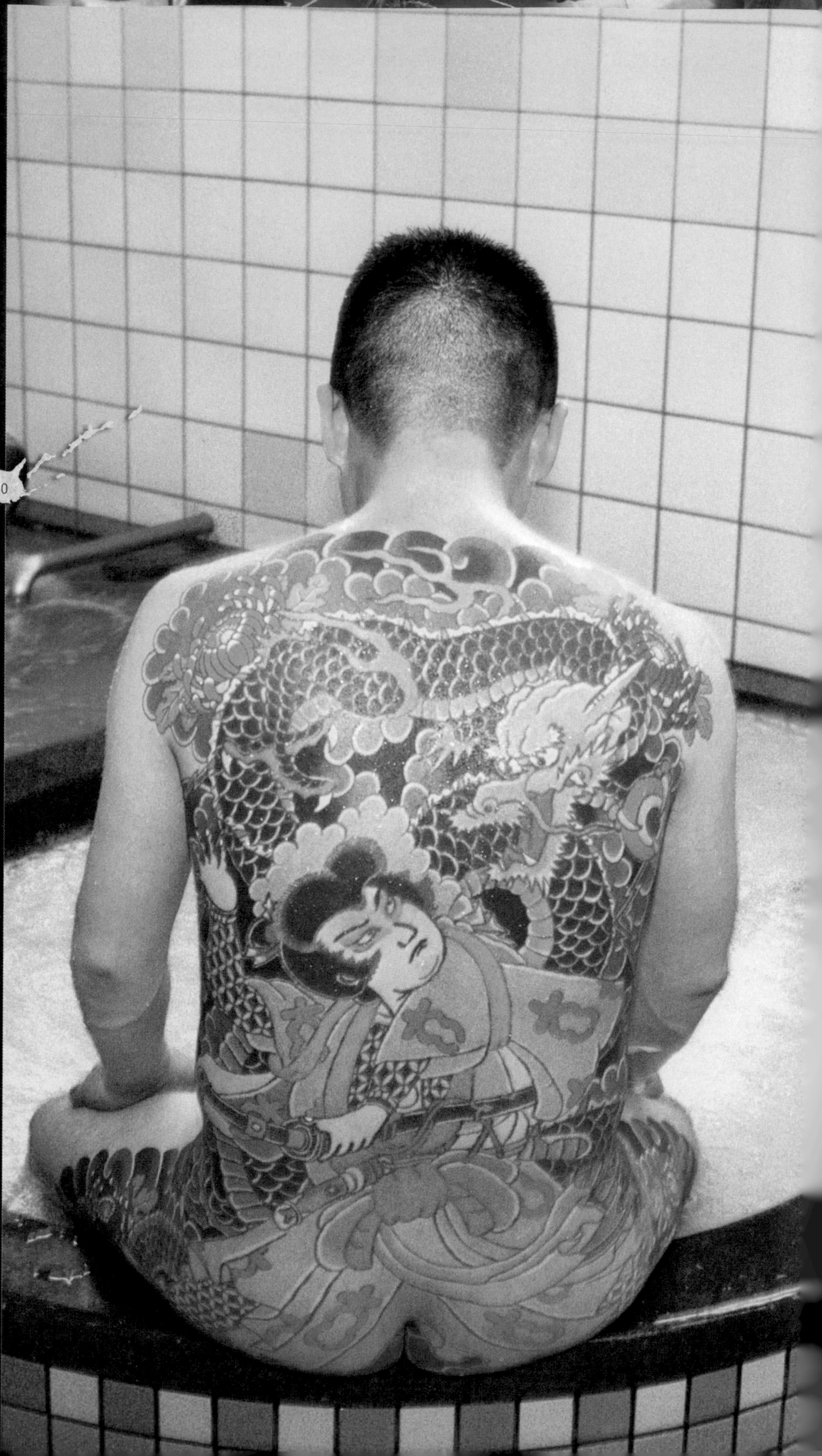

The Yakuza

> " Like other Japanese, the Yakuza greet strangers with a business card showing their organization and rank. The biggest syndicate prints an 18-page internal telephone directory. "

THE ECONOMIST MAGAZINE

Japan has the lowest crime rate of any of the industrial powers. Anyone who has visited Japan can attest to the low incidence of street crime and the security of Japanese cities. Yet Japan has between 100,000 and 150,000 members of 2,500 criminal gangs – collectively known as the Yakuza – dedicated to such illegal activities as strike breaking, labor racketeering, drug running, gambling, prostitution, extortion, and blackmail, in addition to more modern crimes, such as greenmail (*see p*43), money laundering, stock-market fixing, and a host of other lucrative moneyspinners.

Obscure Origins

The name "Yakuza" – basically the Japanese equivalent of the Mafia – did not come into general use until the 20th century, although the phenomenon probably originated in the Edo period (1600–1868). In 1604, Japan was unified by Tokugawa Ieyasu, the first Shogun, ending centuries of civil war. Thousands of warriors found themselves out of work and increasingly marginalized in a society that was becoming mercantile rather than feudal. Wandering bands of unemployed *ronin* (masterless men) began to prey on townspeople and peasants. Some of the bands were known as *kabuki mono* – "the crazy ones" – due to their excessive behavior and extraordinary dress. Townsmen formed gangs to protect the ordinary people. It is from these "chivalrous

Work of art
A Yakuza member in a public bathhouse in Kyoto reveals an elaborate tattoo on his back – once the hallmark of the Yakuza.

commoners" that the Yakuza claim descent, although they also maintain that they are the last section of society to follow the samurai code. Yakuza leaders have devised largely mythological genealogies linking themselves to these past folk heroes. This romantic – and imaginary – link is very important. The Japanese have a deep

Protectors of the poor
The Yakuza claim descent from the ancient "chivalrous commoners" or *okondate*, such as this one, who protected the commoners from the violence of the *ronin*.

reverence for tradition and the ideals of the samurai period, and by identifying with the nation's heroes the Yakuza have put themselves in a different category from common criminals. Much of the Yakuza's behavior is overlooked, because they are perceived as the living link with a nobler world order. While the public is beguiled by tattoos, tales of prowess in the martial arts, and a belief in Robin Hood-type acts, the Yakuza, armed with laptop and cell phone, is asset stripping or manipulating shares in a completely modern idiom. More authentically, the Yakuza developed from the medieval guilds of gamblers (*bakuto*)

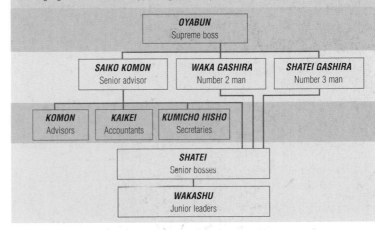

THE YAKUZA POWER STRUCTURE

The Yakuza organize themselves into "families," in which the *oyabun-kobun* (parent–child) relationship is key. The *oyabun* (boss) is a father figure, giving advice, help, and protection to the gang members or *kobun* (children). This simplified chart shows the basic structure:

- **OYABUN** — Supreme boss
  - **SAIKO KOMON** — Senior advisor
    - **KOMON** — Advisors
    - **KAIKEI** — Accountants
    - **KUMICHO HISHO** — Secretaries
  - **WAKA GASHIRA** — Number 2 man
  - **SHATEI GASHIRA** — Number 3 man
  - **SHATEI** — Senior bosses
  - **WAKASHU** — Junior leaders

and street peddlers (*tekiya*). Police still use these two divisions to describe the Yakuza, although the gangs have since branched out into numerous different activities. Many of their traditions, customs, and folklore derive from this background.

The Philosophy of the Yakuza

As was normal in feudal society, the guilds were built on a pyramidal hierarchy, patterned on the family, with absolute obedience and respect given to a father-figure. In this *oyabun-kobun* ("parent–child") relationship, new initiates took the position of children in relation to the leader, and of younger brothers toward senior members of the gang. These relationships are still formally expressed in Yakuza rituals: exchanging cups of saké before a Shinto altar during the "adoption" ceremony, for example. A Yakuza will accept blame when ordered, and is prepared to go to prison, but on his release high-ranking bosses will be at the prison gates, bowing to thank him for his sacrifice.

INSIDE STORY

YAKUZA TERMS

Bosozoku Youthful motorcycle gangs, one of the modern Yakuza's major recruiting grounds.

Burakumin Japan's "untouchables"; a social group that is discriminated against in Japan and a fertile recruiting ground for the Yakuza.

Giri The traditional sense of obligation; a fundamental element in the Japanese social order.

Oyabun-kobun Parent-child relationship, which is the basis of the hierarchy within the Yakuza.

Sangokujin People of three countries – China, Korea, and Taiwan – trafficked into Japan as cheap labor during World War II and now forming an important element in the criminal underworld.

Sokaiya Thugs, blackmailers, and extortionists who break up stockholders' meetings to force decisions in a particular direction; now also used in other contexts.

Yubitsume A traditional ritual whereby a Yakuza gang member who has failed in some way cuts off part of a finger (usually the little finger) and presents it to his *oyabun* to ask forgiveness.

Self-mutilation
A Yakuza member displays hands missing several finger joints as a result of performing the Yakuza ritual of *yubitsume*.

The Yakuza have always recruited from among the rootless or dispossessed, who are probably attracted to the stability of these "family" bonds.

Other qualities approved by Japanese society at large are extremely important to the Yakuza. These include *giri*, a sense of moral duty to exact revenge, and *ninjo*, a sense of compassion, and the ability to empathize with and protect ordinary people. Occasionally the Yakuza have publicly displayed these qualities. After the Kobe earthquake in 1995, for example, Japan's largest organized crime syndicate, the Yamaguchi-gumi, were far ahead of the government agencies in giving assistance. Such public relations exercises have been very helpful in maintaining the positive aspects of the Yakuza myth.

Customs and Rituals

The Yakuza ensure loyalty to the family by draconian measures against any member who is seen as disloyal – and clients, even major companies, who try to disengage from their underworld contacts. The correct form of apology for a Yakuza who offends or fails in some task is to cut off a finger joint – *yubitsume* – and present it to his boss. For really serious offenses, he may be given the option of committing suicide rather than being killed.

Yubitsume is still common. According to a 1993 survey, 45 percent of the Yakuza were missing a finger joint and five percent had performed *yubitsume* at least twice. The new generation operating abroad, however, finds it inconvenient to be marked out in this way; a prosthesis expert in Japan says she has often been consulted by Yakuza or ex-Yakuza wishing to hide their amputations.

Other customs are flamboyantly archaic, such as the Yakuza practice of whole-body tattooing, which dates to the 17th and 18th centuries when it was the fashion among swordfighters, firemen, and members of the "floating world" or pleasure districts. For over a century it was the hallmark of the

The art of the Yakuza
A tattoo artist works on a Yakuza member in 1946. The traditional method using bamboo tools is very painful. It is also a test of endurance, as a back tattoo can take over 100 hours.

Yakuza, a test of endurance, and a proud affirmation of belonging. While nearly 70 percent of Yakuza have at least some tattooing, the traditional whole-body style is going out of favor.

Right-Wing Connections

In 1868, the Meiji Restoration marked the end of the samurai world and the beginnings of reform, democracy, and the opening of the country to outside influences. The changes were resented, especially by those who foresaw losing their ancient privileges.

The Genyosha (Dark Ocean Society) was founded in 1881, and was a model for later ultranationalist movements. Its tenets also included adherence to the national religion of Shinto, a deep reverence for the emperor, a belief in Japan's right to expand overseas, contempt of foreigners, and a hatred of democracy, socialism, and ideas such as the emancipation of women. Terrorism and murder were the preferred weapons to attain their ends, for example, turning the first

> ## "An unwritten rule appears to prevail in highly authoritarian societies: organized crime is successful only when the government allows it to be."
>
> David E. Kaplan and Alec Dubro, *Yakuza*

national election into a bloodbath and assassinating left-wing politicians. Genyosha arose in reaction to Japan's forced opening to Western influence, which led to the upsurge of militarism culminating in Japan's imperialist expansion and Pearl Harbor. Members included the like-minded from many walks of life: ex-samurai and the military, firemen, the police, non-union construction workers, and the Yakuza; and blackmail, extortion, and other rackets provided much of the funding.

Bonds between the right wing and the Yakuza grew even closer with the assassination of the Empress of Korea in 1895 and the occupation of the country. The Yakuza became important in strike breaking on the docks, organizing non-union labor, especially in the construction industry – paralleling Mafia developments in the United States – and, later, trafficking workers from Korea to Japan. Descendants of these Koreans, whose legal status has in many cases never been regularized, are an important element in the Yakuza today.

During the occupation of China and Manchuria, the Yakuza were

Postwar rationing
A man measures out food rations in Tokyo, 1946. The U.S. occupation forces introduced food rationing after the war, which led quickly to a flourishing black market run by criminal gangs.

CASE STUDY

The Class A Criminals from Sugamo Jail

After World War II, many Japanese Class A war criminals were incarcerated in Tokyo's Sugamo Jail. In 1948, the Americans freed a number of them, believing they could be deployed in the war against communism. This created an "old boy" network that was to color Japanese politics for 50 years.

YOSHIO KODAMA

Yoshio Kodama became the greatest of the *kuromaku*, or fixers, who acted as go-betweens between the government and legitimate business and the underworld. Politically he was on the extreme right. He was imprisoned in the 1930s for his part in a plot to assassinate the prime minister. During the Japanese occupation of China

(1936–45), his contribution – looting the country of valuable metals and minerals often obtained at gunpoint – made him a fortune, later used to help fund the Liberal Democratic Party (LDP).

After his release, Kodama worked, among other things, for U.S. intelligence. He tried to put an end to warring among Yakuza gangs to forge them into a single unit as a bulwark against communism. Although he failed, he emerged as a man highly respected by the criminal world and with equal influence in politics, controlling up to a quarter of the LDP representatives through bribes and blackmail, just as his gangs of *sokaiya* kept companies and banks under his control.

Kodama was deeply implicated in the Lockheed scandal that came to light in 1976. He had worked as an agent for Lockheed, a giant U.S. aircraft corporation that had paid millions of dollars in bribes to get various lucrative contracts. The Japanese were forced for the first time to face the links connecting their government, organized crime, and the extreme right wing. The pervasive corruption that was revealed by the courageous investigating media came to be called the *kuroi kiri* – "Black Mist."

Before he could be jailed for his part in the Lockheed affair, Kodama had a stroke.

He spent the rest of his life dealing with failing health, wealth, and influence. He finally died of another stroke in 1984.

RYOICHI SASAKAWA

A passionate admirer of the ultranationalist right, Sasakawa spent three years as a Class A war criminal in Sugamo Jail, where he shared a cell with Kodama. There he made plans to build a multibillion dollar gambling empire and further the cause of the extreme right wing. He liked to boast that eight million Japanese shared his ideals. His hatred of communism endeared him to the U.S. establishment – although he encountered the occasional unpleasant surprise from the United States: for example, that insider trading,

> ## "I am the world's wealthiest fascist."
> Ryoichi Sasakawa, *Time* Magazine, 1974

something he took for granted in Japan, was frowned upon, or opposition to his large-scale money laundering schemes. But such setbacks were rare. Whether it was making a multibillion dollar fortune, taking over much of the shipbuilding industry, or lobbying for the rearmament of Japan (now the world's fifth largest military power), Sasakawa rarely failed in his aims. As an old man he became a philanthropist and gave away perhaps a billion dollars in the hopes of winning the Nobel Peace Prize. Indeed, in 1985 he was nominated, although he did not win.

NOBUSUKE KISHI

Nobusuke Kishi was virtual ruler of Manchuria in China during the Japanese occupation in the 1930s and early 1940s and was imprisoned as a Class A war criminal in Sugamo Jail. Soon after his release in 1948, he entered politics. Supported by Kodama and generally approved of by the Yakuza, who liked his extreme right wing views, he became prime minister in 1957. His links with the Yakuza were close and public.

Leading fixer
Yoshio Kodama was known as "the most powerful man in Japan" until he was implicated in the Lockheed scandal in 1976.

Wealthy fascist
A shipbuilding and gambling billionaire, and friend of several U.S. presidents, Ryoichi Sasakawa combined respectability with longstanding gangland connections.

Prime minister
Kishi became prime minister in 1957, nine years after leaving jail. His attempts to undermine the Constitution were vigorously opposed by the student left.

again very active in trafficking women for the Japanese forces and in pushing drugs to demoralize the locals.

Within days of the U.S. occupation forces' arrival, the Yakuza began organizing a black market. The occupation worked to the advantage of the Yakuza in many ways. The situation in postwar Japan, with four million soldiers returning home to no jobs, food rationing and shortages, made the development of a black market inevitable, and the occupying forces were unable or unwilling to control it. Besides providing food for the Japanese and brothels for U.S. soldiers, the *bakuto* found a new outlet in producing slot machines to give the troops easy-access gambling, laying the foundation for the pachinko (pinball) industry and, eventually, video games.

The Legacy of the War

U.S. political leaders were well aware of the dangers of the Japanese underworld and its political connections with the right wing, and war criminals were initially rounded up. However, they soon decided that the left wing was a much greater threat and considered no price too high to check the spreading influence of communism across Asia. The business community in the United States feared for their interests, and pressure was exerted on the U.S. government to ensure that these were not jeopardized by any serious efforts at regime change by the Japanese. Several major war criminals were freed (*see box, left*) and the Yakuza resumed their role as muscle for the right wing, using intimidation on anyone perceived as left wing. Forty years later, the Yakuza approach had not changed. In 1988, Yakusa leader Masaru Fujii declared on French TV: "We try to teach the Japanese spirit to the Japanese. We break up labor strikes and we march [in] opposition to the leftists."

Partly in exchange for this service, the incoming ruling political party, the Liberal Democratic Party (LDP), like the Americans before them, allowed the Yakuza to continue their activities unchecked.

Two important Japanese cultural factors have greatly facilitated Yakuza activities. One is the need to preserve face – to avoid at all costs being put in an embarrassing position. The other is the desire for peace and quiet, a horror of confrontation. As a result, the Yakuza have found blackmailing banks and companies to be very lucrative. Threatening to reveal something untoward about a company or its executives can bring the Yakuza blackmail payments, insider deals, and access to vast unsecured loans. One branch of the Yakuza, known as *sokaiya* or "stockholder meeting specialists" prey on companies by infiltrating stockholders' meetings, disrupting them and forcing policy in the direction they desire.

Financial Crime and the Yakuza

Most major Japanese companies pay off the Yakuza, and many smaller ones are victimized. The *sokaiya*'s attempts to move into foreign companies based in Japan have not been very successful: to their chagrin, Westerners appear to have no sense of shame. After legal changes in the 1990s, several companies decided that conflict or embarrassment would be better than Yakuza control, but trying to break links with *sokaiya* has resulted in threats, shootings, and bombings. The problem remains unsolved.

The younger generation of Yakuza recruited from the *bosozoku* are not as concerned with public sensibilities as their elders and their antisocial behavior has given rise to complaints – something that requires a great deal of courage in Japan. Violence and street crime have become much more common (although there are still only some 20 gun deaths per year). The old-style Yakuza blame the young, whom they consider lack the proper attitude, and also foreign criminals for drawing attention to crime and destroying the understanding between Yakuza and the general public.

Yakuza violence is mostly aimed at those who resist the extortion rackets or who fail to pay back loans on time. One trick is to force the debtor to insure his life in favor of the Yakuza. He is then murdered, often while abroad, and the Yakuza collect payment.

Red light district
A neon sign advertises a peepshow theater in Tokyo's Kabukicho entertainment district. The Yakuza's control over the area is now challenged by Chinese and Korean gangsters, who are moving into Japan in increasing numbers.

Another branch of the Yakuza with which ordinary Japanese are increasingly likely to have had contact is the *jiageya*. These are thugs who remove unwanted tenants. Harassment, extortion, arson, and even murder are among the methods used. During the artificially induced property boom of the 1980s, increasing numbers of Japanese, victimized by the *jiageya*, became aware of the realities of Yakuza methods. The subsequent collapse of Japan's economy and its effect on banking, jobs, and pensions – all previously considered absolutely stable – served to alert the country to the real costs of allowing national asset stripping on a scale only paralleled in the Soviet Union after the end of communism.

The Yakuza Abroad

The Yakuza's first overseas operations were in China and Korea. They joined forces with right-wing groups in the 1920s and 1930s and were active in Japanese-occupied Asia, trafficking drugs and people. After World War II, the Korean connection continued; the Yakuza were heavily implicated in the kidnapping in Tokyo in 1973 of South Korea's future liberal president, Kim Dae Jung, who was hated by the right wing.

Because Japan had been so unwilling to assimilate the Koreans trafficked by the

Rooftop shrine
Shinto is Japan's national religion. Here a traditional Shinto shrine in Shinjuku, central Tokyo, stands surrounded by modern skyscrapers.

Yakuza as forced labor in the first half of the 20th century, the criminal world provided one of the few career options for those who wanted to move up from jobs at the lowest level. Not only did Koreans become extremely important in Japan's underworld, but, as Korea began to open in the late 1970s, the Korean Yakuza were in an excellent position to provide a bridge.

The Japanese Yakuza began to invest heavily in South Korea, where costs were low, while young Koreans were sent to Japan to learn mob skills. The Yakuza were in a position to speed up greatly the access of organized crime to South Korea, in particular by infiltrating the docks and the construction industry, people trafficking, sex tourism, drug and gun running, and the illegal disposal of toxic waste.

Sex and Drugs

The Yakuza were relatively slow in moving outside Asia, largely for cultural reasons: the older generation felt uncomfortable where they could not speak their own language and where they would not be protected by long-standing networks of favors. This began to change in the 1960s. The new generation, often English-speaking, lightly tattooed, and comfortable in an international environment, fanned out across the world. They set up sex tours for Japanese men to destinations such as Hong Kong and South Korea. Pressure groups soon began to campaign against this form of exploitation, so the Yakuza started trafficking women (often recruited under false pretenses) into Japan to cater for the huge sex industry there. They established links with foreign crime organizations, and, having opened up routes for the trafficking of people, they were able to adapt them for other activities such as gun running.

In the 1930s, Japan held a position similar to that of Colombia today: an aggressive drug producer and distributor, and a major heroin supplier to the United States. During World War II the Japanese government, with the help of the Yakuza, provided its conquered populations with opiates to keep them docile, and supplied its own soldiers and airmen with amphetamines to keep them active and alert. "Speed" and "ice" (crystal methamphetamine) remain the most popular drugs in Japan today, with an estimated two million users. To avoid the possible problems involved in producing methamphetamines at home, the Yakuza established drug factories abroad, in collaboration with local organized crime. South Korea was the preferred location, but at the time of the 1988 Seoul Olympics the Korean government made an effort to clean up the country and drug production moved on, through the same countries that hosted Japanese sex tours – essentially anywhere that law enforcement was lax, policemen underpaid, corruption rife, and where the population was unaware of the dangers of allowing organized criminal groups into their country.

The early communist regime in China had largely eradicated organized crime, but in the 1980s it re-emerged and soon the Yakuza and the Triads (see pp106–117) were working together. Japan needed people, for the sex industry and as cheap labor. Chinese traffickers were happy to provide illegal immigrants, whom

CASE STUDY

The Mystery of the Missing Trillions

In the mid-1980s, the marriage between the Yakuza and the legitimate business world was in a sense officially consummated. The Ministry of Finance noted with dismay that local Yakuza in central Japan were taking over a number of banks, with the result that these banks were in severe trouble. The Minister of Finance appealed, indirectly, to the head of the the Yamaguchi-gumi, Takenaka Masahisa, to come to Tokyo and help rid the banks of the local Yakuza influence. Takenaka agreed to do so, thus establishing a formal relationship between government, banking, and the Yakuza.

The economic slowdown of the 1990s severely affected the Japanese economy. By then, politicians, businessmen, and bureaucrats were inextricably linked to the Yakuza. Scandal after scandal rocked Japan. *No pan shabu shabu* ("No panties hot pot") referring to one notorious restaurant and its waitresses' costume – or lack of it – became code for the lavish entertainment offered to politicians by their underworld contacts. Japan has a tradition of mixing entertainment with business and gift-giving, so many did not realize that it concealed a much more serious threat. Banks and other major financial institutions collapsed and the slowdown turned into recession. During this time, the Yakuza are estimated to have sucked out of the Japanese economy between 30 and 200 trillion yen – a sum in the order of a trillion dollars.

Yakuza leader
Takenaka Masahisa, the leader of the Yamaguchi-gumi Syndicate, was the first Yakuza boss to make a formal agreement with the Japanese government in the 1980s. He was murdered by a rival gang soon afterward.

Booming business
An aerial view of Tokyo's business district, Shinjuku. The Yakuza invested heavily in real estate during Japan's boom years.

"Stockholder meeting specialists" at work
Sokaiya disrupt a stockholders' meeting of Mitsubishi Heavy Industries in 1971. The *sokaiya* use these stockholders' meetings to extort money from companies by intimidation.

the Yakuza could furnish with fake papers and put to work where it suited them. Both China and North Korea are now known to be major drug producers. It can be assumed that the Yakuza are not operative in North Korea, but are taking full advantage of the flow of drugs to act as distributors, as they do with drugs from the Golden Triangle, the major heroin-producing area of Southeast Asia.

The Yakuza Muscle In

From the 1970s, more and more Japanese began to travel abroad. The Yakuza, with the experience they had gleaned from sex tourism, saw no reason why Japanese money should be wasted on the host countries, and began buying into restaurants, hotels, exchange bureaux, shooting ranges, and golf clubs in overseas destinations, providing everything required by Japanese visitors, who found themselves paying wildly inflated prices.

Hotels, gambling joints, and massage parlors were all in a position to provide information that could be very useful to the *sokaiya*. As legitimate Japanese business ventured abroad in the 1970s, the Yakuza exported the extortion rackets that were so successful at home, and Japanese businesses abroad were forced to pay protection in London or Waikiki, just as in Tokyo. There were no complaints, however, and the host countries were largely unaware of what was going on.

By the mid-1980s, the Yakuza was concerned not so much how to make money, as how to launder it. They invested heavily in real estate in the West. This included $10 million in 1988 for a New York golf club with George Bush Senior's brother to act as advisor. In 1991, a bid to build a $300 million casino in the Marianas was temporarily foiled by the astuteness of a

---

CASE STUDY

The Yamaguchi-gumi

The Yamaguchi-gumi is Japan's largest organized crime syndicate, with about 17,500 members. It arose from the gangs who organized labor on the Kobe docks in the early 20th century, paralleling developments under "Lucky" Luciano in New York at the same period. After World War II, Kazuo Taoka (1913–81), transformed a small waterfront gang into Japan's most powerful criminal coalition. Before long, Taoka had expanded into the usual fields, in Osaka as well as Kobe. By 1981, the Yamaguchi-gumi controlled

Yoshinori Wantanabe
After a difficult decade, Yoshinori Watanabe took over the Yamaguchi-gumi in 1989, initiating new policies and alliances.

some 2,500 businesses including language schools and hospitals, with an estimated $500,000,000 annual revenue. Taoka had close relations with such men as Yoshio Kodama and wielded immense political influence. What made the Yamaguchi-gumi so successful, able to ride out gang wars and a temporary split in the 1980s, was Taoka's foresight in combining tradition with innovation. He pioneered forcing legitimate businesses to accommodate the presence of the Yakuza and encouraged seizing new opportunities, including drugs – formally forbidden – both at home and abroad.

Since 1989, the Yamaguchi-gumi has regained strength, surviving both government crackdowns and economic recession. The 1995 Kobe earthquake offered an excellent opportunity for public relations, as the Yamaguchi-gumi provided relief far ahead of the government. Nevertheless, in 2003, a courageous group of Gifu residents were the first to dare to demand the closure of local Yamaguchi-gumi offices because Yakuza behavior was making life intolerable.

Yakuza and the General Public

The Yakuza enjoyed until very recently a high degree of tolerance by the public, in part thanks to their romantic "Robin Hood" connotations. For 50 years Japan has also prided itself on its low crime rate. It was part of the Yakuza ethos that they did not interfere with ordinary people, but let them walk on "the sunny side of the street." No one was particularly worried about what happened to the gambler who defaulted on his debts, as long as the town was safe for women and children. However, violence began to escalate, and by the 1990s it became clear that the Japanese preference for non confrontation was becoming strained. In 2003, a courageous group of Gifu residents demanded that the local Yamaguchi-gumi offices be closed, because their endless fighting with rivals and antisocial behavior were making life intoleratble for the whole neighborhood. The Yakuza also benefit from familiarity and the fact that the Japanese expect a certain level of corruption.

A young Japanese couple setting up a sushi bar will expect to pay protection to local gangsters and will accept it as part of their running expenses, hoping that the amount demanded does not get out of hand. And as Yakuza control becomes more international, the Japanese-Canadian couple in Vancouver will realize that their Canadian passports will not protect them from demands for protection money from local members of the Yakuza and that they would be very ill-advised to call the police.

"Protection" money
A typical sushi bar in Tokyo. Setting up a small business in Japan often involves having to pay protection money to the local Yakuza.

Tourist trap
The Yakuza have moved abroad and exploit Japanese tourists (left) by providing overpriced services specifically tailored to them, such as tours, exchange bureaux, restaurants, and souvenir shops.

U.S. investigator who, however, had to flee for his life. By 1995, an estimated $4 billion of real estate in Australia was in the hands of the Yakuza.

In Europe, the Yakuza again acquired billions of dollars' worth of real estate and also saw the investment opportunities in works of art. For example, Picasso's masterpiece *Noces de Pierrette* was bought for $53 million in 1989. Its present whereabouts is unknown, but it is believed to be in the hands of the Yakuza, like many other works by the Impressionists and post-Impressionists that have dropped out of sight.

Prosperity meant that the Japanese began to be selective about what jobs they were prepared to do. To fill the labor gap, the Yakuza headed to South America, especially Brazil, where there was a large expatriate Japanese colony. Soon 100,000 or more largely illegal immigrants had joined the bottom of the social heap in Japan and the Yakuza had become firmly established in major South American cities such as São Paolo, adding drug and gun running to the human trafficking that had originally brought them there.

International Contacts

Wherever they operate abroad, the Yakuza have had to come to an arrangement with the local criminal structure. In some places, such as the Philippines, Los Angeles, Hawaii, and São Paolo, they have been able to move in. In others, such as New York, China, and Russia, they have largely remained on the outside, essentially as clients of the existing structures, cooperating with them in extremely lucrative deals, whether in gambling, drugs or, for example, shipping stolen cars to Vladivostok in Russia and receiving guns and illegal marine products in exchange. The West was slow to react to the presence of the Yakuza. The Japanese had a reputation as model citizens from an almost crime-free country and those who stood to make money with the Yakuza were pleased at new business opportunities.

The Yakuza's most important overseas opportunities are almost certainly in the United States. The Yakuza's increasing power there was pointed out by former U.S. attorney Michael Sterrett, who said: "There are now shadow governments in the U.S. and Japan that collect their own taxes, make their own rules, and enforce their own laws. An alliance between the Yakuza and U.S. organized crime means that drugs and guns and huge amounts of money will be moving across the world, accountable to no one but the mobs themselves. "

The Yakuza in the United States

Early in the 20th century, the Yakuza's role in the United States was largely connected with Japan's position as a major drug distributor, providing the local Mafias with opium derivatives and amphetamines. Their first bases were in California, especially Los Angeles. More recently, they have tended to come in via Hawaii, where they have reached an accommodation with the local crime syndicates, and combine investment with pleasure in all aspects of the entertainment industry, as well as shaking down Japanese firms and exploiting Japanese tourists.

One aspect of the United States has particular appeal: guns. Introduced from Europe in the 16th century, when Japan rejected Western influence and closed itself to the outside world, access to guns became essentially a government prerogative. This policy, designed to limit violence and concentrate power, was very successful. Still banned after the forced opening by the United States in 1853, guns have great appeal for the Japanese and, with bullets at $15 each, the smuggling of arms, mainly from the United States, constitutes an important Yakuza sideline, with U.S. military personnel often colluding.

As Japan's economy took off from 1970, and the Yakuza became more confident abroad, they turned their attention to Las

Vegas, but without notable success. However, they invested billions of dollars in real estate elsewhere in the United States and in Canada.

Perhaps most serious are Yakuza plans to move into legitimate U.S. businesses and banks with the tactics that worked so well in Japan and on overseas Japanese firms. The *sokaiya* aim for the usual favors: unsecured loans, insider deals, and cooperation over laundering their share of the $50 billion yearly U.S. drug bill, but it is proving tough.

The Yakuza and the Police

The Japanese police have an excellent record in controlling and solving ordinary crime, but their relationship with the Yakuza is difficult and complex. Corruption scandals within the police, particularly in Osaka and Kobe, the home territory of the Yamaguchi-gumi, broke in the early 1980s. Although the corruption was relatively small-scale – traditional gifts, invitations to parties, and bribes in exchange for favors to the Yakuza – the revelations shocked the general public, which had great respect for the police, because they revealed a deeply entrenched web of corruption. A similar, more serious, scandal broke in Tokyo in the 1990s.

The Yakuza's close relationship with business and politics poses a huge problem for the police. A politician may well offer bail for a known Yakuza boss, which puts the ordinary policeman in an impossible situation. There is, therefore, some collusion between the two – the Yakuza save face on occasion by offering confessions or allowing the arrest of expendable members, while the police reciprocate by facilitating the escape of the real bosses and turning a blind eye to, for example, trafficked women and laborers brutally exploited by the gangs.

The Japanese police and the Yakuza tend to share a similar world view: right wing, authoritarian, nationalist, with respect for the samurai tradition and a dislike of foreign influence. It is partly this that has often made the police reluctant to collaborate with foreign law enforcement agencies in tackling the Yakuza, even though only international cooperation can make any impact on transnational crime. The police fear, rightly, that sensitive material may reach the media, and that foreigners will not understand the complexities of Japanese culture. Their loyalties are divided between devotion to law and order and the fate of

Taking on the Yakuza
Ridley Scott's 1989 film *Black Rain* starred Michael Douglas (left) and Andy Garcia as U.S. policemen teaming up with their Japanese counterpart Ken Takakura to fight the Yakuza.

their conationals in foreign hands. There are indications that attitudes are changing. In August 2003, the *Mainichi Shinbun* newspaper reported the police requesting an extra 10,000 men to help battle the worst crimewave since the war, while at the same time, changes in the law have finally made Yakuza bosses responsible for crimes committed by their underlings.

Minbo no Onna: The Gentle Art of Japanese Extortion

It is not surprising that there has been comparatively little protest against the Yakuza, although the number of complaints is rising. Protesters have been swiftly punished by means such as threats to their children, bombs or, in the case of the women's groups providing refuges for trafficked sex workers, rapes and beatings.

Criticism too is apt to be avenged. The first edition of David E. Kaplan and Alec Dubro's book *Yakuza*, the most important work in English on the subject, was shredded on the orders of publisher Robert Maxwell, as a favor to his friend Ryoichi Sasakawa (*see box, p100*). There are many other

Minbo no Onna
Juzo Itami's courageous 1992 film *Minbo no Onna* featured a female lawyer fighting against the Yakuza, who are depicted as common bullies.

examples of Yakuza efforts to intimidate the media both in Japan and abroad.

In 1992, the movie *Minbo no Onna* came out (the title means "Extortion Lady," though the English version was titled *The Gentle Art of Japanese Extortion*). In it, Juzo Itami, one of Japan's top directors, related the adventures of a woman lawyer attempting to deal with a gang of extortionists. Itami did not portray the Yakuza in the heroic role they prefer, but as common bullies preying on ordinary people, who could be dealt with if only society would find the courage. A week later, Itami was waylaid and attacked by a group of men who slashed him viciously across the face and arms.

Itami's movie *Marutai no Onna* (Women of the Police Protection Program) was released in 1997. Itami told the press: "Nowadays everybody is afraid of the Yakuza ... I cannot forgive the Yakuza for the way they humiliate society. Through *Marutai no Onna*, I want people to know that they can fight the Yakuza and win." In December of that year, Itami fell to his death from the eighth floor of a building.

Critic of the Yakuza
Japanese director Juzo Itami working on a film set. Itami died in suspicious circumstances after portraying the Yakuza in an unfavorable light in his movies.

CHINA

THE MEANING OF "TRIAD" AND "TONG"
"Triad" was coined in 1821 by Dr Milne of Malacca in the first English description of the Three Unities Society. A "Tong" originally simply meant a meeting place.

TERRITORY

Hong Kong and Shanghai are traditional centers of Triad activity. Chinese crime groups followed their conationals as they settled across the world. Recently Triads have become active once more in China.

● **HONG KONG**
For 150 years, the main base of the Triads.

● **SHANGHAI**
Triad stronghold at the start of the 20th century.

● **TAIWAN**
Postwar Nationalist stronghold and Triad center.

● **MACAU**
Former Portuguese colony and gambling haven.

● **SINGAPORE**
Site of early Triad activity overseas.

Hong Kong is an important center for narcotics smuggling. In 2002, drug seizures were as follows:

416 lbs/189 kg	Heroin
1,823 lbs/827 kg	Cannabis
216 lbs/98 kg	Ketamine
191 lbs/87 kg	Metamphetamine (Ice)
96,024	Ecstasy tablets

The Triads and the Tongs

" These Asian criminal enterprises adapt easily to the changes around them, have multilingual abilities, and can be highly sophisticated in their criminal operations. "

FEDERAL BUREAU OF INVESTIGATION

The blanket term "Triad" covers a number of different gangs with different names within the international Chinese community, which generally share a common foundation myth, common aims, and similar strategies. Members of a particular Triad form a surrogate "family" and normally come from the same area of China, although they are not related by blood.

Triads are extremely fluid, consisting of groups ranging from half a dozen to 100,000, often changing name and often engaged in vicious gang wars which cause them to vanish and reform. The general nature of the Triads and the political events that have encouraged their growth are of greater importance than the histories of individual gangs, which are notoriously fluid.

The "invincible Triads" are spreading. Checking their spread is not impossible, as the courageous efforts by law enforcement agencies in Hong Kong and Taiwan make clear. They can even be eliminated, as Mao did it in China, but his methods are hardly appropriate to Western democracies. Prevention, however, is better than cure and this is where the West has been slow to respond to the danger posed by the Triads.

The problem is partly that the Triad form of crime has been unfamiliar in most countries for centuries and therefore there

Gang members arrested
Police arrest suspected members of a Triad in a Hong Kong restaurant. They wear masks to protect their identity.

Revered emperor
A portrait of Hung Wu, who became the first emperor of the Ming Dynasty in 1368. The Triads look back on the Ming period as a golden age and trace their origins to the secret societies that supported the Ming.

are often no appropriate legal mechanisms, such as witness protection programs, in place to deal with it. Since Triad activity has until recently been internal within overseas Chinese communities, there has been a tendency to ignore it, a no longer acceptable form of racial discrimination.

Foundation – Myths and Facts
The Triads cannot be viewed in isolation, simply as violent criminals involved in extortion, drugs and slaving. They need to be considered in a political and social context, and also in the light of their own mythology. Otherwise, it is impossible to understand either their view of themselves, or the grip in which they hold their conationals worldwide.

China has a long history of secret societies, thought to go back at least to the T'ang dynasty (619–907) when Buddhism was

proscribed and driven underground, rather like the Falung Gong today. This was probably when the White Lotus sect was founded, which reappeared during the Mongol period, when there is evidence that funds were gathered by extortion and kidnapping. The sect played a major role in driving out the hated foreigners and installing a former Buddhist monk, Hung Wu, as the first emperor of the Ming in 1368. Modern Triads identify with the patriotic and nationalist aspects of the White Lotus, as well as their Buddhist beliefs.

The "First Five Ancestors"
Another myth relates to the 17th century. China was threatened by barbarians, and the second Ch'ing emperor offered to reward anyone who could save the country. The 128 monks of Shao Lin monastery, masters of the martial arts, volunteered their aid and drove back the enemy. The emperor – who was a foreign Manchu – grew fearful of the monks' power and set fire to the monastery. 110 monks died in the flames; only 18 managed to escape the fire, of whom five ultimately reached safety. They are known as the "First Five Ancestors."

The five monks underwent a series of miraculous adventures. They saw an incense burner that blazed with four Chinese characters reading *Fan Ch'ing Fuk Ming* (Overthrow Ch'ing, Restore Ming). In the mythical City of Willows, the monks founded a secret society to avenge the death of their brothers and drive the Manchu from China. The message in the burning incense was to be their oath and elements of their journey became part of the elaborate Triad initiation ritual (*see box, p109*).

Identification with patriots and folk heroes bound Triad members together even if they came from different areas and linguistic groups. In their eyes, the means justified the ends. They were not common criminals – their activities were to raise funds for the ultimate good of China. Today, many martial arts movies propagate the image of Triads as folk heroes, facilitating the recruitment of impressionable youths desperate for status.

The first historical evidence of the Triads comes from 1788, when a merchant tortured by the authorities admitted the existence of

the Tiandihui or Heaven and Earth Society (Triad), then at least 20 years old: "Originally, the reason for people's willingness to enter the society was that if you had a wedding or a funeral, you could get help from the other members; if you came to blows with someone, there were people who would help you. If you met robbers, once they heard the secret code of their own society, they would then bother you no further."

This is an important function of the Triads. They still provide an interface and support system for Chinese immigrants abroad, who are often marginalized in an indifferent or hostile society. There is a price, however. Triad support must be reciprocated and the Triads have always been outlaws, parasitic on their own society. Protection rackets and extortion are the cheapest, easiest, and safest way of raising funds and that is what joining a Triad implies.

"Fan Ch'ing Fuk Ming"

(Overthrow Ch'ing, Restore Ming). Slogan adopted by the Triads

City of the Triads

Hong Kong was a pirate stronghold long before the British arrived in 1842, when China ceded the territory to them. Triads and outlaws quickly took advantage of it

as a place of refuge from the Manchu government and soon Hong Kong was the main Triad city. The British authorities banned membership of secret societies in 1845, but the law had little or no effect. Working to a typical organized crime pattern, the Triads quickly came to control the labor market, then extorted a large part of the laborers' wages. Drugs, gambling, and prostitution, as well as markets and street stalls, also came under Triad control. From the 1850s, however, they realized the advantages of British rule. In China, where they

Fighting monks
A display of the martial arts' prowess of the Shao Lin monks. Triad foundation myths are based on the story of the escape of Shao Lin monks after the Manchu emperor tried to murder them.

INSIDE STORY

THE 36 OATHS

Traditionally, a new recruit to a Triad Society took 36 oaths during his initiation ceremony. The oaths were inscribed on sheets of paper at the Triad lodge entrance, along with the names of initiates, and embroidered on the back of the yellow gauze quilt that hung over the altar before which initiates made their vows.

In the series of oaths the initiate swore to be loyal to his fellow members and never to betray or cheat them. He promised to help them and their families if they needed it, and be hospitable toward them. He swore never to disclose the secrets of the organization.

One penalty for breaking the oaths was to be killed by myriads of swords. This was the famous "death of a thousand cuts," in which all the major muscles and the scalp are cut through, generally with a butcher's knife.

Once a man became involved with the Triads, there was no turning back, as the 13th oath makes clear: "If I should change my mind and deny my membership of the Hung family [Triad] I will be killed by myriads of swords." The 36th oath summed up the Triad's professed aims: "I shall be loyal and faithful and shall endeavor to overthrow Ch'ing and restore Ming by coordinating my efforts with those of my sworn brethren… Our common aim is to avenge our Five Ancestors."

CASE STUDY

Triad Initiation Ceremonies

In 1960, W.P. Morgan, a Hong Kong police inspector, published an account of the elaborate Triad rituals based on his own experience and interviews with imprisoned Triad members.

Initiations took place in the Triad lodge, representing the mythical "City of Willows." The ceremony was directed by the Incense Master dressed in white and the society's leader, dressed in red. All other officials and members dressed in black.

The ceremony began with a ritual dance, then the neophyte approached the east gate, where he was challenged by an official, with whom he exchanged a ritual handshake. He passed beneath an arch of drawn swords. He had to pass through three more entrances guarded by statues of famous Triad generals. Then the neophyte stood before the altar. The walls were hung with records of the lives of the First Five Ancestors and other Hung heroes. When the neophyte approached the altar, he stepped through a bamboo hoop representing the hole through which the monks escaped from the Shao Lin monastery, in a symbolic enactment of rebirth. Before the altar on which are kept ritual objects, the neophyte took the 36 oaths (*see box, opposite*).

During the ceremony, the legendary history of the Hung society is chanted and a cock is beheaded. The neophyte's finger is pricked and dipped in a bowl containing spices, wine, the ashes from burned paper strips, and the blood of the cock. He then licks his finger.

Three days later a face-washing ritual took place, symbolizing purification and rebirth as a member of the Hung. The neophyte was then a full member of the Triad.

Triad Lodge
A plan of a Triad lodge, where initiation rituals took place. The walls were hung with inscriptions, and the lodge was filled with objects symbolizing elements of Triad foundation myths. In front of the altar the initiate re-enacted significant stages of the Shao Lin monks' journey from the monastery to the City of Willows.

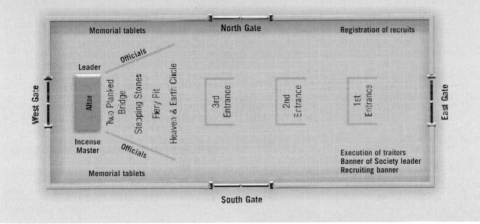

Martial arts hero
Bruce Lee in the movie *Enter The Dragon* (1973). Martial arts films often feature Triad fighters, and are popular in the West.

concentrations of criminals in the world. Filthy and squalid, with an estimated 70,000 people living in an area of roughly 7 acres, it was alive with rats and had no sanitation or amenities of any kind. The main street was known as "Heroin Alley." It was a far cry from the romantic idea of the City of Willows – but it was the Triads' citadel and several of the most important gangs had their headquarters there.

Hong Kong's first "homegrown" Triad was founded by the Nationalist leader, Dr Sun Yat-sen at the start of the 20th century. Called the Chung Wo Tong (Lodge of Loyalty and Righteousness), a high-sounding name typical of the Triads, it is still one of the most powerful Triad groups.

were stirring up rebellion, capture meant death. It suited them to keep Hong Kong and Macau as bolt holes, and more and more Triads poured in. They gave the British relatively little trouble for the next 50 years, apart from infiltrating the police force, but exploited local Chinese in every way possible.

In 1898, China leased Hong Kong and the New Territories to Britain for 99 years, but retained rights over Kowloon Walled City, an enclave consisting of the old Mandarin's residence and a walled compound. Because no police force was responsible for it, the Walled City became one of the densest

Triad suspects
Some of the 435 men suspected of being members of secret societies were rounded up at Kowloon Police headquarters in Hong Kong, during the 1956 crackdown on the Triads.

Triads in the British Empire

The Triads are parasitical, living off the Chinese community wherever they have settled. Triads were operating in the British colony of Singapore by 1830 and their protection rackets affected Europeans as well as the Chinese – indeed this was the only place where Europeans had to join the Triads in order to survive.

As the Chinese poured into Malaysia throughout the 19th century, the Triad problem escalated. British magistrates managed to limit their impact on the foreign community. There remained, however, plenty of scope for preying on Chinese businesses, smuggling in illegal immigrants, providing labor for the plantations and the mines, supplying prostitutes, alcohol, drugs, and gambling facilities to the workers, and finally relieving both the prostitutes and the workers of a large part of their wages. Wherever in the world they are, Triads follow a similar pattern of activities today.

The British authorities tried to prevent the activiies of the Triads from disrupting their commercial interests, but were unable to deal with the root problem. Captain Charles Speedy, an Englishman employed by a local Muslim ruler did succeed in hamstringing the Triads, at least temporarily, using a mercenary force of Sikhs and Pathans recruited from India. Later, when Speedy was appointed Assistant Resident for the area, the position was consolidated by his negotiations with the Triads.

The situation of the British in Malaysia was difficult. The Malays resented being colonized and the Chinese, imported as coolies, literally meaning "bitter labor," were exploited. The Triads hated all non-Chinese on principle and in particular those who tried to limit their criminal activities. At the beginning of the 20th century, however, multi-ethnic Triads were formed for the first time.

In the 1950s, the Triads joined the Malaysian fight for independence. This was a mistake. The British were far more tolerant of the Triads – or incompetent in dealing with them – than the Muslim rulers who took control after Independence in 1957. The Triads of Malaysia began to look for new fields of action.

Triad tamer
Captain Charles Speedy, one of the few who managed to successfully control Triad activity.

At the start of the 20th century, Shanghai was the largest city in China. Policing it was immensely complex because of the foreign concessions, each under the control of a different power with a different law code. It was a city where "anything went" – ideal for Triad activities, such as opium smuggling, slaving, labor racketeering, pimping, and extortion. There were also fortunes to be made from the foreign companies, which required local Chinese agents in order to

trade. The complexity of the situation was exemplified by Inspector Huang, who was both the leader of the powerful Triad, the Green Gang, and one of the local heads of the French Sureté.

Shanghai Network
A leading Green Gang member, Tu Yueh-sheng, or "Big-Eared Tu," was probably the most powerful Triad leader in political terms. Fabulously rich, Tu lived in the French part of Shanghai. Among Tu's friends was Charlie Soong, the protégé of a U.S. millionaire, who funded Soong in the hope that he would preach the gospel in China. Soong set up a printing concern, where he produced both Methodist tracts and Triad initiation certificates. One of Soong's daughters married Sun Yat-sen; another married Chiang Kai-shek, Sun's successor as Nationalist leader. Sun, popular as the overthrower of the hated Manchu Dynasty in 1911, found the Triads to be excellent fundraisers for his cause, particularly in Malaysia and Singapore.

International settlement
Shanghai in the 1920s was a booming international city. It was famous for its many brothels, opium dens, and gambling joints that made local Triads immensely rich and powerful.

It is likely that Tu introduced Chiang to the Soongs. A long-term member of the Green Gang, with a background in art theft, extortion, and armed robbery, Chiang rose through the ranks of the Kuomintang (Nationalist Party) to succeed Sun Yat-sen as leader in 1926.

Communists versus Triads

Chiang called on Tu and the Green Gang when he wanted to break links with the communists in 1927. The Triads, supported by the Kuomintang, began their slaughter of labor unionists, communists, and left-wing intellectuals, killing more than 5,000. These events radically changed the communist leader Mao Zedong's view of the Triads. In 1926, he had said: "The *yu-min* [rural vagrants] consist of peasants who have lost all opportunity of employment as a result of oppression and exploitation... They can be divided into soldiers, bandits, robbers, beggars, and prostitutes. ... They have secret organizations in various places: for instance, the Triad Society in Fujian ... the Green Gang in Shanghai. ... These people are capable of fighting very bravely, and if properly led can become a revolutionary force." Chiang, and with him Tu, became

heroes to the business community and later to Western countries for acting as a bulwark against communism.

The Japanese invasion of China in 1931 changed all the alignments. Some Triads collaborated with the Japanese, while others remained loyal to Chiang, who in 1942 became commander of Allied forces in the region. Tu continued his support, in

particular by providing funds through opium sales. The Green Gang also served as effective enforcers. The U.S. generals accepted every kind of hospitality and lavish gifts from these men, most memorably an armored car, complete with submachine guns, which had originally been made to order for Al Capone.

Home in Hong Kong

At last the Japanese were defeated. Almost immediately civil war broke out between the communists and the Kuomintang. The Kuomintang were defeated in 1949, and Chiang and his followers fled to Taiwan, where he established himself successfully, as did the Triads. He ruled until 1975 and was succeeded by his son. Mao went on to rule China with an iron hand, promulgating in 1952 a fierce campaign against tax evasion, bribery, cheating on state contracts, and the stealing of state economic intelligence.

In World War II (1939–45) most Hong Kong Triads reached an accommodation with the Japanese occupiers, pimping for the troops and serving as enforcers, thugs, and spies. The Japanese encouraged drug use among the non-Japanese to make them

---

Tu Yueh-sheng (Big-Eared Tu)

BIOGRAPHY

Tu Yueh-sheng was born about 1888 near Shanghai in one of the worst slums in China. Tu was viciously brutalized as a child and by the time he was in his teens was a contract killer, as well as a drug runner.

Shanghai was an international city, divided up among foreign powers. Tu forcibly amalgamated or took over the existing criminal gangs, emerging as second-in-command of the now dominant Green Gang by the 1910s. He lived in a mansion on Rue Wagner in the French Concession. His personal fortune was estimated at US$40 million but, as he effectively controlled everything that went on in Shanghai, as well as the Yangtze waterway system as far as the opium-growing areas, he had access to far greater sums of money.

Among Tu's influential friends was Charlie Soong, who had powerful U.S. contacts.

These contacts were important to Tu, in part because their American Christian background was reassuring to the foreign community and lent him the respectability that enabled him to operate with impunity – for example, he was director of the Red Cross – and in part because their support was useful when he came to set up the Shanghai stock exchange, again an excellent source of revenue.

Tu opposed the increasingly powerful communists, who threatened his entire financial empire. Consequently both he and the Green Gang were delighted to oblige when his friend Chiang Kai-shek, leader of the Nationalists, felt that the time had come to sever links with them. Tu's gang beat up or killed thousands of students, communists, and others in 1927. Tu fled the communists and escaped to Hong Kong in 1949, where he died in 1951.

Dates c.1888–1951
Details Tu Yueh-sheng ("Big-Eared Tu") was also known as "The Opium King" and was the most powerful gangster in Shanghai at the beginning of the 20th century.

Opposing leaders
Chiang Kai-shek toasts Mao Zedong in 1946, shortly before war broke out between the Nationalists and Communists. The victorious Mao relentlessly stamped out crime and corruption, forcing many Triads to flee China.

more docile, and consolidated the Triads' position by allowing them to set up opium and heroin dens.

After the war, Hong Kong was returned to Britain. The authorities made the mistake of trying to ban opium. In a city of addicts the result was to make the drug more expensive, which brought bigger profits to the suppliers – the Triads. The Kuomintang set up new Triads expressly to fight communism, just as the Japanese used the Yakuza and the Americans the Sicilian Mafia. One of the most important Triads today, the 14K, was established by a Kuomintang general. The 14K soon had 80,000 members.

Fighting Back against the Triads

The police deported a number of 14K leaders to Taiwan in the mid-1950s. In 1956, the people of Hong Kong rose in protest against the Triads for the first time and demanded action. Some 10,000 more Triads were arrested, new laws were drafted, and there were more deportations to Taiwan. For 10 years, the situation greatly improved. In

Taiwan, however, the exiles, together with Chiang's security guards, formed United Bamboo, still a major gang today.

In the 1960s, the Triads were well placed both geographically and culturally to profit from the expanding drug culture. Suddenly they were entering a new economic league. The Hong Kong Police had long had a problem with Triads among its Chinese members, but in the 1970s British policemen were also discovered to be in the pay of the Triads and serious corruption was uncovered. In spite of police protests, in 1974 the Independent Commission Against Corruption was set up to ensure that officers were not in receipt of "tea money," or bribes. Controls became much stricter and corruption was rooted out, at the price of mass resignations and threats of strikes. At the same time, evidence about the activities of a branch of the 14K led to many arrests. Several other large-scale operations in the 1980s considerably weakened the Hong Kong Triads, in part because the public saw that they were not invincible.

Triad citadel
A view of the Kowloon Walled City in Hong Kong, an area of high crime and a stronghold of the Triads until it was largely pulled down in the 1980s. It is now a park.

Prior to handing Hong Kong back to China in 1997, Britain got permission to level much of the Walled City. The clearance helped to reduce Triad activity, as did the Triads' fear of the incoming Chinese authorities, which led many to emigrate. In fact, the Triads need not have worried so much and everyone else should have been more concerned. China had changed, as a 1993 statement by Tao Siju, chief of the public security bureau made clear: "As for organizations like the Triads in Hong Kong, as long as these people are patriotic, as long as they are concerned with Hong Kong's prosperity and stability, we should unite with them." A worrying omen for the future.

The Sherlock Holmes Connection

The Chinese community in Britain originated largely with sailors who settled in London and other major ports in the 19th century. They formed a closed world, and the Triads settled with them. Little was known of them, but the sinister Chinaman and the opium den became a stock feature of sensationalist literature. The character of the London detective, Sherlock Holmes, was perhaps the most well-known fictional opium addict. Until the 1960s, the Triads remained largely within the Chinese community. Various Triads are now present in Britain: the 14K was one of the first to arrive there, followed by the Wo group, and more recently the Shui Fong. From the 1960s, increased immigration and the rise of the drug culture meant that they had a much greater impact on the general population. Yet a 1980s parliamentary commission declared that the Triads were "not a threat."

In the 1990s, the Triads' impact widened further as they laundered huge drug profits in Britain. The Netherlands has been

London Tong
Chinese Tong headquarters in Limehouse, East London, in the early 1900s. Tongs were originally simply support associations for Chinese immigrants.

similarly affected, as have Canada and Australia, which are battling both Triad and associated Asian youth-gang crime.

The Tongs in the United States

The Chinese began to emigrate to the United States in the mid-19th century, mainly as cheap labor to build railroads and mine gold in California. Often peasants were trafficked into the country unaware of what awaited them. Although conditions were very harsh, many of the Chinese survived and sent money back home to support their families. In 1882, the Chinese Exclusion Act was passed through the U.S. Congress and, until 1965 when the situation was finally normalized, the Chinese had little choice but to live together in Chinatowns. The Triads were already with them, as patriotic societies, "protectors" and exploiters, but this situation, whereby the Chinese could not become part of mainstream America, gave the secret associations enormous power. In the United States, these groups were known as Tongs — literally lodges, or meeting places, of which the On Leung

(Peaceful and Virtuous) was one of the most important. By 1870, there were more than 70,000 Chinese in the United States, most of them on the West Coast, with six Tongs in San Francisco, and another 24 scattered along the Pacific coast. The two leading

Backbreaking work
Chinese laborers in California in the 1890s. Thousands of Chinese were imported into the United States in the 19th century to do the toughest work involved in building the railroads and mining gold.

CHINESE·FREEMASON·SOCIETY

48 CHEE KONG TONG 48

Opium and Politics

The Triads are believed to control the distribution of 80 to 90 percent of the world's heroin and opium derivatives. One estimate of the value of the trade is US$750 billion.

The opium poppy is a hardy and labor-intensive crop, very attractive to desperately poor farmers. For centuries, opiates were seen as a blessing, although the battle with addiction is recorded as early as the 16th century. A hundred years later, the Europeans were avid for Chinese trade goods but, like the Romans, they did not want their gold and silver to flow east. They needed something the Chinese would buy: the answer was opium.

The British brought opium from India, the Americans from Turkey and Iran. The Ch'ing dynasty tried but failed to stop the pushers. By 1900, it was estimated that one third or more of the Chinese were users and 10 percent hopeless addicts. It was not until 1917 that the British agreed to cease importing opium – but that left 150 million Chinese still craving their drug. Criminals such as Tu and the Green Gang moved in.

In 1927, Mao Zedong formed the Red Army, many of whom were to die at the hands of Chiang Kai-shek, who was backed by Tu and also by money from the opium trade. This was to give Mao a lasting hatred of the Triads, whom he eliminated in mainland China when he came to power in the 1950s, causing an exodus to Hong Kong. Mao also drove out the Kuomintang and destroyed the opium fields of China, although he had no objection to drugs reaching the West, hoping they would hasten its downfall.

One of Chiang Kai-shek's generals, Li, fled to the Golden Triangle. Backed by the CIA, Li corrupted local officials and, with the help of his Anti-Communist National Salvation Army, set up a Triad network which dominated opium production for 50 years.

Communist leader
When Mao Zedong (1893–1976) became leader of China he began a concerted campaign to eliminate both the Triads and the production of opium at the same time.

Customs haul
Bags of confiscated Chinese heroin, which has been refined from opium, almost certainly grown in the area of Southeast Asia known as the Golden Triangle.

American opium den
An opium den in New York's Chinatown during the Prohibition era of the 1920s.

19th-century Tongs were the Sum Yops and the Sue Yops of San Francisco. The Sum Yops dealt in gambling, white slaving, and drugs. The Sum Yop leader, Fung Jing Toy, had started out as a "highbinder," or hatchet man, and revived the use of chain mail. However, chain mail was no protection against firearms, and Fung was shot dead in a barbershop by two Sue Yop members. The Sue Yop were then in control, but the Sum Yop were saved by the intervention of the Manchu emperor Kwang Hsu. Chinese government officials informed the Sue Yop that their relatives in China would be executed if any more Sum Yops were harmed. By the beginning of the 20th century, the San Francisco Tong wars were over.

New York Tong Wars

The Chinese in the U.S. spread east, mainly to New York in the late 19th century. New York's Chinatown was located around Chatham Square, Doyers Street, Pell Street, and Mott Street. By 1880, there were 700 Chinese residents, by 1910 more than 10,000. The New York Tong wars began in

Chinatown, New York, Early 20th Century

Chinatown, New York

The largest Chinatown in the United States today and covering about two square miles on Manhattan's Lower East Side, New York's Chinatown grew out of the slums in the Five Points area from the mid-19th century

1899. They were waged over control of the lucrative gambling business. In 1899, there were some 200 gambling establishments in New York's Chinatown, each paying an average $17.50 a week to the police in protection money. Seven percent of all winnings under $25 had to be paid to the Tongs and 14 percent over that sum. The On Leong Tong, led by Tom Lee, ran the gambling. The Hip Sing Tong had to make do with Tom Lee's leavings. Tom Lee controlled the Chinese vote (only six Chinese were qualified to vote at the time), so was made much of by Democratic Party Headquarters and given the office of deputy sheriff of New York County.

In 1900, Lee was challenged by a rival, Mock Duck, leader of the Hip Sing Tong, who sported chain mail and carried two

On Leong leader's funeral

There was a large turnout for the funeral of Tom Lee, the leader of the On Leong and so-called "Mayor of Chinatown" on January 14, 1918, in New York.

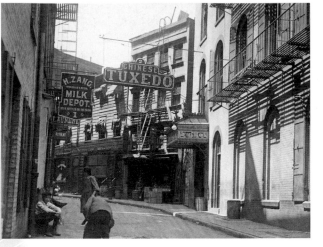

pistols as well as the traditional weapon, the hatchet. His demands for 50 percent of the gambling in Chinatown led to the war. Mock Duck managed to use his political connections to get Lee's gambling dens and whorehouses shut down by the city authorities, then re-opened them all under his ownership. So many men were killed in this first war that Warren W. Foster, judge of the Court of General Sessions, intervened. He arranged a meeting between Tom Lee and Mock Duck and persuaded them to agree a truce in exchange for defining their territories. The On Leongs received Mott

Neutral ground

Doyers Street in New York's Chinatown at the beginning of the 20th century. Doyers Street was declared neutral territory after the first Tong war.

Street, and the Hip Sings had Pell. Doyers Street was to be neutral territory. Within a week, a Hip Sing broke the truce, firing at an On Leong on Doyers Street. This phase of the war was only brought to an end by the intervention of the Chinese government. Mock Duck was eventually tried and convicted.

Fighting Reignites

The next Tong war broke out over a slave girl, Bow Kum. An ally of the Hip Sing bought her in San Francisco for $3,000. When the authorities discovered that he did not have a marriage certificate, Bow Kum was taken away and placed in a Christian Mission house. She later married Tchin Lee, a member of the On Leong, who brought her to New York, where she was recognized. Her original master demanded that Tchin Lee pay him her original purchase price, and when this was refused, the Hip Sing sent a

CASE STUDY

Macau

Leading gangster
Triad boss Wan Kuok Koi, alias "Broken Tooth," sits in a police van outside the supreme court in Macau in November 1999. Wan was given a 15-year sentence after being found guilty of heading the 14K's branch in Macau.

Macau returned to China in 1999 after 440 years of Portuguese rule. Unlike Hong Kong, the people of Macau were relieved to see the Chinese Army. One resident said it was hoped the soldiers would keep the Triads under control.

Triads were battling for dominance over the only 10 legal casinos in the China Sea region. A surge in street crime had seen murders and bombings.

In 1997, for example, 11 children in a video arcade were slashed with knives to punish the arcade owner for not paying protection money. Such incidents became routine, as the gangsters outnumbered the police by at least 3 to 2. The main gangs involved in these turf wars were the 14K, with 5,000 members, and the 3,000-strong Shiu Fong. The Sun Yee On from Hong Kong and the international Big Circle Boys are also trying to move in.

Several newspapers and the TV station received letters stating: "Warning, from today it is not allowed to mention Wan Kwok Koi ... or 14K, otherwise bullets will have no eyes [no specific targets] and knives and bullets will have no feelings." On September 8, 1998, a Triad bomb injured 10 journalists and 4 policemen who refused to be silenced. Students demonstrated against the violence in masks so they would not be recognized.

It is hardly surprising that the Chinese Army was welcomed. Since reunion with China, the situation in Macau seems to have improved, but whether the Triad problem has really been addressed, only time will tell.

letter to the On Leong demanding payment. This was rejected, and a Hip Sing highbinder slipped into Tchin Lee's house on Mott Street one night and killed Bow Kum. This unleashed another Tong war, in which more than 50 men were killed. In 1910, a truce was arranged by a committee of merchants, students, and teachers, under the auspices of the Chinese government.

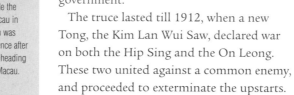

"Plant a tree in America — rest in the shade in China"
Chinese saying

The truce lasted till 1912, when a new Tong, the Kim Lan Wui Saw, declared war on both the Hip Sing and the On Leong. These two united against a common enemy, and proceeded to exterminate the upstarts. In 1913, a new truce was declared, once again at the urging of the Chinese Merchants' Association. Another war between the Hip Sing and the On Leong broke out in 1924, this time with few casualties. The early 1920s saw another serious Tong War on the West Coast, which involved several new

Celebrations in Chinatown
At the colorful New Year celebrations it is traditional for a dancing dragon to collect a "lettuce" or gift from local Chinese restaurants.

Tongs; the Suey Don, Jung Ying, Suey Ying, and Bing Kong. The U.S. situation remained relatively stable from the ending of the Tong Wars in the 1930s until the 1980s.

Extortion rackets often have an innocent face, and have been combined with popular Chinese festivals. The New Year celebrations enjoyed in many Chinatowns across the world, for example, with the splendid dragons from the martial arts clubs and other associations dancing through the streets, can conceal demands for substantial sums of money, along with the "lettuce" fed to the dragons at each restaurant they pass.

One important change for the Tongs was the arrival from the 1970s of a new wave of immigrants from Vietnam and other parts of Southeast Asia. From among these groups arose a new kind of youth gang. Many gang members are no more than children but, brutalized by their appalling experiences, they are capable of reaching levels of violence with which the host countries are ill-prepared to cope. Known as *ma jai* (horse boys), they are ideal for the Triads. They will do anything: rob,

CASE STUDY

The Big Circle Boys

In a recent poll, 91 percent of Canadians see organized crime as a very serious problem; and with good reason. Canada has become, with Australia, the destination of choice for organized crime. Its attractions include a lack of established organized crime groups (and hence a lack of institutions to control organized crime and less competition), liberal immigration, relaxed laws on racketeering and moving capital (which facilitates money laundering), light sentences, and a long, uncontrollable frontier with the United States. Over the past 25 years, Canada has become host to at least 18 active transnational criminal organizations.

LEADING CRIME GROUP

One of the most important of these is the Dai Huen Jai or Big Circle Boys (BCB). This is not a Triad, but an affiliation of loosely organized gangs, originating in mainland China. In the late 1990s, the police thought there might be some 500 in Toronto and 250 in Vancouver, but the general agreement is that there are now many more.

The BCB appears to go back to the purging of Mao's Red Guard from the Chinese Army and their imprisonment in camps, mostly near Canton, marked on maps with a large circle. On their release in the 1970s, they escaped via Hong Kong, many turning to crime. Australia and Canada were their preferred destinations.

The BCB tend to opt for high-yield, high-tech crime, much of which goes unpunished because there are few effective laws to deal with it: credit card fraud, cyber crime, luxury car theft, piracy of intellectual property, and people trafficking, as well as the more traditional activities of organized crime – drug trafficking and prostitution.

The BCB pioneered the technique of "invasion robbery," whereby the victim's house is openly invaded by a gang, who take what they want with maximum violence. Intimidation or even death of witnesses ensures that nothing can be proved against them. Other gangs have copied the technique.

Canadian law enforcement agencies have been infiltrated by the BCB and thus have a new problem: corruption within. A democratic society is extremely vulnerable to these gangs, which by definition do not share any of the premises on which that society is based and therefore cannot be controlled by the means that such a society considers acceptable. It is not surprising that so many Canadians feel they have a problem.

Canadian Chinese
Large crowds gather to celebrate the Chinese New Year in Vancouver's Chinatown.

kill, torture, extort. They are often too young for the law to touch and many, not being Chinese, are perceived by the Triads as convenient and expendable. These youth gangs, although vicious, are generally short lived, swiftly vanishing and reforming. There is more hope that they may vanish with changing social conditions than the Triads.

Modern Triads

Massive efforts to clean up organized crime under New York's mayor, Rudolph Giuliani, including greater police activity, the RICO statute, and generally increased awareness of international crime, led to a number of convictions of Tong members in the 1980s. But by this time the problem was no longer the traditional Tongs. Mao was dead. China was relaxing its controls – and the Triads at once saw an advantage.

The new-style Triads were far more forward-thinking and innovative than the old. The Big Circle Boys in particular, who formed in Hong Kong in the 1970s and then spread to Australia, the Netherlands, Britain, and Canada, following the drug trade, resumed contacts with home; Beijing now had uses for their network and expertise.

Equally worrying is the enormous increase in people trafficking into the United States, Canada, Australia, and Europe (*see p24*). The scale of people-trafficking operations is demonstrated by incidents such as that of the ship *Golden Venture*, which caused a scandal in 1993 when it ran aground in New York Harbor carrying nearly 300 Chinese would-be immigrants from Fujian Province. Ten passengers drowned in the waters of the harbor trying to reach the shore. The immigrants' fee for the smuggling gangs is often paid for by relatives in the destination country. Some estimates are that 100,000 people a year, will owe a "debt" to the Triads. The network continues to grow.

Desperate immigrants
The *Golden Venture* ran aground near New York in June 1993, carrying nearly 300 Chinese immigrants, ten of whom drowned.

NORTH AMERICA

THE MEANING OF "LA COSA NOSTRA"

The phrase "La Cosa Nostra" literally means in Italian "our thing," and was an alternative name for the Mafia first revealed in 1963 by the informer Joe Valacchi. It was a term used by the U.S. Mafia about themselves and their activities. Abbreviated to LCN, it is now standard law enforcement usage when referring to the American Mafia. Organized crime groups refer to themselves by a variety of codenames. In Chicago it is "The Outfit," in Buffalo "The Arm," and in New England "The Office."

TERRITORY

Although New York is considered the base of organized crime in the United States, it is now found across the country. The map shows the major cities where the Mafia operates today, although its tentacles reach far beyond these strongholds.

● **NEW ORLEANS**
First record of Mafia activity.

● **CHICAGO**
Home of "The Outfit," heir to Capone's organization.

● **NEW YORK**
Home of the "Five Families."

● **ATLANTIC CITY**
The home of East Coast gambling.

● **LAS VEGAS**
The gambling city built by the Mob.

New York's "Five Families" have spread their organized crime operations all over North America:

Gambino	Atlantic City, Las Vegas, Chicago
Genovese	New Orleans, Las Vegas
Bonanno	Arizona, Canada (links to Sicily)
Colombo	New Jersey, Florida
Lucchese	New Jersey, Chicago

The American Mafia

"I came to America because I heard the streets were paved with gold. When I got here I found out three things. First, the streets weren't paved in gold. Second, they weren't paved at all, and third, I was expected to pave them."

AN ANONYMOUS ITALIAN IMMIGRANT

Organized crime in the United States is the direct product of the Prohibition era (1920–33), during which the manufacture, sale, and transportation of alcoholic beverages was outlawed by the Eighteenth Amendment. It was the creation of a handful of Jewish–American and Italian–American gangsters, who established a National Crime Syndicate in 1931 that not only outlived its creators but continues its various activities to this day, despite the enormous social and economic changes that have taken place. For an organization born at a precise moment, within a very specific historical context, it is this continuity that is especially intriguing.

For many years the existence of such a nationwide organized crime network was denied by the director of the Federal Bureau of Investigation (FBI), J. Edgar Hoover, even though his agents had been carrying out surveillance of such prominent Syndicate criminals as Benjamin Siegel and Meyer Lansky for years. After numerous Mafia bosses were arrested at the Apalachin "gangland conference" of 1957 (see p159), Hoover was forced to publicly concede the existence of organized crime in the United

Crossing the Mafia code
New York gangster "Dutch" Schultz lies slumped over a table at the Palace Chop House in Newark, New Jersey, in 1935, after being shot by rival gangsters. He died two days later.

Huddled masses
European immigrants aboard a ship to the United States in 1890. It was poor and ill-educated people such as these that organized crime exploited in teeming cities such as New York and New Orleans.

States, although he still refused to accept the term "Mafia," even though it had already entered the public domain. The use of the term, with its hint at an historical link with the Sicilian Mafia, is misleading, because the U.S. Mafia has little in common with the Sicilian apart from its name.

A Nation of Immigrants
Organized crime in the United States came into being by destroying the traditional Old-World elements within its ranks. This process of destruction was completed in 1931, when Salvatore Maranzano, the last of the traditional Mafia dons, was assassinated at the instigation of a group of younger, more Americanized, criminals, who were dissatisfied with the outmoded ways of the older generation (see p148).

On a deeper level, this battle between traditional and modernizing elements was a reflection of the generational conflict that afflicted all U.S. immigrant communities to a greater or lesser extent. Children born or raised in the United States were often ignorant of their parents' values, language, and culture. The New World was born by rejecting the Old, not by transposing it across the Atlantic.

The seedbed out of which U.S. organized crime later grew was laid down before the Civil War (1861-65) in growing industrial cities such as New York and Chicago. It was the political organization of these cities, rather than specific immigrant groups, that made possible the political-criminal nexus characteristic of 19th- and 20th-century American cities. Immigrant communities simply slotted into the system of American city government.

Each wave of immigrants to the United States was caught up in the political organizations that ruled the cities in which they settled. People meant votes, and votes meant political power. This simple equation is the key to an understanding of America's enduring marriage with organized crime.

Corruption at Tammany Hall

The Democratic political organization that ran New York City, known by the name of its headquarters, Tammany Hall, organized new arrivals into voting blocks. The city was divided into political districts, each with its own "boss." The job of these officials was to guarantee that their district voted for candidates selected by Tammany Hall. Political supporters were rewarded with jobs in the city government, in the police and fire departments, even as street sweepers. This system of political patronage created an intricate web that connected even the humblest new immigrant, through the use of his vote, to the political power structure. Tammany Hall could accelerate the process of naturalization, help out in times of need, and provide the chosen few with desperately needed work. The system supplied jobs, protection, and even entertainment. Tammany Hall bosses were lavish spenders, and threw frequent parties. The word "racket" originally referred to these boisterous gatherings of the party faithful, and only later took on its current meaning.

Such a system led inevitably to abuse. Gangs were sponsored or patronized by Tammany Hall in return for repeat voting, ballot stuffing, and discouraging opposition voters by force — usually by the application of a blackjack to the skull, or simply kidnapping rival candidates for the duration of the election — which were long characteristic of the turbulent politics of the larger U.S. cities. In New York City such practices go back to the 1830s and lasted well into the 20th century. Chicago, incorporated in 1837, followed suit slightly later, but ceded nothing to its Eastern counterpart in terms of violent and corrupt local politics.

By the end of the 19th century, Chicago was carved up into 3,000 voting precincts, divided among 50 wards. Each ward sent two alderman and a committeeman to City Hall. This latter official was much more powerful than his name suggests. He could appoint judges and law enforcement officers. He could grant city jobs to favored clients. The committeeman was the lynchpin of the whole system. He remained in power as long he could deliver votes, and although the position was unpaid, many holders retired rich men indeed.

In the 1880s and 1890s, the growth of labor unions and their bitter battles with employers in a highly competitive marketplace created opportunities for members of Irish, Italian, and Jewish gangs. They were recruited, often through the bosses of the political wards, both as strike breakers and union heavies. Many of the famous gangsters of the 1920s got their start in this way. Industrial and labor racketeering have continued to be one of the most fertile fields cultivated by organized crime. It was not until the election of Fiorello La Guardia in 1934 that Tammany Hall's grip on the city was permanently broken.

The Irish Come to the United States

American cities before 1830 were still small, and the earliest immigrants tended to settle on farms or in small towns. The coming of the Irish in the 1840s, however, coincided with the first phase of the industrialization of American cities. Indeed, their labor, like that of the Chinese and Italians who came after them, contributed much to the

Movie history
Martin Scorsese's *The Gangs of New York* (2002) (above), was based on Herbert Asbury's 1927 book of the same title. The film depicts gang life in the Five Points district of lower Manhattan in the 1860s.

Five Points
A painting (left) showing the Five Points area of New York in the 1840s. It became notorious for the gangs that sprang up there, notably the Five Points Gang.

William M. "Boss" Tweed

The links between politics, labor, and organized crime emerged only through corrupt politicians such as W. M. "Boss" Tweed, who epitomized Tammany Hall in 19th-century New York City. He began his political career as an alderman in 1851. He became a member of the U.S. House of Representatives the following year, and joined the New York State Senate in 1867.

He was politically all-powerful in both New York State and City throughout the 1860s. In 1860, he became chairman of the New York County Democratic Party as well as the leader of the Tammany Club, the Democratic Party organization. In 1870, Boss Tweed and his cronies began the systematic looting of the city. He succeeded in passing a city charter that placed control of New York City in the hands of the mayor, the comptroller,

and the commissioners of parks and public works. These officials were all Tweed's friends. By inflating construction costs for public works, the Tweed ring was able to skim between $30 and $200 million in little more than two and a half years.

In 1873, Tweed was sentenced to 12 years in prison as a result of a reforming campaign by the *New York Times* and the efforts of the political reformer Samuel J. Tilden. His sentence was reduced to one year, but he was immediately rearrested and sued by the state for $6 million dollars. He was held in a debtors' prison until he could raise $3 million in bail. He escaped in 1875, fleeing first to Cuba then to Spain, where he enlisted as an ordinary seaman on a Spanish ship. In 1876, he was extradited to New York and died in prison in 1878.

Dates 1823–1878
Details The first and most notorious of the United States's city bosses, Tweed was involved in corruption at all levels of local government. Arrogant and ruthless, he systematically plundered New York City of millions of tax dollars.

the Irish gang, the Whyos, who came to prominence in the late 1860s:

Punching	$2
Both eyes blacked	$4
Nose and jaw broken	$10
Jacked [knocked] out	$15
Ear chewed off	$15
Leg or arm broken	$19
Shot in leg	$25
Stabbing	$25
Murder	$100

The great 19th century Irish gangs such as the Dead Rabbits and the Whyos had long been forgotten until Martin Scorsese's

transformation of the United States from an agrarian to an industrial power. The Irish immigrants settled in the cities on the East Coast and later in Chicago.

Young Irishmen had a talent for politics and rapidly assimilated to their new environment, helped by the fact that they spoke the most prevalent language: English. When the southern Italians and Eastern Europeans arrived in the 1870s, the Irish had long been firmly enmeshed in the political and economic structures of New York, Boston, Chicago, and Kansas City, in both the upperworld of urban politics and the police, and in the underworld of the urban gangs. They were jealous of their hard-won privileges in both fields, and defended them against later arrivals.

New York's Lower East Side

Before the arrival of East European and Italian immigrants, the population of New York City in 1860, the year of the unification of Italy, was 813,669. This was enormous for the time. The city's two biggest ethnic groups in 1860 were the Irish and the Germans, numbering 203,740 and 119,984 respectively. Together, they formed more than one third of the population. Both groups were concentrated in Manhattan, on the East Side. This huge population lived in a very small area. The

number of professional criminals in that year was estimated to be 80,000. It was probably much larger, because in the same year 58,067 criminals were convicted, despite a desperately undermanned police force. Eighty percent of those convicted had been born outside the United States.

New York in the 19th century was a very violent place. Vicious youth gangs fought bitter turf wars with their rivals. They were muggers, pimps, thieves, burglars, hijackers, and hired killers. Some of the more notorious gangs had price lists printed of their services. Herbert Asbury, who chronicled the activities of the Irish, Jewish, and Italian gangs of New York in his book *The Gangs of New York* (1927), published the following example from

Tammany Hall
The original Tammany Hall on East 14th Street, the home of New York's Democratic Party, is decorated for the 1924 Democratic National Convention.

Mafia Lynchings, February 1891, New Orleans

It is hard now to imagine the virulent racism directed against Italian and Jewish immigrants in the late 19th and early 20th century, in the academic as well as popular press. The Italians in particular were widely regarded as unassimilable, ignorant, and prone to crime. In 1891, in New Orleans, 11 Italians were lynched in one of the largest mass lynchings in U.S. history.

New Orleans was a major port of entry for immigrants from Europe and many Italians settled in the city, the great majority hardworking and honest. There was a criminal element, however. Two Mafia clans from Sicily, the Matranga family and the Provenzano family, controlled the New Orleans docks. Open warfare broke out between the two groups and there were a number of killings. The chief of police, David Hennessey, was thought by the Matranga family to favor their rivals, and it is probable that a member of their organization was responsible for the shotgun murder of Hennessey on October 15, 1890.

A grand jury indicted 19 men but only three were eventually charged. There were later claims of witness intimidation and bribery of jury members. In the course of the trial, the grand jury announced "the existence of a secret organization known as the Mafia has been established beyond doubt." It was the earliest official recognition of the existence of the Mafia on American soil.

Two days after the end of the trial, a mob of New Orleans citizens marched on the jail where the prisoners were still awaiting their release, hanged two of them, and shot and killed nine more. As a result, Italy severed diplomatic relations with the United States, which was eventually forced to pay compensation to the victims' families.

Intimidation
A cartoon showing a New Orleans jury being intimidated by the Mafia (in the guise of a woman) during the trial of the suspected murderers of Police Chief David Hennessey, 1891.

Lynch mob
The lynching of the Italian Mafia suspects in New Orleans in 1891. The citizens break down the door of the parish jail where the suspects were being held.

film *The Gangs of New York* (2002), which was based on Asbury's book. But this Irish pre-history of American organized crime is of great importance, for such crime cannot exist without political protection. It was the Irish gangs of New York and Chicago that laid the groundwork for organized crime in the 1920s.

Italian and Jewish Immigrants

More than 25 million immigrants arrived in the United States between 1885 and 1926. About four million of these were of Italian origin, overwhelmingly from Naples, Calabria, and Sicily, regions impoverished by centuries of neglect, agricultural over-exploitation, and absentee landlordism. The vast majority were young men, between 18 and 30, seeking work and a better life. Many were brought in as contract laborers and worked on construction projects and in mines all over the United States, often returning to Italy when they had saved enough money to do so.

These same years saw the arrival of large numbers of immigrants from Russia and Eastern Europe, many of them Jewish. In cities like New York, the port of entry for the vast majority of immigrants, Italian and Jewish neighborhoods were contiguous or intermingled, the new arrivals settling in the poorest areas. The average Italian immigrant arrived in New York with no more than $12. More than half were illiterate.

These immigrants began their lives in their new country with the great disadvantage of not speaking the language. This limited their prospects for employment and explains their natural wish to live alongside people with whom they could communicate. The fact that most of them had arrived with almost no money also meant they could not move beyond their ports of entry. The Italian and Jewish enclaves in New York were the result. In these neighborhoods, however foreign the architecture, the sights, sounds, and smells, at least the language was familiar. Both the Jewish and Italian communities had theaters that performed works in Yiddish or Italian, and they also had Yiddish and Italian newspapers.

Not only did the Italians and the Jews from Eastern Europe share linguistic disadvantages and neighborhoods; both groups were the object of considerable prejudice from those immigrants groups that had preceded them. They were preyed upon by the Irish street gangs and in self-defense formed their own. These Italian and Jewish gangs were ideal training grounds for men like Charles "Lucky" Luciano (*see p148*) and Meyer Lansky (*see p151*), who were the true architects of syndicated organized crime in the United States.

The Black Hand

Because of their linguistic isolation, the new Italian immigrants were easy prey for their criminally inclined compatriots. Suspicious of authority, new arrivals were at the mercy of groups like "La Mano Nera," the Black Hand, a secret society said to terrorize Italian neighborhoods. In fact, the "society" was simply a collection of criminals, and the name itself the creation of journalists, but the very notion inspired real terror.

The system was simple. The blackmailer sent a letter to his victim demanding money and threatening death if the demand was not met. Originally, the letter was signed by the imprint of a hand in black ink. Later, with the advent of fingerprinting techniques, this "signature" was discontinued. Anyone within the Italian community who was prosperous was at risk. The police files of cities like New Orleans, New York, and Chicago were filled with samples of these threatening letters, typically crudely written and inscribed with the black hand — hence our term "blackmail." In New York, a total of 424 cases of Black Hand extortion were reported in 1908. The letters were not merely idle threats. In Chicago alone there were 110 Black Hand killings between 1910 and 1914, few of them ever solved by the police. In the first three months of 1915, there were 55 Black Hand bombings of shops and homes, presumably of victims slow to pay up.

Black Hand Hitmen

In New York, the most famous Black Hander was Ignazio Saietta, known as "Lupo the Wolf" (*see box, above right*). Originally from Sicily, Saietta belonged to the earliest New York Mafia family, the Morello family. He is thought to have murdered at least 60 people. Many of these were tortured to death in the infamous "Murder Stable" at 323 East 107th Street, in the cellars of which many human bones were later discovered.

Chicago had its nightmare Black Hander as well, the famous "Shotgun Man." He was an unidentified contract killer, known to have killed at least 15 men between 1911 and 1912. Many of these killings took place on the corner of Milton and Oak Streets in Chicago's Little Italy, which became known as "Death Corner." Thirty-eight people were murdered here in a single 14-month period, beginning in January

1910. The choice of a single killing ground reinforced the popular belief that the Black Hand was an all-seeing organization with tentacles everywhere, rather than simply a group of extortionists.

With the coming of Prohibition in 1920 (*see p127*), when alcohol could not longer be sold legally, Black Hand extortion almost vanished in favor of more rewarding careers in "bootlegging" — the production and

Ignazio Saietta

BIOGRAPHY

Some early immigrants provided a direct link between criminal organizations in southern Italy and their emergence in the United States. Ignazio Saietta (known as "Lupo the Wolf") was born in 1877 in Scaccia, a town on the southern coast of Sicily. In 1898, he emigrated to the United States to escape a murder charge in Palermo. He opened a store in East Harlem, then moved to Brooklyn, and in 1901 back to Manhattan, this time to Prince's Street, where he opened a saloon and a store. Despite these legitimate business, Saietta was involved almost from his arrival in Black Hand extortion schemes and counterfeiting, in association with the Morello gang. The police were never able to convict him for murder, although he was suspected of being

involved in at least 60, many of them carried out in the infamous "Murder Stable" at 323 East 107th Street. Saietta was one of the suspects in the "Barrel Murder" of 1903, in which an unidentified mutilated corpse was found stuffed in a barrel. Lieutenant Joe Petrosino (*see p125*) was involved in the investigation, which turned up evidence that Saietta and Morello were also involved in importing counterfeit dollars from Sicily.

In 1908, the leader of the Sicilian Mafia, Vito Cascio Ferro, visited Saietta in New York, probably to discuss the killing of Petrosino. Saietta was arrested in 1909, and in 1910 was imprisoned for counterfeiting. Granted parole in 1920, in 1936 Saietta was jailed again for racketeering. He died in 1944 in Brooklyn after serving a short sentence.

Dates 1877–1944
Details Ranked as one of the most fearsome *mafioso* of all, Ignazio Saietta was proficient and deadly. A specialist in torture, his methods later became obsolete when bribery proved a more effective tool.

The territory of the Black Hand
The Italian–American neighborhood of New York in 1900. It was on streets such as these that the Black Hand operated, preying on newly arrived immigrants from the Old Country.

CASE STUDY

The Gangs of New York

At the end of the 19th century, the two biggest gangs in New York were the Five Points Gang and the Eastman Gang. The Five Pointers, based, as their name indicates, in the Five Points district, were led by Paolo Antonini Vaccarelli, also known as Paul Kelly. His adoption of an Irish name is significant; as a young man he was a welterweight boxer and it was probably then that he began calling himself Paul Kelly. Prejudice was so strong against Italians that the public was unwilling to accept an Italian fighter. James DeMora, also a boxer as a young man, would do the same: he took the name Jack McGurn, later becoming known as "Machine Gun Jack."

At its height, the Five Points Gang numbered some 1,000 members, almost all Italians but including a few Jews, notably Nathan Kaplan, who was known as "Kid Dropper," and all bitter enemies of Monk Eastman's equally large Jewish gang. In August 1903, when East Pointer's went to crash an Eastman-sponsored crap game a particularly savage gunfight broke out between the two gangs on the Lower East Side. Three men were killed and seven

wounded and police reserves had to be summoned to break up the fight. Given the number of men involved, the duration of the battle, and the weapons they all carried, the casualties were surprisingly light. There were several arrests, but Paul Kelly escaped and Monk Eastman was released without charges after the intervention of his political protectors at Tammany Hall. Tammany Hall also arranged a meeting between the two leaders, mediated their quarrel, and defined their territories, insisting that such public gunfights were bad publicity and must be stopped. Both gangs were clients of Tammany Hall, so it was only natural for the politicians to step in to resolve their differences.

The Five Points Gang was a direct link between old New York with its ethnic youth gangs and territorial battles, and the new world of criminal consortiums that would take shape with the coming of Prohibition in 1920.

The streets of New York
New York in 1888 was a city of ruthless street gangs that ruled their territories with brutal violence.

---

supply of illicit liquor. Many extortionists smoothly made the career transition, among them men like Frankie Yale (*see p138*) and the Genna brothers of Chicago. There is no doubt that the Black Hand, popularly believed to be a sinister, worldwide Italian criminal conspiracy, prepared the public's mind for the idea of the all-embracing power of the Mafia that was to come.

A notorious Black Hander was probably the first real *mafioso* to establish himself in New York. Antonio Morello headed a large family from Corleone, in Sicily. The town remains the base of the most powerful Mafia family on the island, and was made famous in Francis Ford Coppola's 1972 film *The Godfather* (*see p171*). Morello is said to have killed up to 40 people in the 1890s. Members of his family continued to operate until the 1930s, and some of his descendants are said to be involved in U.S. organized crime to this day.

Crime Organizer: John Torrio

The most famous graduate of New York's Lower East Side (*see box, above*) was John Torrio, the first man to endeavor to rationalize and syndicate organized crime.

Torrio was born in Orsara, Italy, in 1882 and came to New York with his family in 1884. The family settled on the Lower East Side. While still in his early teens, Torrio led his own gang and gained a reputation for viciousness, but during his later criminal career it was his intelligence and ability to conciliate that gave him his authority. He never carried a gun, a fact that speaks volumes at a time when even lowly street criminals usually packed more than one firearm, often prominently displayed.

Torrio eventually convinced Paul Kelly to join forces with him. Torrio went on to own his own bar and whorehouse by the age of 22, and he soon added drug dealing to his portfolio of illegal activities. He was also

experienced in local politics. In 1904, he and his gang were instrumental in the election of the mayor of New York, George Brinton McClellan, by stuffing ballot boxes with forged papers and violently preventing citizens from exercising their democratic right to vote for his rival.

Diamond Jim
Jim Colosimo rose from humble beginnings as a street cleaner to become the most powerful mob boss in Chicago.

Torrio: organizer
John Torrio, the mentor of Capone, with whom he ran the Chicago South Side in the 1920s. Capone eventually took sole control.

Crime Wave in Chicago

Torrio had a cousin in Chicago named Vittoria Moresco, the leading brothel-keeper in a city with numerous whorehouses. In 1902, she married the flamboyant Jim Colosimo (later to be known as "Diamond Jim"), a Calabrian who had worked his way up from cleaning the streets to head the Street Laborers' Union and the City Streets Repairers' Union. At this point in his career Colosimo was taken under the wing of the two most powerful political bosses in Chicago: the First Ward committeeman Michael Kenna and Alderman John Coughlin. Within their political bailiwick, the First Ward, lay the notorious Levee district, an area filled with brothels, saloons, and bookie joints. Kenna and Coughlin employed Colosimo as their collector in return for the block vote of his union. Colosimo was appointed Democratic precinct captain, a post with guaranteed police immunity. He collected $60,000 a year in payoffs from the Levee for Kenna and Coughlin, who paid a percentage to the city's mayor, "Big Bill" Thompson.

The "New York–Chicago Pipeline"

Colosimo's marriage to Torrio's cousin Vittoria prospered too. By 1912, he and his wife owned more than 200 whorehouses, catering to all income levels. He was earning around $600,000 a year, almost $10 million today. His base of operations, Colosimo's Café, decorated in the most lavish style, was the place to be seen in Chicago. Enrico Caruso, the Italian tenor, was a visitor, along with other showbusiness names. Colosimo wore white linen suits sewn with diamonds. The pockets were filled with diamonds too. When conversing, he liked to pour them from hand to hand and watch them glitter.

Colosimo, wealthy and powerful, was a natural target for Black Hand extortionists. Three different attempts were made to relieve him of part of his fortune, but each time he succeeded in killing the Black Hander. In 1909, however, he received a demand for $50,000. This time Vittoria advised him to call her cousin in New York, John Torrio. Torrio took the train to Chicago, initiating what came to be called the "New York–Chicago Pipeline," by which numerous gangsters shuttled between the two biggest mob cities in the United States. He dealt with the three Black Handers by subcontracting the task to two gunmen, who shot them dead at the money drop.

CRIMEBUSTER

Joe Petrosino and the Italian Squad

Giuseppe (Joe) Petrosino (1860–1909) was a famous New York police officer and is the only one to be killed in the line of duty on foreign soil. He was born in Padula, Italy, in 1860. In 1873, he emigrated to New York, learned English, and joined the New York Police Department in 1883. In 1905, he was put in charge of the Italian Squad, newly formed in response to the growing number of criminals in Little Italy. It was vital to have Italian-speaking officers who understood Italian culture and who could win the trust of the recent arrivals from the Old Country.

In the next four years thousands of Italian–Americans were arrested and hundreds were sent to prison. Black Hand crimes were halved and many Sicilian criminals were deported back to the Mediterranean. During this period the squad discovered the terrible secrets of the Morello family's "Murder Stable" in Italian Harlem. In 1908, Petrosino had a run-in with Ignazio Saietta (see p123), who publicly insulted his mother. Petrosino beat Saietta senseless before an admiring crowd and tossed him into an ash can.

In 1901, while still just a detective, Joe Petrosino had arrested a new arrival from Sicily named Vito Cascio Ferro, while investigating a Morello barrel murder. (The Morello custom was to stuff their victims in a barrel and toss them in the river or send them by rail to imaginary destinations.) Cascio Ferro fled to New Orleans, and in 1904 returned to Sicily, taking with him Petrosino's photograph.

In 1909, Petrosino went secretly to Palermo, Sicily, to gather records of known criminals who had emigrated to the United States. On the night of March 12, two men approached him. He waved them away, then followed them into the Garibaldi gardens. Unknown assassins then shot him four times, killing him instantly. The crime was never solved, but was almost certainly ordered by Vito Cascio Ferro, who was by now the all-powerful leader of the Sicilian Mafia. Petrosino's body was returned to New York, where 250,000 people attended his funeral. The school in his native Italian town is named after this heroic fighter against organized crime.

Giuseppe (Joe) Petrosino was the first U.S. police officer to recognize the need for U.S.–Italian cooperation in defeating Mafia-led crime in the United States. His pioneering work led to his death but pointed the way for future law enforcement.

Jumping-off point
The port of Palermo, Sicily, in the early 1920s. It was from here that the Sicilian Mafia exported organized crime to the United States. Members emigrated on transatlantic liners to exploit their countrymen in the new Italian-American neighborhoods of New York and other cities. It was to Palermo that Petrosino came to further his investigations into the Mafia's activities in the United States.

In 1915, grateful for Torrio's help, Colosimo put him in charge of his empire of saloons, whorehouses, and gambling dens. Colosimo also gave Torrio permission to set up his own criminal organization. Torrio bought a building at 2222 South Wabash Avenue, known thereafter, from the number of its address, as the Four Deuces. Torrio set up a brothel on the top floor, gambling operations on the second and third, and a saloon at street level. The Four Deuces rapidly became the headquarters for a criminal empire beyond anything Diamond Jim Colosimo had ever envisaged. Within a short time, Torrio controlled 1,000 enterprises, all devoted to three things for which there is a constant and unlimited demand: gambling, drink, and sex. His gunmen eliminated anyone who protested at the extension of his empire.

The age of the automobile had begun, and Torrio had the foresight to see that the future of vice in Chicago lay not in its traditional center, places like the Levee, but in the suburbs. The vice-ridden city had

always spasmodically generated reform movements, but as the Prohibition era drew near, they gathered momentum and effectiveness. There were protest marches against everything from prostitution to the use of tobacco. At one point, protesters even invaded the Levee district of the city, where they succeeded in closing down most of the whorehouses.

However, it was alcohol that the protesters saw as the root of all evil, and far-sighted men like John Torrio knew that it was only a matter of time before the Prohibition movement succeeded in banning the sale of alcohol entirely.

The "New York–Chicago Pipeline"
An advertisement for the Lake Shore and Michigan Southern Railway and New York Central Railroad, promoting a 20-hour trip between New York and Chicago – a journey often taken by Mafia hitmen.

CASE STUDY

The Eighteenth Amendment and the Volstead Act, January 17, 1920, Washington, D.C.

Prohibition (the ban on the sale of full-strength alcohol) came about as a result of the Eighteenth Amendment to the Constitution of the United States of America, and the Volstead Act, which empowered the American Treasury Department to enforce it. Drunkenness was a big social problem in 19th-century America, as it had been in Europe since the invention of spirits in the early 18th century. In an attempt to combat this, the American temperance movement began in 1824. The Women's Christian Temperance Union (WCTU), founded in 1874, and the Anti-Saloon League (ASL) of 1893 turned the movement into a national force for political reform, supporting anti-alcohol candidates in both state and national elections.

The WCTU and later the ASL were extremely effective in their attacks against the public sale of alcohol. The Anti-Saloon League (later renamed the Anti-Saloon League of America) was non-denominational, but successfully solicited funds in churches throughout the country. A number of prominent industrialists, including John D. Rockefeller and Henry Ford, were supporters of

the Prohibition movement. The liquor industries seriously underestimated the amount of public support for a ban on alcohol.

The Eighteenth Amendment was passed on January 16, 1919, when two-thirds of American states voted for Prohibition. It became law on January 17, 1920. The Volstead Act of 1919

authorized the Treasury Department to enforce the amendment. The golden age of the American gangster was born. Overnight, the criminal fraternity was presented with a huge and lucrative new market for illicit whiskey and beer.

The Volstead Act
Andrew J. Volstead penned the Volstead Act, which, in conjunction with the Eighteenth Amendment, banned the sale of liquor in the United States.

Enforcing the law
Huge posters were pasted up on premises closed by the federal courts for violations of the Volstead Act.

PUBLIC NOTICE
THESE PREMISES HAVE BEEN
CLOSED
FOR ONE YEAR
BY THE UNITED STATES DISTRICT COURT FOR
VIOLATION
OF THE NATIONAL
PROHIBITION
LAW

PALMER E. ANDERSON   EDWIN A. OLSON

Contraband liquor
U.S. revenue agents during a raid on a speakeasy in Washington, D.C., on April 25, 1923.

America Runs Dry

When Prohibition came in 1920, Torrio was determined to profit from the opportunities it presented. He soon realized that the only way for his organization to operate was by sitting down with rival criminal groups and marking out territory, otherwise the battle to supply illicit alcohol to the thousands of "speakeasies" (illicit drinking dens) that sprang up would lead to chaos. To his astonishment, his mentor, Colosimo, distracted by a love affair with a young singer, seemed unaware of the need to defend his own territory from major rivals like Roger Tuohy and Dion O'Banion.

Torrio saw only one solution. His cousin Colosimo had to be eliminated. Four weeks after Prohibition was officially proclaimed, "Diamond Jim" was gunned down in the Colosimo Café by an unknown assassin.

This was the first gangland slaying of the Prohibition era. The triggerman was Frankie Yale, former member of the Five Points Gang and now the most prominent gangster in New York. He was also the patron of Alphonse Capone (*see* p129).

Colosimo's funeral was a major event. His coffin was carried by three

Chicago night life

Chicago's Wabash Avenue at night. This district of the city was a popular center for speakeasies, where drinkers would rub shoulders with mobsters.

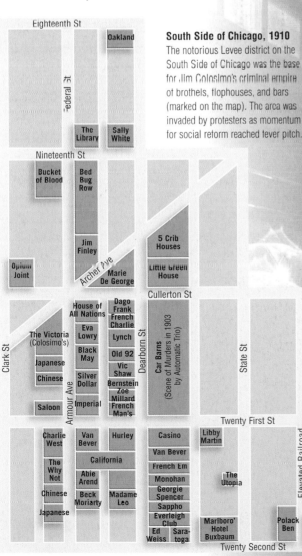

South Side of Chicago, 1910

The notorious Levee district on the South Side of Chicago was the base for Jim Colosimo's criminal empire of brothels, flophouses, and bars (marked on the map). The area was invaded by protesters as momentum for social reform reached fever pitch.

judges, an assistant state's attorney, nine aldermen, and a representative of the state government. They were flanked by Torrio and his henchmen. Colosimo's funeral laid bare the true power structure of Chicago — with the gangsters firmly at the top.

The Torrio Syndicate

Torrio immediately assumed the leadership of Colosimo's empire. He took over a number of breweries, and then began to organize the major Chicago gangs, assigning each their own territory. In return, the gangs forced saloons to stock Torrio alcohol, and protected shipments and distribution. The North Side fell to Dion O'Banion. The West Side was divided between Torrio and partners Terry Druggan and Frankie Lake, leaders of the Valley Gang. Torrio controlled part of the South Side, and the rest was divided among gangleaders Ralph Sheldon, Danny Stanton, Frank McErlane, and Joe Saltis.

Two gangs left out of Torrio's syndicate were the Klondike O'Donnell gang, based in Cicero, and the unrelated O'Donnell brothers led by Spike O'Donnell, who at the time was in prison for bank robbery. When he got out, Spike began hijacking Torrio's delivery trucks, and moving in on the territory of Frank McErlane and Joe Saltis. McErlane killed five of Spike's men, and drove Spike himself out of Chicago.

The Rise of Al Capone

Capone's 21st birthday coincided with the first full day of Prohibition: January 17, 1920. Capone had known John Torrio since he was 14 years old in Brooklyn, New York. In 1921, Torrio invited Capone to come to Chicago. Torrio's organization was already very lucrative, earning $10 million a year from beer, gambling, and prostitution. Torrio had an army of between 700 and 800 men working for him.

Capone began on the bottom rung in Chicago, working as a promoter outside one of Torrio's whorehouses. It was probably at this time that he met Jack Guzik, a member of a large Jewish family involved in prostitution. They became friends and Guzik went on to become treasurer for the Torrio–Capone organization. Capone's esteem for Jack Guzik was vividly shown in 1924 when Joe Howard, a hijacker,

Alcohol raid
Government agents raid a speakeasy during Prohibition. In Chicago, Torrio and Capone's operation was severely curtailed by the election of a hardline mayor, William E. Dever.

made an anti-Semitic remark to Guzik. Capone shot him six times in front of witnesses in a saloon on South Wabash Avenue. Capone was interrogated by Assistant State Attorney William McSwiggin, but discharged for lack of evidence. All the witnesses had suffered from sudden memory loss.

In 1922, Capone was joined by his brother Ralph. Al became manager of the Four Deuces and rose to become Torrio's partner, receiving a basic salary of $25,000 a year. In 1923, Torrio and Capone, motivated by the election of the reform mayor, William E. Dever, who closed down 7,000 speakeasies, moved their base from the Four Deuces in downtown Chicago to the Hawthorne Inn in the industrial suburb of Cicero. An independent township, it was outside the jurisdiction of the mayor of Chicago.

The area was dominated by the Western Electric plant, which paid its 40,000 workers well, meaning that the local population had plenty to spend in Capone's saloons and betting shops. Cicero also had a large number of Czech inhabitants, accustomed to thick Bohemian beer. This was supplied by the West Side O'Donnells, who had not joined the Torrio–Capone syndicate, and who regarded Cicero as their territory. Without informing them, as courtesy demanded, Torrio probed the extent of their power in Cicero by setting up a whorehouse on Roosevelt Road. The Cicero police, acting for the O'Donnells, promptly closed it. The O'Donnells disapproved of prostitution. They did allow gambling, however, but only slot machines, which were controlled by a local politician named Eddie Vogel. Torrio, in retaliation for the closing of his brothel, sent out the Cook County Sheriff to confiscate Vogel's slot machines. Torrio then sat down with the O'Donnells and Vogel and arranged a truce.

Vogel's slot machines were returned and Torrio agreed not to open any whorehouses in Cicero. In addition, Torrio allowed them to continue to supply beer to some areas of Cicero. In exchange, the Torrio syndicate was granted the right to sell beer everywhere else in Cicero, and to run gambling joints and cabarets wherever it wanted.

Alphonse (Al) "Scarface" Capone

Alphonse Capone was born in Brooklyn, New York, on January 17, 1899. In 1900, the family moved to Park Avenue, still in Brooklyn, then later to Garfield Place. When he was old enough, Al attended the nearby Public School 7, which he left at the age of 14 after striking a teacher. It was at this time he first began doing errands for a neighbor, John Torrio, who ran the local Italian lottery, as well as a chain of gambling joints and whorehouses. Torrio introduced Capone to Frankie Yale, who ran the Harvard Inn on Coney Island. Yale was the leading figure in the New York underworld, and gave Alphonse a job at the Harvard Inn. It was during a quarrel over a girl at the inn that Capone received the three prominent knife scars that disfigured his face.

In 1918, Capone quit his job with Frankie Yale and went to work in Baltimore. When his father died in 1920, Torrio contacted him and told him that Chicago was wide open, urging him to join him there. Capone arrived in 1920, and, working with Torrio, he began his climb to the top of organized crime

Although Capone's control of the illicit market for alcohol in Chicago was never total, he became the most prominent bootlegger in America between 1925 and 1931. The organization he set up became the framework for the Chicago Outfit.

Capone was sent to jail for income tax evasion in 1932, first to the Atlanta State Penitentiary, then to Alcatraz. He was released in 1939, seriously ill from syphilis. He died at home in Florida in 1947.

Dates 1899–1947

Details Al Capone (above in a police "mug shot") was the most notorious American gangster of the Prohibition era. Undoubtedly a murderer, nevertheless it was his failure to pay income tax that led to his imprisonment in 1932.

Torrio, having gained entry to Cicero, turned it over to Capone and left for Italy with his mother and several million dollars. He bought his mother a villa and deposited the remainder of the money in an Italian bank. He then returned to Chicago.

Capone's Chicago

The first challenge facing Capone was to take over the city government. His chance came with the mayoral election of 1924 between Democrat Rudolph Hurt and Republican Joseph Z. Klenha. The election took place on April 1. Capone threw the weight of the Syndicate behind the Republican candidate, Joseph Z. Klenha. By now, Capone had brought his family to Chicago, and his brothers Ralph and Frank and his cousin Charley Fischetti helped bring out the vote for Klenha and other Syndicate candidates. They were assisted by 200 gunmen. Stationed at the polling booths, they prevented anyone voting for opposition candidates, usually violently, and in Democratic precincts emptied ballot boxes, refilling them with ballots favorable to their candidates. News of the violence and fraud reached County Judge Edmund K. Jarecki, who ordered a force of 70 policemen to go into Cicero and stop it. They wore plain clothes and arrived in unmarked cars. As they drove by the

Western Electric plant, the first person they saw was Frank Capone. They braked and piled out of their cars. Frank, thinking it was a hit, reached for his gun, but was cut down by a hail of shotgun blasts before he could pull it. The police then emptied their guns at leisure into his body as he lay in the street. He was 29 years old. Frank was given a superb gangland funeral. He was placed in a silver-plated casket and the

modest Capone house on South Prairie Avenue was festooned with $20,000 worth of flowers. A procession of 100 cars took the casket to Mount Carmel Cemetery. Al Capone had lost a brother, but won the election. He was now in control of Cicero.

Capone's Empire

Capone's base of operations in Cicero was The Hawthorne Inn at 4833 22nd Street. The police attack that had led to his brother's death had made him security conscious, and he fortified the inn, posting gunmen in the lobby and putting up bulletproof shutters on the windows.

Capone now controlled 161 speakeasies in Cicero. He also had 150 gambling joints. Just one of them, the Hawthorne Smoke Shop in the Hawthorne Inn, saw a daily turnover of $50,000. Capone also ran 22 brothels, since there was no longer any need to adhere to the agreement with the O'Donnells. These were downmarket establishments where men waited their turn on pine benches and girls cost $5.

Capone's empire was grossing about $105 million a year, but its overheads were high. Bribing police officers alone was costing

Modest abode
Al Capone's family residence at South Prairie Avenue, Chicago. The house was the scene of his brother Frank's lavish funeral in 1924.

INSIDE STORY

THE SPEAKEASY

As soon as Prohibition came into effect, illegal drinking establishments, or "speakeasies," sprang up across America. There were soon 32,000 in New York City alone, and 20,000 in Chicago. It is estimated that the number of drinking establishments in the United States, never small, doubled with Prohibition. It was easier to get a drink during Prohibition than it had been before.

It was during Prohibition that the modern United States, along with American organized crime, was born. Class, racial, and gender barriers began to erode in the fellowship of the speakeasy, where everyone present shared the camaraderie of breaking the law. Politicians, attorneys, and policemen rubbed shoulders with blue collar workers, gangsters, and entertainers. Al Capone's Cotton Club in Cicero hired black jazz musicians and by 1927 Chicago had become the jazz capital of America.

In New York, Meyer Lansky and Charles Luciano were paying out $100,000 a week in bribes to the police to keep their operation running. Since their clientele was largely from the traditionally law-abiding classes, a contempt for the law and the men who enforced it spread from gangland to the middle classes. Even U.S. president Warren G. Harding served his guests bootleg whiskey.

Joining the club
In Prohibition-era New York, a membership card from a well-known speakeasy would permit entrance to any other drinking club in the city.

$30 million annually. However, profits were still enormous. Men who worked for Capone were earning up to $250 a week. Compared with the workers at Western Electric, the gangsters were rich. Capone took to wearing $5,000 suits. He was 25 years old.

Capone's Rivals

Dion O'Banion was a throwback to the earlier days of the ethnic Chicago gangs, making no secret of his dislike of Italians (except for "Schemer" Drucci), particularly Sicilians, although he didn't mind selling them flowers for their funerals. O'Banion owned a half interest in Schofield's Florist Shop and was a serious and competent florist, almost always working a full day at the store. He abhorred prostitution, and refused to sell homemade whiskey, only dealing in the real thing, imported from Canada. He delivered the vote for the 42nd and 43rd Wards and led a team of ruthless gunmen — men like George "Bugs" Moran and Frank Gusenberg. The police reckoned that O'Banion had committed 25 murders.

O'Banion was a member of the Torrio–Capone Syndicate, but in 1923 he began behaving in an increasingly irrational manner, occasionally hijacking his own partners' liquor. Torrio tried to reason with him, pointing out that they were all in the same business, but to no avail.

O'Banion's dislike of Sicilians was increased by the inroads a family of Sicilian brothers from Taylor Street in the 19th Ward were making into his profits. These were the six Genna brothers: Angelo, Mike, Pete, Sam, Jim, and Tony. The Genna brothers were members of the Syndicate, like O'Banion. They had obtained a license to produce industrial alcohol — legal under the Volstead Act — and under its cover subcontracted the actual distillation to Sicilian families in Little Italy, Chicago.

The Paradise Club, Harlem, New York
During Prohibition, many American women began to enjoy themselves in public. Drinking and dancing became common.

This cottage industry was a godsend to poor families. They were paid $15 dollars a day (a princely sum) to run their stills, and once a week the Gennas collected the product, which they artificially colored and sold. The average home still could make 350 gallons a week, and cost the Gennas $1 a gallon to produce. This was earning them $300,000 a month.

North Side Hijack

Because of their low overheads, the Gennas were able to market their liquor for less than the Torrio-Capone syndicate. They started selling it on the North Side of Chicago, O'Banion's territory, in a clear infringement of the Syndicate agreement. O'Banion complained to Torrio, who was reluctant to intervene. The Gennas were extremely violent and politically well connected, and Torrio did not want to provoke them. Impatient, O'Banion hijacked one of their delivery trucks, with a cargo worth $30,000. Torrio had to use all his diplomacy to restrain the Gennas from retaliating. As the Gennas flooded other territories with their cheap whiskey, it was clear that the Torrio truce was breaking down. It was at this delicate point that O'Banion pushed Torrio and Capone too far. The three men had equal shares in the Sieben Brewery, which with Prohibition had been leased to the George Frank Brewery for the making of non-alcoholic beer. The George Frank Brewery was undoubtedly a front for the Torrio-Capone Syndicate. In 1924, O'Banion told Torrio and Capone that he had had enough of bootlegging and quarreling with the Gennas. He was going to retire to Colorado. He would sell his share of the Sieben Brewery to Torrio for $500,000. Torrio and Capone leaped at the chance. With O'Banion out of the way, the North Side would be theirs. They agreed to meet at the brewery on May 19 so that O'Banion could load his last shipment of beer.

It was a setup. O'Banion had learned from contacts in the police department that Prohibition

agents were planning a raid on the Sieben Brewery that night. Torrio and 29 others, including O'Banion, were arrested as they were loading beer for distribution throughout the city. Torrio, who had a previous conviction, was liable to a sentence of nine months. He posted bail and was released pending trial. Ominously, Torrio did not post bail for O'Banion and the others. O'Banion paid his own bail and was released because he had no previous criminal convictions.

O'Banion Meets His Maker

Torrio's suspicions of O'Banion's treachery were confirmed within a week. Torrio heard that O'Banion was bragging to his friends that he had taken Torrio for $500,000. It was typical of Torrio that he kept this knowledge to himself. Meanwhile, Torrio and Capone informed the president of the Unione Siciliana, Mike Merlo, that they had had enough of O'Banion, and planned to kill him. Merlo urged restraint as he was unwilling to precipitate a gang war. Merlo was much respected and Torrio agreed to do nothing. He knew that Merlo was dying of cancer and out of respect would wait till after his death to take his revenge. Merlo died seven months later, in November 1924.

Hired gun
George "Bugs" Moran was a member of Dion O'Banion's gang on the North Side of Chicago, eventually taking over after the demise of O'Banion and Hymie Weiss, who both fell to Capone hit men. Capone tried to have Moran killed on St. Valentine's Day in 1929.

O'Banion's fate was sealed. Two days later, John Scalise, Albert Anselmi, and Mike Genna entered the Schofield Florist Shop. O'Banion assumed they had come to pick up a wreath ordered the previous day. As he reached out his hand to greet them, one of the gunmen grabbed it and pulled him off balance, while the others shot him six times. His funeral was a magnificent affair. The Chicago Symphony Orchestra played as

Bootlegger's truck
A bootlegger's vehicle ingeniously disguised as an innocent load of lumber. Prohibition agents discovered a trapdoor of board ends leading to the interior where 70 cases of contraband whiskey were stashed.

mourners viewed the corpse. The funeral procession was a mile long, and a crowd of some 20,000 people assembled at the grave site in Mount Carmel Cemetery, among them Torrio and Capone. Public killings like this, carried out in broad daylight, were carefully orchestrated to send a message to a gang's competitors. However, the North Side gang were determined to hold on to their territory and to avenge the murder of their leader.

Weiss Takes Over

Earl "Hymie" Weiss, whose real name was Earl Wajciechowski, took over the leadership of the North Siders. Born in Poland in 1898, he had known O'Banion since they were boys. Despite his nickname, Weiss was a devout Catholic. He was determined to avenge his friend. Together with Vincent Drucci and George Moran, he set out to do

so with the help of some recently-available .45 caliber Thompson submachine guns. It was the first time this characteristic weapon was used on the gangland scene.

Torrio had left Chicago after O'Banion's funeral, leaving Capone in charge of operations in Chicago. On January 12, 1925, two months after O'Banion's murder, Weiss, Drucci, and Moran machine-gunned Capone's car, which they found parked outside a restaurant on State and 55th Street. The driver was hit but not killed. Capone's two bodyguards fell to the floor and were unharmed. Capone was inside the restaurant and escaped unscathed.

Capone stepped up his security, only moving at night, and always with his bodyguards. Torrio returned to Chicago a few days after the attack. On January 24, he went shopping with his wife. On his return to his apartment, Weiss and Moran jumped out of a car, Weiss with a sawn-off shotgun, Moran with an automatic pistol. First they fired at Torrio's car, thinking he was still in it, and wounded the driver. Then they spotted Torrio in front of his apartment and shot him twice, hitting him in the neck and chest. While he lay in agony, they shot him twice more. Moran attempted to deliver the *coup de grace*, but his clip was empty. A truck drove by and the assassins panicked. They ran away, thinking it was the Capone gang. It was a delivery truck.

Remarkably, Torrio survived and was rushed to hospital. Capone was informed and mounted a 24-hour guard on Torrio's room. Torrio and Capone refused to answer any questions about the attackers. Torrio spent four weeks in hospital.

Immediately on his release Torrio was tried for the Sieben Brewery incident and sentenced to nine months in the Lake County Jail in Waukegan, Illinois, where he became a close friend of the warden. The local sheriff even provided a number of his deputies to guard Torrio and prevent another assassination attempt. The time passed pleasantly enough, but Torrio

realized that his attempt to rationalize gangland Chicago had been a failure. He summoned Al Capone for a prison visit. Torrio said that he was planning to retire, and that he would leave the Chicago operation to Capone. On his release from jail, Torrio left for his beloved Italy.

Funeral procession
The funeral of Angelo Genna on June 1, 1925. Genna, who was a member of the Capone Syndicate, was murdered by Earl "Hymie" Weiss (inset) and the North Side gang. The funeral was a major public event.

Scene of the crime
A crowd gathers at Schofield's Flower Store, where Dion O'Banion was shot. The store remained the headquarters of the North Side gang after his death.

The Beer Wars

After John Torrio had left Chicago, Capone moved his headquarters to the Metropole Hotel at 2300 South Michigan Avenue. He conducted his by now far-ranging and complex business dealings from Room 406. It was here that he received visitors from all walks of life, including many politicians and journalists.

Capone was now faced with defending Torrio's legacy. The coalition he had formed had been shattered by the decision to kill O'Banion. Weiss, who had taken O'Banion's place as leader of the North Side gang, was supported by the O'Donnells from the West Side and the Saltis–McErlane gang. Capone was supported by the Genna brothers and several other Italian gangs. Chicago had returned to the days when gangs were motivated as much by ethnic rivalry as by competition for markets.

Weiss, Drucci, and Moran struck first, killing Angelo Genna on May 26, 1925. Mike Genna was killed by the police a month later, as he, John Scalise, and Albert Anselmi were about to ambush Moran. Scalise and Anselmi killed two police officers before escaping. Tony Genna was murdered soon afterward by the Gennas' own gunman, Giuseppe Nerone, who may have been in the pay of Capone. Nerone himself was killed a few days later. The surviving Gennas left for Italy. Scalise and Anselmi joined Capone.

The Massacre at the Adonis Club

In December 1926, Capone went to New York to negotiate with Frankie Yale over the purchase of Canadian whiskey. Business successfully completed, Yale invited Capone to stay for a Christmas Eve party at the Adonis Social and Athletic Club in Brooklyn. Yale warned Capone that there might be trouble. The White Handers, an Irish gang led by Richard "Peg Leg" Lonergan, had threatened to attack the party. The issue was control of the Brooklyn docklands, traditionally an Irish stronghold

Capone's politician
William Hale Thompson became mayor of Chicago in 1927, sponsored by Capone. During the next four years gangsters operated openly in the city, largely unhindered by the police.

but now threatened by Yale's gang. Capone immediately sent to Chicago for gunmen Scalise and Anselmi.

Lonergan and his men duly arrived at the club on Christmas Eve, demanding drink and making insulting remarks to the assembled Italians. As they stood at the bar, the owner simultaneously turned out the lights and buried a meat cleaver in the skull of one of the Irishmen. Shots rang out and when the lights were turned back on three more Irishmen lay dead. Lonergan, who had

lost his wooden leg, was hiding under the piano. He emptied his gun at Capone, who walked over and shot him three times in the head. Capone was charged with murder, but the indictment was quashed and Capone was back in Chicago by the New Year.

What was later called the Adonis Club Massacre changed the balance of power not only on the Brooklyn docks, now under the control of the Italians, but also between Brooklyn and Chicago. Both Torrio and Capone came out of Brooklyn, and in some respects their operation in Chicago was a Brooklyn subsidiary. By killing Lonergan, Capone had established the priority of his Chicago organization over Brooklyn.

Capone Under Fire

Back in Chicago, Capone moved into a new area, the largely Italian suburb of Chicago Heights, which was controlled by a group of Sicilians who ran a protection racket on home distillers. Capone's men killed off the Sicilians one by one, and Capone took over their operation.

Another murder charge was brought against Capone in 1926. Assistant State Attorney William McSwiggin was out drinking in Cicero with Klondike and Myles O'Donnell. Furious that the O'Donnells were in his territory, Capone ambushed them, machine-gunning them on the street. McSwiggin was killed, and a warrant was sworn out for Capone. He fled but eventually gave himself up. The case against him was dismissed for lack of evidence. The killing was headline news and made Capone notorious in a way he had never been before. From now on, every killing in Chicago was laid at his door.

And there was still Weiss to deal with. On September 20, 1926, while Capone was eating lunch at the Hawthorne Inn,

a convoy of North Siders slowly drove by and machine-gunned the restaurant. Sixty customers were present. More than 1,000 rounds were fired. Amazingly, no one inside the restaurant was hurt, although several bystanders outside were injured.

Even with this provocation, Capone tried yet again to make peace with Weiss. They were unable to reach an agreement, and so Capone decided to remove Weiss from the scene. Weiss still used Schofield's Flower Shop as his headquarters. Capone rented an apartment across the street and installed a hitman armed with a submachine gun. On October 4, 1926, Weiss, his driver, a fellow bootlegger, a politician, and a lawyer crossed the street and were machine-gunned by Capone's hired killer. Weiss and the bootlegger were killed, the others wounded. This time Capone did not attend the funerals. With Weiss out of the way, Capone tried once more to make peace. He called a conference of gang leaders at the Hotel Sherman and suggested an amnesty. Previous murders would go unavenged. Everybody would start with a clean slate. Moran, Weiss's successor, would keep his territory, and Capone would keep his. This time everyone agreed, and for 70 days no one was killed.

In April 1927, Mayor William E. Dever lost the election to gangland's candidate, William Hale Thompson. Capone had sponsored Thompson to the tune of $250,000.

The Sullivan Law

A month later, in May 1927, as a result of the court case *U.S. vs. Sullivan*, the Supreme Court of the United States passed an unusual law. From now on profits from the illegal sale of alcohol would be taxed like any other income. Although at first sight the law was absurd — why would someone engaged in an illegal activity declare it? — it proved to be a powerful tool against the bootleggers. They could now be sent to jail if they did not file income tax returns. If they did file, they implicated themselves in an illegal act. The U.S. Attorney's office in Chicago estimated that in 1927 Capone's gang had grossed $105 million from bootlegging, gambling, vice, and other rackets. He had paid no tax.

CRIMEBUSTERS

Eliot Ness and the "Untouchables"

Eliot Ness was born in Chicago in 1903. His parents were Norwegian and lived on Prairie Avenue, where, oddly enough, Al Capone's family later also lived. Ness graduated from the University of Chicago and in 1928 he joined the Bureau of Prohibition, working under the District Attorney, George E.Q. Johnson. Soon Ness was working undercover, posing as a corrupt official. The operation resulted in the indictment of 81 men, and the breakup of a bootlegging ring that pulled in $36 million a year.

Ness was promoted and began to try to dismantle the Capone organization in the suburb of Cicero, which had become its home territory. At the time Capone was serving a year's prison sentence for illegal possession of a concealed weapon, and his brother Ralph was in charge. Ness managed to tap Ralph's phone and located some of the secret breweries that supplied the Capone organization. He raided a major brewery on South Wabash Avenue, ramming through the front door with a snowplow, a technique he pioneered.

Chicago's Prohibition Bureau was so riddled with corruption that it had made little progress against bootlegging. Ness selected and led a small team of honest agents whose resistance to Capone's attempts to buy them off led to them being dubbed the "Untouchables" by the newspapers. The team

> ## "Reliable in every respect, a clean young man; morally a fine fellow"
> FBI report on Ness in 1928

originally consisted of just nine agents: By tracing beer barrels on their journey from speakeasy to brewery, the team were able to locate and raid six Capone breweries and five distribution plants, seizing 25 delivery trucks and confiscating beer with a value of $9 million. To humiliate his adversary, Ness paraded the beer trucks down Michigan Avenue past Capone's headquarters at the Lexington Hotel, having called him to tell him to look out of the window.

Ness managed to arrest 69 Capone bootleggers, and his raids caused damage to the organization. He survived several attempts on his life, once discovering a bomb in his car. But by 1932, Capone was facing a much more serious threat: The indictment for income tax evasion that

would finally send him to Atlanta and Alcatraz. In the end, Ness's efforts did not cause Capone's downfall. Meanwhile, his success antagonized the director of the Federal Bureau of Investigation (FBI), J. Edgar Hoover, who subsequently did everything he could to hamper Ness's career. Hoover not only refused Ness's application to join the FBI, but opened a file on him. At the bottom of one page Hoover wrote: "Beware of Eliot Ness."

In 1935, Ness became Director of Public Safety in Cleveland, Ohio, a post he held until 1942. He successfully purged the corrupt police department and disrupted organized crime in

Eliot Ness
Eliot Ness shortly after he was appointed Director of Public Safety in Cleveland in 1935. During his seven-year administration the city's law enforcement agencies were dramatically improved.

the city. However, his failure to capture the "torso" murderer, a serial killer who terrorized Cleveland, dented Ness's reputation. He ran for mayor of the city in 1947. He was defeated and never recovered from this blow to his self-esteem. This, coupled with marital problems, led him to drink excessively.

In the 1950s, Ness collaborated on the story of his life with Oscar Fraley. *The Untouchables* was published in 1957, but Ness died of a heart attack before the book came out. Ness's battle against Capone was made into a television series in 1959, and several film versions of their rivalry have also been made in the years since then.

The Untouchables
Eliot Ness's memoirs (ghost written by Oscar Fraley) were the basis for a major TV series, *The Untouchables* (1959–62) starring Robert Stack, and Brian de Palma's film (1987) with Kevin Costner (above).

Gangsters' hangout
A 1930 photograph (left) of the Montmartre Club, one of the many clubs and bars that flourished in Capone's stronghold in Cicero, west of Chicago.

Mean streets
New York gangster Rosario Riggio, dead behind the wheel of his car in Brooklyn, New York, on March 1, 1935. He had been shot to death by members of a rival gang in a showdown over territory. Bullet holes can clearly be seen in the car windows.

Then the killings began again. Soon after Thompson took office there were four unsolved murders, each of the victims dressed in "gangster chic" and each found clutching a nickel in one hand. Rumor had it that the perpetrators were out-of-town assassins, sent to kill Capone but taken out before they could do so by Capone's favorite gunman, Vincenzo Gebaldi, also known as "Machine Gun" Jack McGurn. They had come to Chicago hoping to collect a $50,000 bounty put on Capone's head by Joseph Aiello, a Sicilian from Castellamare. Aiello and his brothers Antonio, Dominick, and Andrew had a number of rackets going, including levying a tax on Californian grapes unloaded in Chicago railroad sidings. They supported the Castellamare side in the war between Maranzano and Masseria that was beginning in New York, while Capone helped finance Masseria. When he was a boy, McGurn's father had been killed by the Gennas and he had sworn revenge. When he grew up, each time he killed a Genna gunman, he left a nickel in their hand as his own personal calling card.

Aiello next tried to bribe one of Capone's cooks $10,000 to poison him. The cook prudently informed Capone. When Capone discovered that Aiello had set up a machine gun position across the street from the store where Capone made payoffs, Capone told friends on the police force, who arrested Aiello and advised him to leave town. Capone later had him gunned down in New Jersey.

In early January 1928, Capone and his family left Chicago for Miami, Florida. Toward the end of the previous year, Capone had repeatedly publicly stated that he was going to retire from bootlegging, even calling a press conference to announce his intentions to an incredulous group of reporters. He purchased a large house for $40,000 in the name of his wife Mae on Palm Island, near Miami. The purchase attracted the attention of the Internal Revenue Service (IRS), which was determined to go after Capone for non-payment of income tax. The relentless IRS agent Elmer Irey investigated the sale, but, because the house was in Mae's name, he was unable to use it to indict Capone. It seems incredible, given Capone's lavish lifestyle, that an income greater than the allowable exemption of $5,000 could not be traced, but Capone did all his business through front men and it was difficult to link him to the rackets that were generating such colossal sums. However, the IRS did not give up easily.

The "Pineapple Primary"

Mayor William Hale Thompson's first year back in office had been a disaster, and widespread discontent with his corruption and incompetence was growing. The city of Chicago was $300 million in debt. Primary elections for city offices were scheduled for April 8, 1928, but election violence began in January with a bomb attack on the home of a city controller. In February, Judge John Sbarbaro's home was bombed. Sbarbaro had strong connections to Capone because, in addition to his position as judge, he had long been involved in bootlegging, and he also owned gangland's preferred

Frankie Yale

Frankie Yale started out as a member of the New York Five Points Gang, along with John Torrio. In 1908, he graduated to join John Torrio's Black Hand extortion racket. In 1918, having proved his mob credentials, he took over the Unione Siciliana, which had become a criminal organization under Ignazio Saietta, rather than the fraternal association it had been originally.

Based at the Harvard Inn in Coney Island, New York, Yale took to bootlegging when Prohibition was declared in 1920, and he also ran a "legitimate" business selling cigars. In actual fact, this too was a scam, as he forced tobacco dealers to stock his inferior merchandise or risk reprisals.

Yale supplied Capone's liquor needs in Chicago and also was on call to perform assassinations for the Chicago crime boss. He was also the prime suspect in the murder of "Diamond Jim" Colosimo (see p127).

Yale and Capone eventually fell out when Capone suspected Yale had been hijacking shipments of bootleg whiskey that were intended for Chicago. Yale was hit on July 1, 1928. Having been lured out of a Brooklyn speakeasy, Yale drove off down 44th Street, when another car pulled alongside him, riddling Yale and his car with a hail of bullets. Yale slumped over the wheel and was pulled dead from the wreckage when the car hit a nearby house.

Frankie Yale's funeral was a typically extravagant affair, with 10,000 mourners, 28 carloads of flowers, and a procession of some 250 automobiles.

Dates (1885–1924)
Details Trusted by Al Capone, Yale was an ideal killer – cold-blooded and efficient. When asked by the police what he did for a living, Yale replied "I'm an undertaker." In broad terms, he was telling the truth.

The wages of sin
The palatial estate of Al Capone near Miami, Florida, which he bought in 1928. After a lengthy prison spell in the 1930s, Capone returned to the house, where he died in January 1947.

funeral home, which, it was said, dealt with inconvenient corpses by burying them in "double-decker" coffins. There were 62 bomb attacks in total, most against politicians and city officials who opposed Thompson. The hysteria that gripped Chicago was fanned by not knowing who was responsible, although Capone in far off Miami was inevitably blamed. The election came to be known as Chicago's "Pineapple Primary" — "pineapple" being slang for hand grenade. When the election finally came, Thompson remained as mayor but lost control of the city government. However, the bombings were counter-

Hitman
"Machine Gun" Jack McGurn (above) was implicated in the murder of Frankie Yale and in the St. Valentine's Day Massacre.

productive. One of those who received threats was George Johnson, the U.S. Attorney in Chicago, who was now leading the investigation into Al Capone's finances.

The Death of Frankie Yale

Capone was responsible, even from the distance of Florida, for the most significant gangland assassination of 1928. A combination of reasons convinced him of the necessity of eliminating New York's most prominent gangster and bootlegger, Frankie Yale, who with John Torrio had given Capone his start. Yale was trying to take control of the Chicago Unione Siciliana, which controlled the home distilleries in the Italian community. Not only that, Yale's whiskey shipments to Capone were being hijacked, and Capone suspected Yale himself was responsible. He sent four killers, probably including Jack McGurn, Scalise, and Anselmi, to Brooklyn, New York. On July 1, 1928, they followed Yale's bulletproof car and shot-gunned him through the window. They then finished the job with a Thompson submachine gun (*see* p149), the first time the weapon was used in New York. Yale was given the most lavish funeral gangland had ever seen, better even than Dion O'Banion's in 1924 (*see* p131).

Yale was placed in a $15,000 nickel-and-silver coffin and the procession was followed by 38 carloads of flowers. Yale's killers had thrown their weapons away after the job, as was the custom. The police traced the guns back to Capone, who denied any knowledge of the crime. The evidence was only circumstantial and Capone escaped indictment.

In the summer of 1928, Capone went back to Chicago, leaving his wife and child in Miami, Florida. He set up new headquarters in the Lexington Hotel, on 22nd Street and Michigan Avenue, at first renting 10 rooms, then taking over the entire hotel.

Capone was still not free of the ongoing repercussions of the killing of Frankie Yale. His candidate for the presidency of the Unione Siciliana, Antonio Lombardo, was believed to have connived with Capone in the killing. Lombardo was shot in the head while out walking on September 8. Lombardo's successor, Pasqualino Lolardo, also a friend of Capone, was killed in January 1929, and this too was thought to have been in retaliation for the death of

Death of a hoodlum
The body of Frankie Yale lies beside his car at 44th St., Brooklyn, New York, on July 1, 1928, after being shot to death from a pursuing automobile. Yale's car crashed into a house and he was ejected.

Capone's headquarters
The notorious Lexington Hotel in Chicago, the headquarters of Capone's organization. This photograph was taken in 1984 when the hotel was boarded up. It was demolished in 1995. Capone occupied the hotel from 1928 to 1932.

Frankie Yale. In late 1928, Capone returned to Miami. He was now in control of the Chicago political machine, and virtually invulnerable to the law. There were 367 murders in Chicago in 1928.

January 1929 saw the first successful federal raid against a Capone stronghold. In December 1928, the police chief of Chicago Heights was shot by two men as he sat reading in his front parlor. He had been scheduled to testify against two bootleggers. U.S. Attorney George Johnson, in cooperation with the Chicago Police Department, raided Chicago Heights — first having arrested the entire police department who were thought to be on Capone's payroll — and broke up stills and breweries. They found ledgers recording profits from slot machines at the home of the manager of one of Capone's Cicero gambling dens. Careful scrutiny of the documents led to the indictment for income tax evasion of Capone's brother, Ralph. Meanwhile, in Miami, Florida, Al Capone did not seem worried by this development, but he should have been.

St. Valentine's Day, 1929

There remained the unfinished business of the North Siders, now led by George Moran. Two of his gunmen, the brothers Frank and Pete Gusenberg, attempted to kill Jack McGurn, shooting him as he was making a telephone call from a public booth. McGurn survived. He went to Miami and told Capone the time had come to eliminate all the North Siders. This time Capone agreed. The result was the St. Valentine's Day Massacre, when seven of Moran's men — but not Moran himself — were murdered (*see box, opposite*).

The St. Valentine's Day Massacre, as it became known, shocked even Chicago. Gangland was in turmoil and hundreds of gangsters fled the city, fearing the same fate. McGurn's solution to the Moran problem had attracted so much publicity that everything Capone had achieved was now

threatened. The press had a field day, and although Capone's alibi was unbreakable, it was common knowledge that he had authorized the worse gangland slaying in Chicago's history. His relative anonymity in Miami was at an end. He was now the most notorious man in America. McGurn was arrested, but police were unable to break his alibi and he was released. However, McGurn was then cold-shouldered by Capone. He was shot dead on February 13, 1936. One of the killers put a nickel in his dead hand.

In March 1929, Capone was summoned to appear before a federal grand jury in Chicago. He falsely claimed sickness as a reason for not attending. He was cited for contempt, but escaped prosecution. The federal government, however, now had him in its sights and even Capone should have been concerned at what they might do next.

Justice, Mob-Style

Capone returned to Chicago in May 1929. Informants told him that Scalise, Anselmi, and Joseph Guinta, the new president of the Unione Siciliana, had allied themselves with Capone's old enemy, Joseph Aiello. Capone acted swiftly, first corroborating the rumor, and then throwing a dinner party at a roadhouse in Hammond, Indiana, inviting Scalise, Anselmi, and Guinta along with 100 other guests. After dinner was over Capone savagely beat the three "traitors" with a baseball bat. Then his gunmen shot them to pieces. Capone, perhaps as a result of mental deterioration caused by syphilis, was clearly losing control of himself.

Three days later, on May 10, Capone went to Atlantic City, New Jersey, accompanied by 23-year old Anthony "Joe Batters" Accardo, who would later head the Chicago Outfit. In Atlantic City they met with crime leaders from all over the country, concerned about the heat and publicity generated by the St. Valentine's Day Massacre.

The Atlantic City Conference

The roll call of invited guests at the conference was impressive: Jack Guzik, "Boo-Hoo" Hoff, and Nig Rosen from Philadelphia, Abe Bernstein representing the Purple Gang from Detroit, Leo Berkowitz,

CASE STUDY

The St. Valentine's Day Massacre, February 14, 1929, Chicago

In February 1929, the Capone gang set up a typically elaborate operation, probably thought up by Jack McGurn, to eliminate George Moran and the key members of his North Side gang. Capone left Chicago for Florida, leaving the execution of the plan to McGurn, while giving himself the perfect alibi.

Moran's headquarters was the SMC Cartage Company Garage at 2122 North Clark Street. Capone had to make sure Moran and his henchmen were there. To set them up, he arranged for a Detroit hijacker to offer to sell Moran a truckload of contraband whiskey. Moran agreed to the buy, and said to deliver the truck to the SMC garage at 10.30 a.m. on February 14 – St. Valentine's Day.

At the appointed time, instead of the promised truckload of whiskey, three men in the uniforms of the Chicago police department and carrying Thompson submachine guns, accompanied by two men in plain clothes, drove up to the main entrance of the garage. There were seven men inside, six of them members of the North Side gang and one a respectable Chicago optometrist

who got a kick out of hanging out with known criminals. The gangsters were not alarmed, assuming this was just another police shakedown. They were ordered to line up facing the wall. Then the "police" (in reality Capone gunmen) opened fire, killing them all. Ballistics experts later recovered between 80 and 100 .45 slugs.

The murdered men were identified as James Clark, Frank Gusenberg (who survived for a few hours) and his brother Pete, Al Weinshank, John May, and Adam Meyer. The optometrist was Dr

"Only Capone kills guys like that!"

George "Bugs" Moran, after the massacre of six of his men in the SMC Cartage Company garage

Reinhardt H. Schwimmer, who paid a heavy price for his fascination with the underworld.

Surprisingly, neither the *Chicago Daily News* nor the *Chicago Herald Examiner* coined the obvious "St. Valentine's Day Massacre" headline. They did publish photographs of the corpses, cleaned up for public consumption, but nevertheless still very shocking. It is indicative of the times that, when

news of the massacre first broke, many, including the Prohibition administrator Frederick Silloway, thought it had been carried out by the police. The *Herald Examiner* knew better, saying: "Gangland Garbs Its Executioners in Police Uniforms. Massacre Wipes Out Last of Powerful O'Banion Gang." This headline was not quite accurate. Moran was not among the dead. He had overslept, arriving just as the "policemen" were entering the garage. He held back, and when he heard the sound of the Thompsons, made himself scarce. But he was finished as a power in Chicago. He allied himself with Capone's enemies, the Aiello clan and Jack Zuta's Jewish gang, but Capone wiped out the leaders before they could organize. George Moran eventually served two long prison terms, dying in 1957 at Leavenworth Penitentiary. No one was ever arrested for the St. Valentine's Day Massacre.

Mistaken identity
Crowds quickly gathered outside the SMC building after the St Valentine's Day Massacre. Because the killers wore police uniforms, many Chicagoans thought at first that the killings had been carried out by policemen involved in the hijacking of illicit whiskey.

| Adam Meyer | John May | Al Weinshank | James Clark | Frank Gusenberg | Pete Gusenberg |

The carnage
Photographs of the machine-gunned victims of the St Valentine's Day Massacre shocked the public and led to a nationwide outcry for law reform.

In cold blood
The victims of the St. Valentine's Day Massacre, all members of George Moran's North Side gang. The only survivor was John May's dog.

Murder in the movies
The climactic scene in Roger Corman's 1967 movie *The St. Valentine's Day Massacre*, starring Jason Robards as Al Capone and George Segal as Pete Gusenberg. A version of the massacre also featured in Billy Wilder's comedy *Some Like It Hot* (1959).

MENS CELLROOM

Masseria and Salvatore Maranzano, rival Mafia leaders in New York, at war over which one would be "the boss of bosses." For Luciano and Torrio, this was a hangover from the days of the ethnic gangs. They wanted a Syndicate in which each member controlled his own territory and no one was subservient to anyone else. They envisioned a federation, not a kingdom. Masseria and Maranzano had to be eliminated. The old Sicilian Mafia would be replaced by a new U.S. version, open to non-Sicilians. It would be corporate, with a board of directors, not run as a family business.

It was also agreed that it would be good public relations if Al Capone went to jail. Hoff arranged for him to be arrested in Philadelphia on a charge of carrying a concealed weapon. Two detectives were paid $10,000 each to arrest him in the lobby of a cinema, charge him, and get him sentenced as quickly as possible. They did so in the record time of 16 hours. It was the first time Capone had served a prison sentence. He was delighted to do so. A year in jail was just what he needed to take the heat off. His brother Ralph would look after the rackets in Chicago. Al was duly sent to serve his time at Eastern State Penitentiary in Philadelphia, now a museum where his luxurious cell, carpeted and furnished with fine antique furniture, may still be visited.

Public Enemy Number One

Capone was released in March 1930 after serving 10 months. He returned to The Lexington Hotel in Chicago, ignored the Atlantic City Commission rulings, and picked up the reins where he had left them. The only major changes he found were that the young Prohibition agent, Eliot Ness (*see box, p*135), was making a nuisance of himself, and that his brother Ralph had been indicted for income tax evasion, along with Frank "The Enforcer" Nitti, who had assisted Jack Guzik while Capone was in jail. However, Capone discounted the difficulties

The Milk Monopoly

In 1930, as the end of Prohibition became more likely, Capone associate Murray Llewellyn Humphreys suggested another source of income. Murray said that the markup on milk was higher than that on bootleg whiskey, and that the market was bigger. After all, it included children. Capone loved the idea. Humphreys kidnapped the president of the local Milk Wagon Drivers' Union, collecting $50,000. He used the ransom money to set up Meadowmoor Dairies, and undermined the competition by using non-union deliverymen. Prices dropped and soon Meadowmoor had a monopoly of the market. It was a rare example of a gangland takeover that created a social benefit.

Chicago's children
Al Capone's Meadowmoor Dairies fixed the price of milk in Chicago and pioneered the concept of "sell-by" dates.

and Moe Dalitz from Cleveland, John Lazia from Kansas City, Longy Zwillman from New Jersey, and Daniel Walsh from Rhode Island. The New York contingent was even more formidable and very angry: Lansky, Luciano, Dutch Shultz, Albert Anastasia, Louis Buchalter, Ben Siegel, Joe Adonis, and Frank Costello. With them came John Torrio. He and Lansky could not forgive Capone for killing Frankie Yale on their home territory without permission.

For three days the delegates talked, walking on the beach far from prying ears. They adopted a series of resolutions, some designed to cut Capone down to size, others to lay the groundwork for organized crime after Prohibition. The delegates formed a Commission, with Torrio as its head, which would deal with disagreements between members. Capone's organization was to be disbanded immediately and his gambling joints taken over by the Commission. There was to be no more killing. The new head of the Chicago Unione Siciliana would be Capone's enemy, Joseph Aiello.

Other resolutions were to have serious consequences for organized crime in the future. There were two conspicuous absences from the conference: Joe

his brother was having. It seemed unlikely that anyone would be convicted of so small a crime as not paying income tax. But the government's strategy was the right one. Juries that would never dare convict a gangster of murder for fear of retaliation had no hesitation in bringing in a conviction for what was, after all, seen as little more than an error in bookkeeping. Capone was astonished when Ralph was convicted and faced 22 years in prison.

To make matters worse, a citizens' group called the Chicago Crime Commission published a list of the most prominent criminals in the city. The first name on the list was Al Capone, followed by his brother Ralph. The idea of "public enemies" was picked up by newspapers across the country, and J. Edgar Hoover, head of the Federal Bureau of Investigation (FBI), created the "Most Wanted" lists that still adorn all U.S. post offices today.

In Chicago, the federal government was pressing ahead with its income tax evasion

investigations. Frank Nitti, who had fled after being indicted with Ralph Capone, was finally found in the suburb of Cicero and arrested. Jack Guzik was found guilty and sentenced to five years in Leavenworth Penitentiary.

The year 1930 saw Capone at the height of his power. The Atlantic City Commission never enforced its sanctions against him, and when Capone returned from jail he was able to take control of a smoothly working organization. The Commission's appointee as head of the Unione Siciliana, Joseph Aiello, was shot and killed in October, almost certainly on Capone's orders, and the Commission took no action. At 31 years of age, Al Capone was now the most powerful man in Chicago. The *Chicago Daily News* estimated his weekly take from the rackets and prostitution at more than $6 million dollars. And this was at the beginning of the Great Depression, with fortunes being lost on Wall Street and businesses closing across the country.

Machine-gun bullet holes
The bullet-riddled coat worn by crime boss Joe Aiello when he was slain by Capone hitmen on October 25, 1930, in Chicago. The coat has 37 holes in it. Struck by between 50 and 100 bullets, Aiello's body was cut almost in two.

CRIMEBUSTER

J. Edgar Hoover and the FBI

From the 1920s to the mid-1950s, while organized crime grew from local bootlegging operations to a National Crime Syndicate, J. Edgar Hoover and the Federal Bureau of Investigation (FBI) concentrated their energies on fighting communism, on bandits like John Dillinger, and on other perceived threats to the American way of life.

Not only that, but until the comic-opera conclusion of the Apalachin conference of 1957 (*see p*159), which received wide press coverage, Hoover publicly denied the existence of organized syndicated crime in the United States, and specifically denied the existence of the American Mafia.

Privately, the Bureau was not as uninformed as Hoover made it sound. Its files contain a long and detailed

history of the Mafia, dating from the early 1950s. Even earlier, in 1946, the Chicago FBI had bugged Outfit headquarters in the Morrison Hotel and had had *mafiosi* followed.

After Apalachin, and at the relentless urging of Attorney General Robert Kennedy, Hoover employed the vast resources of the FBI in the fight against organized crime. The testimony in 1963 of informer Joe Valacchi allowed detailed charts of the various crime families to be drawn up, and law enforcement officers formed an idea of the structure, extent, and membership of the National Syndicate. The lives of leading Syndicate members became increasingly difficult and it was harder for them to do business.

Hoover seized on a phrase used a number of times by Joe Valacchi in his

Badge of office
The official seal of the Federal Bureau of Investigation (FBI).

testimony before the Senate Investigative Committee, and used it to counter press criticism of his refusal to admit the existence of the Mafia. The phrase was "La Cosa Nostra" (Our Thing), which Valacchi used when referring to the five crime families of New York. Hoover claimed that the FBI had always been aware of the existence of La Cosa Nostra, but he still insisted that the Mafia did not exist.

Many attempts have been made to explain why Hoover, always so ready to find communist conspiracies in the most unlikely places, should have taken so long to admit the Mafia existed. One explanation is that he was aware of the difficulties of convicting organized crime leaders, with their political connections. Another idea is that he knew how easily organized crime corrupted those with whom it came in contact and wanted to keep his agents clean. A more convincing theory is that Hoover saw organized crime as part of the power structure and, through its control of key unions, as an ally in fighting communism and socialism.

J. Edgar Hoover
For nearly 50 years, from 1924 until 1972, Hoover was the Director of the Federal Bureau of Investigation. His reluctance to admit that the Mafia existed made some think that he was more closely involved. There is also the fact that Hoover loved betting on horse races and received tips from his friend the columnist Walter Winchell, who in turn received them from gangster Frank Costello.

The Great Depression and Rural Bandits

What the Depression did to urban economies, the "Dust Bowl" did to rural America. As the wind blew away the topsoil, hundreds of thousands of farmers and farm laborers throughout the Midwestern states lost their livelihoods when banks foreclosed on loans and took over farms. Men and women migrated west to California or to eastern cities, desperate for work.

Prohibition had been the expression of the will of rural America, whose population was largely of German, Scandinavian, and Scottish background. They were devout Christians and suspicious of cities, their immigrant populations, and their attendant vices. Cities were sinks of iniquity, and the open flouting of Prohibition in places like Chicago and the doings of gangsters like Al Capone confirmed them in their views.

Armed and dangerous
Notorious criminal John Dillinger, poses with a Thompson submachine gun in one hand and a .38 Colt handgun in the other.

AMERICA'S MOST WANTED

The Dust Bowl shattered the myth of the purity of rural America, just as it shattered its prosperity. Bandits like Bonnie Parker and Clyde Barrow, John Dillinger, Charles "Pretty Boy" Floyd, the Barker family, and George "Machine Gun" Kelly were just as vicious as their urban counterparts but much less competent. They came from small towns no one had ever heard of in states like Oklahoma and Texas, beyond the experience of most easterners. Rural bandits also had fewer options than the criminals in big cities. They

Soup kitchen
Capone's soup kitchen in Chicago handed out free meals for the unemployed. During the 1930s, many rural workers headed for the cities only to find there was no work.

robbed stores, gas stations, and, above all, banks. Some law-abiding people silently cheered them on. Hadn't the banks robbed them? Charles Floyd, born in Oklahoma, used to tear up peoples' mortgage papers when he robbed a bank. He was eventually killed by agents of the Federal Bureau of Investigation (FBI) in 1934. Ten thousand people attended his funeral.

Bonnie Parker and Clyde Barrow, known simply as Bonnie and Clyde, operated for only four years, between 1930 and 1934, killing 13 people and robbing many banks. They died in a hail of bullets from a police ambush outside Arcadia, Louisiana, in 1934. Thirty thousand mourners paid their respects at Barrow's coffin.

The most famous rural bandit was John Dillinger from Indiana. Released from prison in 1933, he carried out a number of bank robberies and killed several police officers. Dillinger caught the public imagination by a number of daring prison escapes and gunfights against the forces of law and order. In 1934, his movements were betrayed to the FBI by a girlfriend, and he was killed as he left the Biograph Theater in Chicago, having just seen Clark Gable in the movie *Manhattan Melodrama*.

J. Edgar Hoover, head of the FBI, built his reputation on his success against rural bandits, whose exploits Hoover exaggerated to enhance his own. In truth, the real danger to America came from the much more highly organized city gangsters.

Bonnie and Clyde
Bank robber Bonnie Parker playfully points a shotgun at her lover Clyde Barrow in 1932.

The U.S. stock market had crashed on October 29, 1929. By early 1931, as the Great Depression worsened, armies of the unemployed appeared on the streets of Chicago. Capone fought back against his "Public Enemy" image by opening a soup kitchen on South State Street during the winter months. On Thanksgiving Day he fed 5,000 people. The goodwill generated did a great deal to mitigate Capone's reputation in the eyes of ordinary Americans. The gesture did nothing to help his image with the federal government, which wanted to know where he got the money to pay for it.

Capone Finally Goes to Jail

Unable to find proof of murder, bootlegging, and racketeering that would stand up in court, investigators instead concentrated on Capone's expenditure, comparing it with his declared income. Internal Revenue Service (IRS) agents combed the stores of Chicago and Miami, calculating the cost of Capone's furniture, tableware, rugs, and even his underwear. After interviewing hundreds of people, it was clear that his income was vastly greater than he had stated. Government agents could now prove that his income between 1924 and 1929 totaled $1,038,654.84, and they calculated that he owed $215,080.48 in taxes. Capone offered to pay off the tax but his offer was rejected. On June 5, 1931, he was indicted for income-tax evasion. He was brought to trial on October 7, 1931, and convicted. He was sentenced to 11 years and fined $80,000.

After serving eight months in the Cook County Jail in a luxuriously furnished cell from which he continued to run his empire, Capone was transferred to Atlanta State Penitentiary. In 1934, he was sent to Alcatraz. In 1939, seriously ill as a result of syphilis, he was moved to the Federal Correctional Institution at Terminal Island, near Los Angeles. Released to the care of his family in 1939, Capone died of a heart attack at home in Miami on January 25, 1947.

Shackled and silent
Heavily armed police officers (right) escort manacled rural bank robber and kidnapper George Kelly on October 2, 1933, in Memphis, Tennessee. He later joined Capone in Alcatraz jail.

Mae Capone
Capone's wife, Mae, uses her mink coat to hide her face from press cameramen after visiting her husband in Alcatraz Federal Penitentiary in 1938. Mae received a monthly pension from the Chicago Outfit until her death in 1986.

The Chicago "Outfit"

When Al Capone arrived in Chicago in 1921, the city was a patchwork of ethnic gangs, battling for territory. Ten years later, when Capone was jailed, the situation had completely changed. After Prohibition was repealed in 1933 (*see p151*) the old ethnic gangs vanished, their members absorbed into the Capone organization, the legitimate world, the prison system — or the cemetery. It might have been expected that with Capone in Alcatraz, his organization would break up. The press created the false impression that Capone was a criminal mastermind, solely responsible for political corruption and the violence and mayhem on Chicago's streets. His prosecutors also thought that, once he was jailed, organized crime in the city would disappear overnight. It was only gradually that they realized that things were not going to be so simple.

Capone had inherited an efficient organization from Torrio, and transformed it into something like a modern corporation that would outlive its creator. Prohibition had given the organization the money to diversify and also to create a network linking the Chicago mob to other crime groups in New York, New Jersey, Buffalo, Cleveland, Kansas City, and in Canada and the Caribbean. These places had all been part of the network of illicit liquor production, smuggling, shipping, and trucking. Groups that would otherwise scarcely have known of one another were now in constant contact. The car and the interstate highway system, the telephone and telegraph, had all greatly facilitated these contacts and created a web of organized crime.

Chicago After Capone

In Chicago, with Capone gone, the mob was taken over by a "board of directors" made up of Jack Guzik, now out of jail, Johnny Roselli, Paul Ricca, Murray Llewellyn Humphreys, and headed by Joseph Accardo. These men were insulated from the operational end of the business by a layer of "managers," each with an area of authority, from bootlegging to prostitution. At street level were the collectors, enforcers,

Members of the board
Paul Ricca (left) and Jack Guzik (right) became members of the Chicago Outfit's "board of directors" when Capone was jailed in the early 1930s.

and gunmen. The organization was called simply the "Outfit," and is still in business today, although downsized and diversified.

The Outfit drew up certain laws. It tried to discourage flamboyant dress or so-called "gangster chic," and members dressed well but soberly in business suits. They worked 12-hour days. Drug dealing was banned, and those who broke this rule were killed. Although mild social drinking was tolerated, anything more was similarly sanctioned. Wives and families were sacrosanct and, if possible, kept in ignorance of Outfit doings. Widows of Outfit members were paid pensions. Capone's widow Mae, for example, received monthly payments of $25,000 until her death in 1986.

The Castellammarese War

In April 1931, Giuseppe Masseria, boss of the leading Mafia family in New York had been killed. Masseria's death had been ordered by Luciano during the "Castellammarese War," named after Castellamare del Golfo in Sicily, the home town of Masseria's rival, Salvatore Maranzano, who had been sent to the United States by Vito Cascio Ferro, the foremost Mafia boss of Sicily. Maranzano's task was to organize all the main American crime groups, both Italian and non-Italian, under his leadership. His boss, Cascio Ferro, would then rule an empire spanning New World and Old. Leaving Cascio Ferro's unrealistic scheme aside, Maranzano had an enormous impact on the structure of

American organized crime. He established himself in Brooklyn in 1927, and allied himself with other *mafiosi* from his home town. These included men like Joe Profaci in Brooklyn, Joe Bonanno, Stefano Magaddino in Buffalo, Gaspar Miliazzo in Detroit, and Joe Aiello, Capone's old enemy in Chicago.

the Castellammarese War, because during Prohibition there was no lack of other reasons for murder. The best estimate is around 50 dead.

Masseria and Maranzano were fighting a typically Sicilian war, motivated by regional pride but in an environment where the

Giuseppe Masseria

Giuseppe "Joe the Boss" Masseria emigrated from Sicily to New York in 1903, fleeing a murder charge. He began to work for the Morello family as an enforcer under brutal gangster Ignazio Saietta (*see p*123).

By 1913, most of the leaders of the Morello organization were in prison or dead. Masseria seized his chance to take over. He began killing members of the Morello clan and taking over their rackets. By 1920, he was in control.

Peter Morello, a surviving clan member, joined with Umberto "Rocco" Valenti to try to kill Masseria in 1922. Valenti caught up with Masseria on 2nd Avenue, and shot his bodyguards. Masseria ducked into a store; Valenti followed, emptying a clip at

Masseria. Out of ammunition, Valenti retreated. Masseria was unhurt, and became known as the "man who could dodge bullets."

Masseria then arranged a meeting with Valenti. When Valenti showed up with three gunmen, Masseria's crew ambushed them. Valenti fled, but was picked off by a young Masseria gunman named Salvatore Lucania, later known as Charles "Lucky" Luciano.

Just as Masseria took power by betraying the Morellos, Luciano took over by arranging the assassination of "Joe the Boss" in 1931, when the Castellammarese War was still going on. Luciano took Masseria out to a restaurant on Coney Island, and then went to the bathroom, leaving his friends to enter the restaurant and shoot Masseria dead.

Dates (1879–1931)
Details Giuseppe "Joe the Boss" Masseria held power on New York's Lower East Side for more than a decade before his murder in 1931.

Common culture, a shared dialect, and the uncanny ability to communicate by a mere gesture formed a bond between them that was accentuated by living among strangers.

The War Begins

Masseria watched the growing power of his rival with concern. His own organization contained a number of redoubtable names — not only Luciano, but Albert Anastasia, Vito Genovese, Frank Costello, Willie Moretti, Carlo Gambino, and Joe Adonis. In 1929, the wars began, with Masseria's supporters killing Maranzano's and vice versa. Nobody knows exactly how many gang deaths between 1928 and 1931 were soldiers in

The ace of spades

Giuseppe Masseria's body lies on the floor of the restaurant in Coney Island where he was murdered in April 1931. His dead hand holds the ace of spades, placed there by a resourceful photojournalist.

> ## "You need just as good a brain to make a crooked million as an honest million."
> Charles "Lucky" Luciano

thing that really mattered was money, their war was interfering in making it. Young men in both groups were disaffected. They were dying for a code that they did not share. Led by Luciano, these men began to meet secretly, finding they had more in common with each other than with their bosses. Luciano then decided to eliminate his own boss first, setting up Masseria in a Coney Island restaurant. On April 15, 1931, the two men dined and then played cards. When the restaurant had emptied, Luciano got up to use the lavatory. Ben Siegel, Albert Anastasia, Joe Adonis, and Vito Genovese burst into the restaurant and shot Masseria dead. All four killers were members of Masseria's own organization.

Luciano quickly made his peace with Maranzano, who in return made Luciano his second in command. Maranzano then summoned the leading mob bosses to a

Maranzano had drawn up a list of prominent Mafia figures to be eliminated. Luciano himself was on the list, as were Genovese and Costello. With Maranzano out of the way, the last of the traditional Sicilian Mafia, was gone. Later legend had it that new boss Luciano had had between 40 and 90 of the old guard assassinated around the country on the same day Maranzano was killed: September 10, 1931. Although untrue, the legend encapsulates a historic change that really did take place. The old guard, with their ancient vendettas, secret rituals, and concepts of honor and shame imported from Sicily, were supplanted by an Americanized leadership to whom these feelings were no longer relevant. Meanwhile, in Italy, fascist leader Benito Mussolini had put Maranzano's mentor, Vito Cascio Ferro, in jail, thus severing the link between the Sicilian and American Mafias.

September 10, 1931, witnessed the birth of modern American syndicated crime. Luciano and Lansky had long realized that close cooperation between criminal groups led to greater profits for all. However, one other man should also be given his due: Arnold Rothstein.

The National Syndicate
Rothstein first began thinking of a National Crime Syndicate in the early 1920s. He saw that the vast profits from bootlegging had changed forever the relationship between

Coney Island, Brooklyn, New York
Crime boss Salvatore Maranzano set up his operation in Brooklyn in 1927 and established rackets among the fairground attractions of Coney Island. Maranzano had his rival Giuseppe Masseria murdered in a Coney Island restaurant.

meeting. Speaking in Italian before an audience of 500, he said that from now on the Italian crime groups of New York would be divided into five "families," each with a simple structure: boss, underboss, lieutenants, and soldiers. Maranzano then declared that he would be the *capo di tutti capi*, or "boss of bosses, "and his empire would be called "La Cosa Nostra" (Our Thing). Maranzano held his title for only four months. On the orders of Luciano, he was killed on September 10, 1931, by four Jewish gunmen. Luciano had acted quickly once he discovered that

Charles Luciano

Charles "Lucky" Luciano was the most important gangster to emerge from the 1920s in America. It was Luciano who co-founded the New York Syndicate in 1931, a structure that has guided the Mafia ever since.

Salvatore Luccania (also known as Charles "Lucky" Luciano) was born in Leucara Friddi, Sicily, and arrived in the United States in 1906. When Prohibition came in 1920, Luciano began bootlegging operations and soon he began working for Giuseppe Masseria, who ran New York's biggest crime family. Masseria was very much of the Old World, with its emphasis on Sicilian traditions. Luciano began to see that the Mafia of the future would embrace the multi-ethnic, multi-cultural world in which they

now lived. When the Castellammarese Wars broke out (*see* p146), Luciano took his chance and seized control of the New York mob. The "old Mafia" was replaced by the "new" American Syndicate, embracing all ethnicities and controlling bootlegging, prostitution, narcotics, and gambling.

In 1936, Luciano was convicted on a prostitution charge and jailed. He maintained control of the Syndicate while behind bars and assisted the U.S. government during World War II, making use of his contacts in Sicily to help the Allied invasion in 1943 (*see* p157). As a "reward," Luciano was released and deported to Italy in 1946. In the 1950s, Luciano's influence waned. He died of heart attack at Naples airport in 1962.

BIOGRAPHY

Dates 1897–1962
Details "Lucky" Luciano was the first of a new breed of American *mafiosi*. Determined to modernize the mob in New York, he organized the elimination of the old-fashioned Mafia Dons.

INSIDE STORY

THE TOMMY GUN

The classic weapon of the rural Mafia in Sicily was the *lupara*, a double-barreled shotgun carried by estate guardians to shoot wolves. Urban *mafiosi*, both in Sicily and in the United States, clung to this lethal weapon that needed little skill to use, but cut down the barrels and often hinged or truncated the stock for ease of concealment. Loaded with buckshot, this was long the weapon of choice against moving targets or when faced with more than one enemy. The downside was collateral damage and slow reloading.

Although a wide variety of instruments of death have been used – garrottes, knives, ice picks, baseball bats, double action revolvers and automatics, carbines, Kalashnikovs, grenades – one Mafia weapon defined the image of the gangster in the 1920s. This was the Thompson submachine gun, familiarly known as the Tommy Gun and sometimes nicknamed the "Chicago Piano." The weapon was named after its co-inventor, General John Thompson, who developed it during World War I (1914–18). It was originally designed for sweeping the German trenches, killing everyone in its path. The weapon used the easily available .45 ACP cartridge. The early models took not only a 20- or a 30-round box magazine, but a 50-round drum was dispensed with later models. Although it could deliver bullets at a rapid rate of fire, the gun was only really effective at close range. It was the ideal weapon for urban warfare, if you didn't mind killing bystanders. George Moran's gang was the first to use it, but gangsters everywhere soon took it up, paying as much as $2,000 per weapon. The Chicago Police then adopted it, fearing they were being outgunned. The Thompson was later used by the U.S. military in World War II (1939–45).

Capone's car
An FBI agent poses with a Thompson submachine gun in Al Capone's car. This 1938 photograph was taken while Capone was in Alcatraz. Automobiles were often used by gangsters for "drive-by" shootings.

THOMPSON GUNS
MODELS 1921—1923
Manufactured by Colt's Patent Fire Arms Mfg. Company
FOR THE
Auto-Ordnance Corporation
302 BROADWAY
NEW YORK, N.Y., U.S.A.
Cable "AUTORDCO—N.Y."

Weapon of choice
The Thompson submachine (left) was the classic gangsters' weapon. The Thompson, manufactured by the Colt Company, was later taken up by both the U.S. police and the U.S. military, as depicted in the maker's advertisement (above).

the underworld and the upperworld. The underworld now controlled enough capital to be able to buy protection directly from the politicians. Criminal groups were an economic force to be reckoned with. Indeed, they were vital to the economy. Rothstein's political connections in New York were so good that he could get almost any court case dismissed. Indeed, until 1928, when he was killed over an unpaid gambling debt, almost every bootlegging case that came before the New York courts — more than 6,000 in all — was thrown out through his intervention.

The New-Look Mafia

Rothstein financed Meyer Lansky's first enterprise, a trucking rental firm on the Lower East Side of New York. Lansky's vehicles were in great demand during Prohibition, and he was joined by Luciano in a number of bootlegging ventures. Rothstein also financed some of Luciano's drug deals. In addition, Rothstein was financier and mentor to Louis Buchalter and Jacob Shapiro, organizers of labor unions in the New York garment district and later star members of Murder, Incorporated (see p153). Another of his protégés was Arthur Flegenheimer, also known as "Dutch" Shultz (see p150).

> ## "Money talks. The more money, the louder it talks."
> Arnold Rothstein

Arnold Rothstein was as much the godfather of organized crime in the United States as John Torrio, who often relied on Rothstein's judgment. Rothstein's Syndicate model was a loose confederation, with clearly defined territories and a board of directors. There was little in the way of hierarchy. Although law enforcement agencies, following Valacchi's testimony before the McClellan Committee in 1963 (see p163), devoted much time to drawing up hierarchical organizational charts of New York crime families, Rothstein's model is closer to reality. The idea that there is an all-powerful single Mafia controlled by a handful of men whose word is law and whose orders are carried out without question anywhere in America has, however, proved much more seductive than the reality of a loose network of independent groups, each with its own power struggles and commercial concerns.

The National Syndicate set up by Luciano and Lansky used many of Rothstein's ideas, dispensing with the old "boss of bosses" concept in favor of a National Commission made up of six men who would adjudicate disputes and act as an advisory board. Maranzano's five New York Mafia families were retained, with Luciano taking over the Masseria operation, which is now known as the Genovese family.

Conspicuous consumption was to be avoided. Journalists and politicians were not to be killed because of the attention it would draw.

New York gangster Dutch Shultz came close to breaking this last rule. Shultz not only controlled a vast bootlegging empire, but in 1931 formed his own crime syndicate and took over the Harlem numbers racket. In many ways, Shultz was New York's answer to Chicago's Al Capone, controlling a key politician, James T. Hines, as well as a corrupt district attorney and other city officials. Hines, for example, was paid a retainer of up to $1,000 per week, depending on the take from Schultz's numbers racket. The business grossed $20 million each year.

When Special Prosecutor Thomas E. Dewey (*see p152*) began his clean-up campaign against organized crime, Shultz was one of his main targets. In 1935, Dewey confiscated thousands of Shultz's slot machines and publicly smashed them. Shultz went to the newly formed National Commission and asked for permission to kill Dewey. It was refused. Luciano said that the publicity would damage the Syndicate's operations.

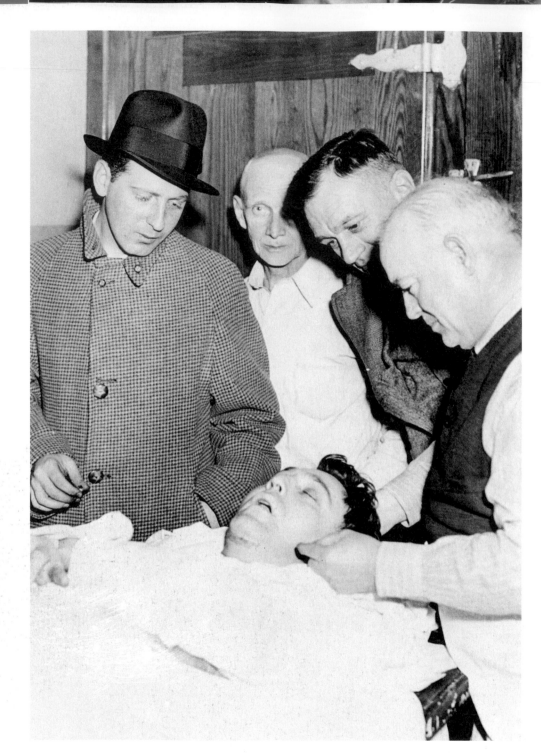

The other New York families are now known as the Colombo, Gambino, Lucchese, and Bonanno. The Syndicate included 24 Mafia groups in 24 other cities across the United States and was made up of Jewish and Protestant members as well as Roman Catholics. The New York families retained the tradition of Italian descent as a prerequisite of membership and some of the old rituals, including oathtaking.

Death of Dutch Schultz
Gangster "Dutch" Schultz laid out on the mortuary slab. He was gunned down on the orders of Luciano after Schultz had threatened to kill Special Prosecutor Thomas E. Dewey.

Mob Rules

There were certain rules, aside from the law of *omertà* (keeping silent about mob business). As with the Chicago Outfit, a man's family was off-limits. Anyone making approaches to another man's wife was killed.

THE NEW AMERICAN MAFIA

The structure of the U.S. Mafia in the 1930s is shown below. The National Commission was set up in 1931 and was the sole body to sanction murders and to mediate disputes between rival Mafia groups. The Five New York Families and the Chicago Outfit had a major influence on all Commission affairs. The most important Mafia states of the time are also shown. States like Nevada were not exploited until the 1950s, when Las Vegas became the biggest mob city outside of New York and Chicago.

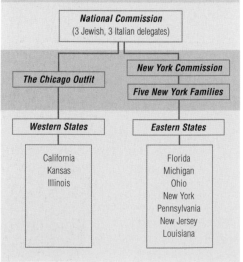

National Commission
(3 Jewish, 3 Italian delegates)

New York Commission

The Chicago Outfit

Five New York Families

Western States

Eastern States

California	Florida
Kansas	Michigan
Illinois	Ohio
	New York
	Pennsylvania
	New Jersey
	Louisiana

Meyer Lansky

Maier Suchowljansky, also known as Meyer Lansky, was born in 1902 in Grodno, in what is now Belarus. His father emigrated to the United States in 1909 and, like so many other immigrants, shortened the family name. In 1914, the family moved to the Lower East Side of Manhattan, where Meyer met Ben Siegel and Charles "Lucky" Luciano. Throughout the 1920s, Lansky and Siegel were involved in bootlegging and hijacking, and the occasional contract killing.

Influenced by Arnold Rothstein, Lansky and Luciano co-founded syndicated crime in the United States, which they achieved by organizing the assassinations of Giuseppe Masseria and Salvatore Maranzano, dividing the Italian crime families of New York into five groups, and forging an alliance with Jewish gangsters and other Italian crime families (see p149).

Lansky was the first to see the possibilities of Cuba and Las Vegas, pointing out that legal gambling would be more cost effective than illegal. So influential did he become that he was consulted on all major mob operations, both by the Chicago Outfit and the New York Syndicate.

The U.S. government finally charged him with income tax evasion in 1970 and he fled to Israel, where he attempted to claim citizenship. Pressure was put on Israel by the U.S. government, and Lansky was deported in 1972. He was tried in 1973 in Miami, Florida, and acquitted. He died in 1983.

Dates 1902–1983
Details One of the founderss of modern syndicated crime in the United States, Meyer Lansky restructured the Mafia and amassed an estimated fortune of $400 million by the time of his death.

Shultz left, swearing that he would kill Dewey himself. Luciano asked for and received permission to eliminate Schultz. On October 23, 1935, Schultz was shot in the Palace Chop House in Newark, New Jersey, by Charles "The Bug" Workman and Emmanuel Weiss. He died a few days later. Although Dewey never knew it, he owed his life to Luciano.

The End of Prohibition

Prohibition was repealed on December 5, 1933, by the Twenty-first Amendment to the U.S. Constitution. Repeal had been bitterly contested by the "drys," who only capitulated when the Democratic government agreed to a heavy tax on alcoholic beverages. This meant that former bootleggers could continue to produce and smuggle illicit liquor, which could

be sold tax-free. There was also a lucrative subsidiary for some criminals in forging tax stamps. Meyer Lansky, for example, set up two distilleries, one in Ohio and one in New Jersey, each turning out 20,000 bottles of 190 percent proof alcohol per day. These were raided in 1935, and Lansky turned to the gambling rackets. He went into the casino business

in Saratoga Springs, in upstate New York, in a joint-venture partnership with Frank Costello and Joe Adonis. Soon Luciano joined them. By this time, Luciano was living in the Waldorf Astoria Hotel in New York, taking a cut from every racket going in the city, from gambling and extortion to prostitution. He was running 5,000 prostitutes nationwide, and reputedly earning $12 million a year. This was at the height of the Depression.

The casino in Saratoga Springs, and later "carpet joints," were the precursors of Havana and Las Vegas (see p158). Lansky and his friends domesticated gambling by creating the safe, luxurious, and enticing road houses that sprang up all over the United States from 1933 onward. The fact that it was against the law only made the carpet joints more attractive to the American public. The lean years of Prohibition had taught a whole generation contempt for the law. In addition to their ventures in the North, Lansky and Jimmy

Let the good times roll
A group of women celebrate the end of Prohibition in December 1933. With the rise of organized crime in the United States during the 1920s, Prohibition had created more problems than it solved.

"Blue Eyes" Alo opened up Florida, establishing carpet joints in Hallendale. From there, in 1938, he expanded to Cuba, advising Batista on the proper way to run a casino (see p164).

In New York, the numbers game, labor racketeering, and prostitution were the big moneyspinners for the Mafia. The strong links forged with City Hall during the Prohibition era provided the necessary political protection. Until the formation of the National Syndicate, prostitution in New York had been largely the preserve of various Jewish gangs. Charles Luciano's two areas of expertise were prostitution and drugs, and it was he that suggested the mob should take over the sex trade in New York. The Syndicate paid off the police, who notified them of impending raids. Madams (brothel-keepers) were charged $15 a week to stay in business, plus $10 for each prostitute they employed. The brothels of those who refused to pay were destroyed and the women beaten. In 1936, Special Prosecutor Thomas E. Dewey brought Luciano to trial on a charge of compulsory prostitution. He was convicted and sentenced to 30 to 50 years in jail. After World War II, Luciano was released and deported to Italy in 1946 (see p157).

Death in the Electric Chair

Special Prosecutor Dewey had another mobster in his sights. Louis Buchalter controlled the New York garment makers' unions, becoming rich and powerful in the process. He and his partner, Jacob Shapiro, next moved into the bakery delivery drivers' union, collecting a penny a loaf tax on all

CRIMEBUSTERS

Thomas E. Dewey

In 1935, New York governor Herbert Lehman appointed Thomas E. Dewey to be Special Prosecutor for the investigation of organized crime in New York. Dewey's appointment was a direct result of the 1930s' reforms that had made a concerted attack on corruption in Tammany Hall, the Democratic Party machine that for so long had controlled public appointments, particularly in the boroughs of Manhattan and Brooklyn.

The first of three inquiries into police corruption and political racketeering began in 1930. It was headed by the prominent lawyer, Samuel Seabury. The public was appalled at the web of corruption that existed at almost every level of city government. Democratic Party officials had used a $10 million Depression relief fund for their own uses, the sheriff of New York County and other officials were involved in illegal gambling enterprises, and corruption governed the granting of city permits, franchises, and leases.

Dewey extended the parameters of the investigation to known racketeers, including some of the most prominent names in organized crime. He won 72 convictions out of 73 prosecutions. Among those convicted was Charles Luciano, who was sent to prison in 1936 for 30 to 50 years on 90 counts of compulsory prostitution, the longest sentence ever handed out for such a charge.

In fact, Dewey owed his life to Luciano. In 1935, Dewey was investigating mobster Dutch Schultz. Schultz had threatened to kill Dewey but Luciano knew that such a high profile killing would attract unwanted attention. Two days later Schultz was shot by Luciano's men. He died in hospital soon afterward (see p150).

DEWEY TARGETS THE MOB

Dewey's successful investigations led to his appointment as district attorney in 1937. He continued his racketeering investigations, convicting politician Jim Hines of running a numbers game to the tune of $1 million per year. Most notably, Dewey went after Louis "Lepke" Buchalter and Jacob "Gurrah" Shapiro, the two most prominent labor racketeers in the New York garment district. Lepke was electrocuted in 1944 on an ancillary charge of murder.

Dewey went on to become governor of New York state (1943–55) and he twice ran for U.S. president, losing both in 1944 and 1948. His reputation was hit by revelations that he owned stock in a company that was involved in building Meyer Lansky's casinos in the Carribean. This, his authorization for the early release of Luciano from prison, and his refusal to answer questions before the Kefauver Hearings (see p162) destroyed Dewey's political credibility.

Crusading lawyer
Thomas E. Dewey led the fight against organized crime in New York in the 1930s and secured a notable list of convictions against racketeers and gangsters. He was governor of New York State from 1943 to 1955, but his reputation was questioned when he released Luciano in 1946, ostensibly for his help during World War II.

Captured mobster
One of Dewey's many successes was the jailing of Luciano, seen here arriving at the Supreme Court in 1936. He was convicted as head of New York's vice syndicate and sentenced to 30 to 50 years in prison.

Hotel Riviera
This hotel in Havana, Cuba, was one of the casino complexes built by gang boss Meyer Lansky. Dewey held stock in a company that was found to have a stake in Lansky's gambling resorts.

Murder, Inc.

Murder, Incorporated was the name given to the enforcement arm of Luciano and Lansky's National Commission. The term was coined by Burton Turkus and Sid Feder, authors of a sensational book published in 1951 titled *Murder, Inc.: The Story of the Syndicate.* Dutch Schultz's killers, Charles Workman and Emmanuel Weiss (*see p151*), certainly carried out that job for the Commission, but between 1935 and 1940 they also killed a lot of men who had nothing to do with the Syndicate, but who were simply business rivals or potential police informers. They and their associates, Abe "Kid Twist" Reles, Harry "Pittsburgh Phil" Strauss, Louis Capone (no relation to Al), and Martin "Buggsy" Goldstein were engaged in a

Escape route or false trail?
A detective examines the improvised rope of wire and bed sheets that police say mob informer Abe Reles used in a fatal attempt to escape from the Half Moon Hotel in 1941.

number of different rackets in Brownsville and were part of the network of neighborhood-based criminal groups that were a feature of 1930s' New York. They had business and social relationships with two other members of Murder, Inc.: Louis "Lepke" Buchalter, who was heavily into labor racketeering, and Albert Anastasia, who controlled the New York docks.

THE MIDNIGHT ROSE

Both Anastasia and Buchalter were high up in the Luciano–Lansky Syndicate, and Buchalter was on the Commission. Buchalter and Anastasia subcontracted Syndicate killings to the Brownsville association, who hung out in Midnight Rose's Candy Shop in Brooklyn, where they could be contacted at any time, day or night. The store was also the headquarters of Reles' loan-sharking operation. Its owner, 69-year-old Rose Gold,

was charged with 17 counts of perjury, but because of her political connections she was only given a suspended sentence.

The recruiting of Abe Reles was done by Buchalter on the orders of the Commission. The Syndicate wanted killers from outside their own

"The canary could sing, but it couldn't fly."
Frank Costello on Abe Reles

organization, who could not be traced and who were unknown to the mob world. The only Syndicate members in direct contact with the killers at the Midnight Rose were Anastasia and Buchalter.

In exchange for their services, the Syndicate granted Reles and his gang a free hand in East New York and in Brownsville. They received the crap game concession in Brooklyn, and retainers of $250 per week. Between 1933 and 1940, Murder, Inc. is thought to have carried out between 400 and 500 killings, settling mob differences from New York to Los Angeles. All the murders would have had to have been cleared through Lansky, Luciano, and the members of the Commission. The decision was then passed to Anastasia or Buchalter, who called the Midnight Rose. It is doubtful if Reles was even aware of the existence of the Commission that made the decisions. As early as 1928 he had killed several men as favors to Anastasia and Louis Capone. However, the most prolific killer at Midnight Rose's was Harry "Pittsburg Phil" Strauss. A brutal and competent killer,

Destination "Death Row"
Louis Buchalter (right) with a federal agent, having been convicted of murder. He died in the electric chair on September 15, 1943.

he would travel anywhere to carry out a contract. Only once in 100 hits had he failed.

In 1940, Reles and a number of other Brownsville colleagues were arrested on suspicion of murder. Reles decided to save his own skin. He did the unforgivable and broke the code of *omertà*, making a deal for immunity by revealing the details of 200 murders he had taken part in. His testimony convicted Harry Strauss and Buggsy Goldstein among others. All were electrocuted. Reles also identified the killers of Dutch Schultz: Workman and Weiss were sentenced to life.

From the Syndicate's viewpoint, these men were all expendable, but when Reles implicated Anastasia, Buchalter, and Siegel in first degree murder something had to be done. To protect Reles, the police kept him under 24 hour guard in a hotel room on the sixth floor of the Half Moon hotel on Coney Island. On November 12, 1941, his body was found on the ground outside the hotel. The police were unable to explain how this had occurred. Lansky and Luciano in their later years claimed that the police had been paid $100,000 by Frank Costello to demonstrate that although the "canary" could sing, it could not fly.

The case against Anastasia was dismissed, although Prosecutor William O'Dwyer had plenty of evidence to get a conviction. The failure led to much criticism, but did not prevent O'Dwyer from later becoming mayor of New York City.

$25,000 REWARD
DEAD OR ALIVE

Reward poster
A New York City Police Department poster from 1939 offers $25,000 for the capture of Murder, Inc. Louis Buchalter, wanted for conspiracy and extortion.

The Rise of the Gangster Film

When Al Capone was tried for income tax evasion in 1931, movie actor Edward G. Robinson attended the trial. The previous year he had starred in one of the most famous gangster films in cinematic history, Warner Brothers' *Little Caesar*, in which he played the role of Caesar Enrico Bandello. He now wanted to study the model for his character Nick Scarsi, also based on Capone, in his upcoming play *Broadway*.

Gangster films had been produced since the silent era of the 1920s. Several of them, like *Me, Gangster* and *Underworld* starred Joe Browne, a former gangster who was a friend of Al Capone. However, it was not until the 1930s that gangster

Gangster movie great
Edward G. Robinson's portrayal of a killer in *Little Caesar* (1931) has been much imitated but never bettered.

movies caught the American imagination. The films were the urban answer to the Western, and created a rival and darker mythology. The lone cowboy hero battling for the triumph of law and order was replaced by the gangster, operating in an amoral world of violence in which no quarter is given. The Western gunman, who faces his enemy and gives him a chance to draw first, was replaced by the hit squad firing machine guns from a moving vehicle.

In 1931 alone, Hollywood produced more than 50 gangster films. Those made by Warner Brothers had a gritty authenticity that won them a huge following. The most famous was probably *Scarface* (1932), starring Paul Muni as Tony Camonte, loosely based once again on Capone, and the mob-connected George

Raft. The film depicts 43 murders, and the Motion Picture Production Code (MPPC) refused to approve it. Producer Howard Hughes was forced to add a subtitle, *The Shame of the Nation*, and a new ending. In the original, Camonte is gunned down by other gangsters. In the new finale he is hanged by the authorities after being told that crime does not pay. By this time, however, everyone in America knew that it did. Nobody ever gunned down the real Al Capone. He died quietly and without ceremony in his luxurious home in Florida.

The popularity of the gangster films of the 1930s is understandable. The movies were made when the Depression was at its worst, and depicted the hopelessness of the time, the sense that the American Dream had ended, and that the world was, in reality, a cold, lonely place where the only law that counted was the gun.

Scarface (1932)
Paul Muni starred as mobster Tony Camonte, a thinly veiled version of Al Capone, in Howard Hawks' dark and violent movie exposé of the criminal underworld. The film was passed by the censors only after changes were made.

> ### "Mother of Mercy, is this the end of Rico?"
> Rico, played by Edward G. Robinson, in *Little Caesar*

Top Gangster Movies (1930s)

Little Caesar	1930
The Public Enemy	1931
Scarface	1932
The Petrified Forest	1934
G-Men	1935
Bullets or Ballots	1936
Kid Galahad	1937
The Last Gangster	1937
Racket Busters	1938
I Am the Law	1938
Angels with Dirty Faces	1938
The Roaring Twenties	1939

bread deliveries and a similar tax on flour. Working with Tommy Lucchese, they branched out into a number of other protection rackets, involving everything from handbag makers to restaurants. Buchalter was well connected as a member of the Commission, and a close friend of Lansky, Luciano, Costello, and Joe Adonis.

Dewey was determined to get Buchalter, and he concentrated on his activities in the bakery racket. Meanwhile, several other government agencies were investigating Buchalter for restraint of trade and drug smuggling. Getting wind of these

investigations, Buchalter went into hiding for two years, moved by Anastasia from safe house to safe house in Brooklyn. A nationwide search was on. Luciano and Lansky decided Buchalter must turn himself in to take the heat off the Syndicate. They informed him, through one of Buchalter's most trusted friends, that a deal had been arranged with J. Edgar Hoover. If Buchalter turned himself in, he would only be charged with drug smuggling and would be out of prison in five years. In 1939, Buchalter gave himself up to Hoover himself. While he was in jail, gangland informer Abe Reles

implicated Buchalter in murder and he was sentenced to death. Despite frenzied last-minute attempts to cut a deal, Buchalter was sent to the electric chair.

Moving into the Movies

During the Depression, the movie business was the fourth-largest industry in the United States. This was enough to attract the attention of the Chicago Outfit. The Outfit had begun to control the entertainment industry in Chicago, where many films were shot in the 1920s and 1930s. The Outfit began taking over trade unions like the

Motion Picture Operators' Union, and at the same time ran a protection racket on movie theater chains, demanding up to 50 percent of their take. An ex-pimp named Willie Bioff, who became the Outfit's bagman in Hollywood, ran the racket. Another Chicago gangster, Johnny Roselli, broke into Hollywood as a result of the 1933 strike by the International Alliance of Theatrical Stage Employees (IATSE). The studios went to Roselli to break the strike, which he did by hiring thugs to intimidate the strikers.

The Chicago Connection

Meanwhile in Chicago the board of the Outfit summoned George Browne to a meeting. Browne was a candidate for the next president of IATSE. The Outfit guaranteed his election in return for control of the union. Browne, already in trouble with the Outfit for running a protection racket in their territory, readily agreed. He was duly elected president. No other candidate was nominated.

Browne and Bioff were then sent to New York, where they were introduced to Luciano and Frank Costello. Soon afterward Browne was able to demonstrate his power by calling a strike against the RKO and Loew theater chains. He then went to the chairman of RKO and offered to call it off in exchange for $87,000, which was immediately handed over. The president of Loew, Nick Schenk, then paid Browne and Bioff $250,000 for a no-strike deal for a period of seven years. In exchange, Browne agreed to reduce worker wage-increase demands by two-thirds.

Bioff was put in charge of the Hollywood branch of IATSE in 1936. He and Browne then levied a 2 percent surcharge on paychecks for strike insurance. This levy generated more than $6 million, two-thirds of which went to the Outfit.

Now the mob moved against the film studios. Again, the procedure was simple. By controlling the unions, they could cripple any studio that refused to pay protection against strikes. They could close down all the theaters in the country with a single telephone call. They went to Nick Schenk and demanded $2 million, finally settling for $1 million in cash.

The Mob in Tinseltown

The Outfit now controlled Hollywood. Unfortunately for them, Bioff was the weak link in their organization. He made a down

"I had Hollywood dancing to my tune."
Willie Bioff

payment on a piece of property with a $100,000 dollar check from Twentieth Century-Fox, run by Nick Schenk's brother Joe. The check proved to be Bioff's undoing. A breakaway organization from IATSE, the

The road to Hollywood
The famous gates to Paramount Studios in the 1920s. Paramount were forced to pay the Chicago Outfit an annual "protection" premium of $50,000 in order to ensure that movie production ran smoothly.

International Alliance Progressives, began to convince workers to defy Bioff. They were determined to remove underworld control of the union. At the same time, Bioff tried to take over the Screen Actors' Guild, which started to investigate Bioff's activities. The California State Legislature became interested as well. The $100,000 check and Bioff's past as a pimp in Chicago came to light. The case against Bioff was put on hold, but Joe Schenk was prosecuted, and his explosive testimony began to unravel the Mafia's Hollywood operation.

Worse was to come. The press discovered from Chicago police files that, in 1922, Bioff had been convicted of beating a prostitute. He was still wanted on the charge. A warrant for his arrest was issued and Bioff served five months in jail.

In New York, Joe Schenk was indicted for fraud. In return for a reduced sentence, he agreed to tell everything he knew about Bioff and Browne. They were indicted in 1941 for tax evasion and racketeering. Desperate to keep their names out of the case, the Outfit sent their lawyer Sidney Korshak to Hollywood. He told Bioff to admit to being Schenk's bagman, but to say nothing else. To Korshak's horror, when he took the stand, Bioff pleaded "Not guilty," which meant he would be questioned — the last thing the Outfit wanted. Bioff was sentenced to ten years, Browne to eight.

During the trial, Bioff had let slip a reference to Chicago. This was the clue the government had been waiting for. Terrified of being murdered for his error, Bioff decided to co-operate with the government. On March 18, 1943, Johnny Roselli, Frank Nitti, and Paul Ricca were indicted for extortion and conspiracy. At the trial in October, a number of studio

heads testified and Bioff backed them up. Bioff also said that Nick and Joe Schenk had been stealing from their stockholders. The trial lasted 73 days. Found guilty, Roselli, Nitti, and Ricca were each given 10 years in jail. Nitti committed suicide rather than face prison. The Outfit's Hollywood dream was shattered.

Vito Genovese

Vito Genovese (1897–1969) rose to become the most feared Mafia boss of his generation. Originally from Naples, he emigrated to New York in 1913, where he met "Lucky" Luciano in 1917. Together they committed robberies and progressed to brothel-owning, bootlegging, and drug peddling, in the process meeting Arnold Rothstein, who assisted and financed their activities. Fleeing to Italy in 1937 to escape a murder charge, Genovese fell in with Italian dictator Benito Mussolini but when the Americans arrived, Genovese switched sides, becoming involved in lucrative blackmarketeering. Returned to America to face a murder charge, Genovese was acquitted and then sought control of the New York Syndicate. Genovese spent 10 years building up a narcotics racket as a power base from which to launch a bid for leadership of the five New York famnilies. He engineered a series of murders, including those of rivals Willie Moretti, Steve Franse, and Albert Anastasia. However, his plot to kill Frank Costello failed. It was Genovese who called the Apalachin Conference (*see* p159), a meeting that ended in disaster. Genovese was blamed, little knowing he had been setup by Costello, Luciano, and Lansky, who wanted his brutal methods curtailed. These three then dreamt up a narcotics sting in 1959 that saw Genovese sentenced to 15 years in prison. He died behind bars in 1969.

Dates 1897–1969
Details Ambitious and cold-hearted, Genovese betrayed almost everyone in his attempts to seize the ultimate position in the Mafia: the boss of bosses. In the end, Genovese was setup by.Luciano and jailed.

Organized Crime during World War II

When the United States went to war in 1941, shortages brought new opportunities for organized crime. The black markets in sugar, coffee, butter, automobile tires, shoes, and other hard-to-get items flourished. The economy boomed. Many more women were working in factories and earning good wages. They were desperate for luxuries like soap, stockings, and scent. The New York Mafia were able to corner the market in these items because they controlled the docks and thus could control the supply to stores. In addition, Mafia control of the dockers' and truckers' unions meant they could foment strikes and then "mediate" them, an extremely lucrative activity during wartime. Hijacking, pilfering, and hoarding meant that the war years were extremely profitable for the Mafia.

The Rise of Vito Genovese

When Luciano took over Masseria's crime organization in 1931, Vito Genovese (*see box, above*) served as his underboss and expected to succeed him when Luciano was imprisoned in 1936. However, Luciano overlooked him. It was at this point that Special Prosecutor Thomas E. Dewey, who

Tomorrow's news

A police officer stands over the dead body of newspaper editor Carlo Tresca on a New York street on January 11, 1943. The murder was organized by Vito Genovese as a favor to Benito Mussolini, the Italian dictator.

The Mafia and World War II

During the first six months following the Japanese attack on the U.S. naval base at Pearl Harbor on December 7, 1941, German U-boats sank 272 ships off the Atlantic coast of the United States. In February 1942, the French liner *Normandie*, in the process of being converted into a troop ship, caught fire and capsized at her moorings on the New York docks. U.S. Naval Intelligence was convinced the fire was set by German saboteurs.

THE INTELLIGENCE WAR

Lieutenant Charles Radcliffe Haffenden set up a Naval Intelligence operation in New York, controlling 150 agents. The New York fishing fleets were largely manned by Italians, and the docks and Fulton Fish Market along with their unions were controlled by Tony Anastasia, brother of Albert, and Joseph "Socks" Lanza respectively. Haffenden got contacted by Lanza, head of a local branch of the United Seafood Workers and asked for his help in the search for enemy agents both in the New York docklands and in coastal waters. Lanza agreed, but said that higher authority was needed to ensure everyone's cooperation in the war effort. The higher authority was Luciano, still serving out his sentence in Dannemora Prison.

The head of Special Prosecutor Thomas E. Dewey's rackets bureau, Murray I. Gurfein, was contacted for suggestions on how to put the project to Luciano. Gurfein got in touch with Luciano's lawyer, who prudently said he did not know Luciano well enough to broach such a delicate matter. An intermediary, someone Luciano knew and trusted, was needed, and he suggested Luciano's old friend and partner Meyer Lansky.

Lansky agreed to talk to Luciano, but said he couldn't face the journey to Dannemora, a forbidding place almost on the U.S.–Canadian border. Luciano was soon moved closer to New York, to Great Meadow, a much more relaxed prison, in Comstock, New York State. Lansky met with Luciano at Great Meadow a number of times, as did Joseph Lanza. Luciano told Lanza: "I will have word out and you won't have no difficulties."

LUCIANO KEEPS HIS WORD

Soon afterward eight German agents were arrested in New York and Chicago. They had been landed on the U.S. coast by German submarines and carried maps and plans for strikes against coastal defenses and other targets. Much of the information that led to their capture was supplied to Haffenden by Lanza, who was in turn informed by dockers and fishermen. Luciano's influence also helped in settling a number of dockland strikes that impeded the American war effort. Many years later, Lansky claimed that the sinking of the *Normandie* had been carried out by Anastasia as part of an elaborate plot to get Luciano out of jail, the idea being to give Luciano political leverage by helping the government in wartime, and in exchange get his sentence reduced or even win

"The Syndicate is bigger than U.S. Steel."

Meyer Lansky

early release. The government investigation into the *Normandie* attributed the disaster to worker carelessness.

As the Allied armies made progress in North Africa, and in 1943 began to make plans for an assault on Sicily, Haffenden's agents in New York gathered detailed information on the island from Sicilians resident in the New York area, who cooperated through respect for Luciano. Agents interviewed men from coastal towns, collecting photographs and information about tides and coastal defenses. It is very possible that Sicilian Mafia groups in Sicily itself cooperated. The Sicilian Mafia had suffered greatly under Mussolini, a large number of their leaders and members having been been incarcerated or exiled.

Four of Haffenden's Sicilian informants accompanied the Allied invasion fleet in 1943. Local contacts on the island led the Allies to the secret headquarters of the Italian Naval Command, where they found maps of Mediterranean minefields and the disposition of Italian and German forces throughout the Mediterranean.

After the war, in 1946, Luciano was released from jail and deported to Italy. He had never bothered to become a naturalized citizen. Frank Costello and a few friends gave him a last supper on board ship. Luciano briefly returned to

Leucara Friddi, the poverty-stricken village where he was born, and then established his base in Naples. He never returned to the United States, but within a year he was with Lansky organizing casinos in Batista's Cuba (*see p*162).

The Allied military government relied on local Mafia groups, sworn enemies of Mussolini, during their occupation of Sicily. The Allies needed non-communist anti-fascists to run the infrastructure, and at the time the only men who fitted this category were members of the Honored Society. Don Calogero Vizzini, soon to be boss of the Sicilian Mafia, was made an honorary colonel. The Mafia emerged as a major political force after the war, regularly bringing in the Sicilian vote for the Christian Democratic Party. This relationship between the Mafia and the dominant post-war political party, which originated in U.S. concern to stop a postwar communist takeover of the Italian government, is still a key factor in Italian politics today.

Syndicate godfather
Luciano was jailed by Special Prosecutor Thomas E. Dewey in 1936 for a period of 30 to 50 years. However, during World War II he agreed to arrange Mafia cooperation in U.S. military operations in the invasion of Sicily in 1943. As a "reward" he was released from jail on condition he leave the country, which he did in 1946, returning to Italy. He retired from crime in the 1950s.

***Normandie* Sinking**
The troop ship *Normandie* on fire in New York Harbor in 1942 following alleged sabotage by German espionage agents.

Benjamin Siegel and Las Vegas

Gambling was legalized in Nevada in 1931, at a time when it was prohibited almost everywhere else in the United States. Reno and Las Vegas were both small-time gambling towns in the 1930s, but their clientele was local. This was the height of the Depression and most people had neither money to gamble nor cars to get to the casinos.

The New York Syndicate moved on Las Vegas during World War II. Meyer Lansky, looking for new money-making schemes, already had old friend Benjamin "Bugsy" Siegel on the West Coast, running the Syndicate's bookmaking service. Siegel saw the potential that lay in Las Vegas. Gambling had always been a main moneyspinner for the mob. It was something they understood, and even when the mob branched out into lucrative new areas like narcotics and stock-market fixing, straight gambling operations were never abandoned. Siegel and Lansky also realized that legal gambling meant fewer overheads. In Nevada there was no necessity to pay off police and politicians. Legal gambling was also the perfect setup for laundering money.

SIEGEL HITS TOWN

In 1943, Siegel convinced the New York Syndicate to loan him $2 million dollars to build a casino in Las Vegas. El Rancho Vegas, run by Thomas Hull, was already in place on the Strip, but Siegel wanted to build a really luxurious place. Costs quickly rose, and soon he owed the Syndicate $6 million. Siegel named his casino the Flamingo, after his nickname for his favorite mistress, Virginia Hill. She helped skim the construction money for the casino and made frequent trips to deposit money in Swiss banks for the Syndicate as well as for Siegel.

It was only a matter of time before the Syndicate realized that their trust had been abused. If the Flamingo had enjoyed the success it had deserved, Siegel could probably have paid off his debt and lived, but the casino opened before it had built up a clientele. The Flamingo was at last beginning to show a profit as World War II ended, but when Siegel missed the deadline for repayment of his loan the Syndicate decided the time had come to eliminate him. The decision was made in 1946 at a conference in Havana. Siegel was hit while sitting in the living room of Virginia Hill's Beverley Hills mansion in May 1947, with two head shots through a window. Virginia Hill was in Switzerland at the time, and was later prevailed upon to return Siegel's money to its rightful owners.

However, Siegel had left an enduring legacy. He had pioneered the luxury casino in Las Vegas. Popular performers appeared at Las Vegas casinos and did much to make gambling and the city respectable. Meyer Lansky took over the running of the Flamingo and within a year had made a profit of $4 million. Lansky also held shares in the Sands Hotel, along with singer Frank Sinatra, who, with the "Rat Pack," put Vegas on the map

The 1940s and 1950s were the heyday of Las Vegas as a Mafia-run enterprise. The casinos were immensely lucrative, but, in the wake of the Kefauver Hearings (*see p*162), it became more difficult to conceal illegal activities, and in the 1970s and 1980s mob influence in the city began to wane.

Las Vegas boss
Casino owner and gangster Ben "Bugsy" Siegel (left) with his long time friend, Hollywood star George Raft. Siegel was the first mob boss to move into Las Vegas with his hotel and casino called the Flamingo. Siegel was murdered in 1947.

The resort
One of the first Las Vegas casinos, El Rancho Vegas was run by Thomas Hull, who was not a member of the Mafia. His hotel, however, became a model for the mob casinos that came later, such as Siegel's Flamingo.

Hollywood meets Vegas
The original "Rat Pack" of top Hollywood stars: (from left) Frank Sinatra, Dean Martin, Sammy Davis Jr, Peter Lawford, and Joey Bishop. Popular entertainers such as these put Las Vegas on the map.

"We only kill each other."
Benjamin "Bugsy" Siegel

was convinced that Genovese had succeeded Luciano as boss, indicted Genovese for organizing a murder in 1934. Genovese fled to Italy, where he became close to Italian dictator Benito Mussolini. He ingratiated himself with Mussolini further in 1943 by organizing the assassination of editor Carlo Tresca in New York because Tresca's newspaper, *Il Martell* , was critical of the Italian leader.

When the Allies invaded Sicily in 1943, Genovese switched sides to work for the Americans as an interpreter. Genovese became wealthy in the black market, but was suspected of illegal activity by a 24-year-old sergeant named Orange C. Dickie, who worked with the U.S. Army's Criminal Investigation Division in Italy. Dickie eventually arrested Genovese and returned with him to New York to face a charge of murder. The case was dismissed because of the death by poisoning of a witness, Peter La Tempa, while in police custody.

Power Struggles

Frank Costello was boss of the Masseria-Luciano crime family while Luciano was in exile from 1946 onward. Costello was very popular, largely because of his solid political connections and the fact that his complex deals with Lansky and Luciano meant that members of his family were granted unusual autonomy, many of them becoming very rich indeed. Costello was protected not only by his friendship with Lansky and Luciano, but by his enforcer, Albert Anastasia. No one messed with Anastasia. Vito Genovese was determined to take Costello's place, however, and patiently built up a war chest by dealing in drugs. He also cultivated supporters within the family, including Carlo Gambino, who recruited Joe Profaci. It was obvious that for Genovese to succeed he had to remove both Costello and Anastasia, and neutralize both Lansky and Luciano.

Frank Costello

Frank Costello was born Francisco Castiglia in 1891 in Calabria, Italy. His family came to the United States in 1895 and settled in New York. In his early twenties Costello met Luciano, Lansky, and Siegel. The four bootlegged together during Prohibition and later were founding members of the National Syndicate. It was during the 1920s that Costello developed his legendary network of political contacts. After Prohibition, Costello moved into gambling, slot machines, and bookmaking. When Luciano was deported to Italy in 1946, Costello took over the old Masseria-Luciano New York family.

Costello's appearance before the Kefauver Hearings on March,13, 1951 (*see p*162), effectively ended his usefulness to the mob. Threatened with deportation and under constant watch by the police, he was forced to answer questions rather than taking the Fifth Amendment. Even so, Costello was found guilty of contempt and sentenced to 18 months. He was then prosecuted again and imprisoned for tax evasion in 1956, but was bailed after serving just 11 months.

Soon after his release, on May 2, 1957, Costello was shot by Vincent Gigante as he entered his apartment building. He was only grazed, but the police found an incriminating note in his pocket listing his take from various gambling operations. On October 26, Costello's main supporter, Albert Anastasia, was killed at the instigation of Vito Genovese. Costello decided to accept "retirement" as head of the Masseria-Luciano family, which Genovese took over. Costello died in 1973.

Dates 1891–1973
Details One of Costello's triumphs was effectively neutralizing J. Edgar Hoover, the chief of the Federal Bureau of Investigation, by supplying him tips on horse races. For years, Hoover refused to investigate organized crime.

Genovese struck at Costello first. In May 1957 Costello was shot as he entered his apartment building on Central Park West. The bullet grazed his skull, not causing serious damage. The gunman was Vincent Gigante, who was identified by the doorman and certainly known to Costello. Gigante was brought to trial, but both doorman and Costello now claimed they had never seen him before and the case was dismissed.

Genovese did better with Anastasia. He gave the contract to Joe Profaci, who in turn subcontracted the hit to the three Gallo brothers: Joe, Larry, and Albert. On October 25, 1957, the Gallos shot and killed Anastasia in the barbershop of the Park Sheraton Hotel. Luciano and Lansky almost certainly authorized the

killing; Anastasia had been behaving increasingly erratically and knew where too many bodies were buried. After the killing Costello decided he had had enough, and retired, turning the family over to Genovese.

The Apalachin Gangland Conference

Vito Genovese's killing of Albert Anastasia and his attempt on the life of Frank Costello in 1957 created a very unstable situation that affected not only the uneasy balance of power among the five New York organized

Apalachin, New York

The country home of gangster Joseph Barbara (inset) was the scene of the infamous Apalachin crime convention in November 1957.

Barbershop rub out
The corpse of hitman Albert Anastasia lies on the floor of the barber shop at the New York Sheraton Hotel on October 25, 1957. Anastasia had been trying to move in on Meyer Lansky's Cuban operation, so Lansky had him shot

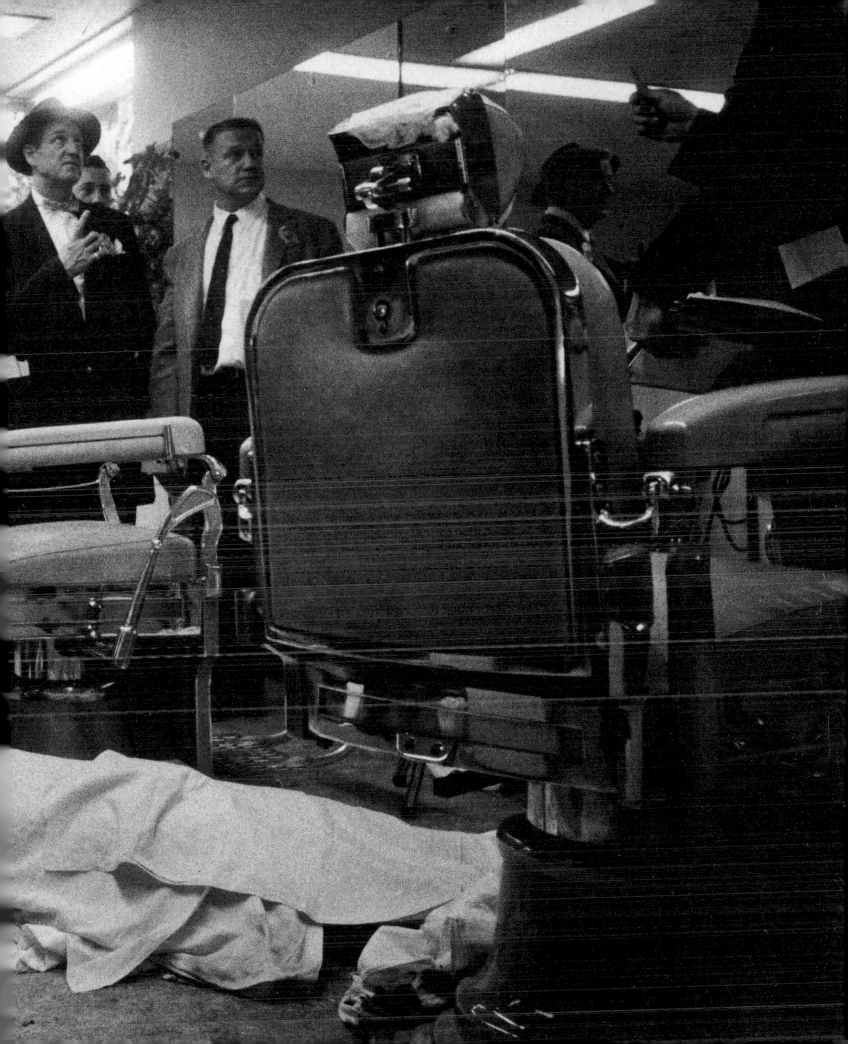

crime families, but the Chicago Outfit and the other organized crime families scattered throughout the United States. Costello's retirement left Genovese the *de facto* head of the most powerful Mafia family in New York, the family that Luciano had taken over after killing Masseria in 1931. Genovese urgently needed confirmation as the new head of the family, and to get this he needed to explain his motives and convince the National Commission to accept his leadership.

On the recommendation of Steve Magaddino, Mafia boss of Buffalo, Genovese arranged for the conference to be held at the estate of Joe Barbara in the little town of Apalachin in upstate New York. Barbara, who came from Sicily, had worked in Buffalo with Magaddino during Prohibition, and now had a legitimate business distributing soft drinks in upper New York State. His house in Apalachin had apparently been used for a number of previous Syndicate meetings, including one the previous year, with no trouble from the local police. But this, one of the largest gangland conferences ever convened, ended in a complete fiasco.

The Mob Meets Up

More than 100 delegates were invited and Barbara made reservations for them in hotels and motels in the surrounding area. He ordered prime steak from Chicago for a barbecue. His guests began to arrive on November 14, 1957, three weeks after the Anastasia killing. A New York State Police sergeant named Edgar Croswell had noticed the arrival of large expensive cars with out-of-state license plates and, accompanied by his partner and two agents of the Alcohol and Tobacco Tax Agency, went to Barbara's estate to take a look. As soon as the guests, who were gathered around the barbecue, sighted the officers they took to their heels, dashing into the surrounding woods or diving for their cars, emptying their pockets of money, guns, and other incriminating evidence. They were wearing expensive city clothes, and were no match for the terrain. The Outfit's Sam Giancana and 30 or 40 others got away; 58 others were arrested, but could not be held. Only nine of those arrested were without a criminal record. They were collectively carrying $300,000 in cash. They came from California, Florida, Texas, Ohio, Colorado, Illinois, New York, New Jersey and Philadelphia. They were some of the most famous names in organized crime: Joe Profaci, Carlo Gambino, Santo Trafficante Jr., and Vito Genovese. Genovese was the first to be caught, stopped at a roadblock as he drove

CRIMEBUSTERS

The Kefauver Hearings

The Kefauver Hearings began in May 1950 and were held in 14 U.S. cities. More than 800 witnesses were subpoenaed to testify. Some of the proceedings were televised, attracting 20 to 30 million viewers. Audiences were fascinated, especially by the New York hearings in 1951.

Estes Kefauver was a Democratic senator from Tennessee and chairman of the Special Committee on Organized Crime in Interstate Commerce, always subsequently called the Kefauver Committee. The main focus of the Committee was gambling. The witnesses came from all walks of life: politicians, policemen, state governors, gamblers, and racketeers.

Not all of the hearings were public. Members of the Outfit subpoenaed in Chicago were able to preserve their anonymity. The cameras rolled, however, in New Orleans, where Carlos Marcello testified, and in New York, where Frank Costello and Willie Moretti appeared, although in the case of Costello, only his hands were shown on TV. Outfit leader Murray Humphreys spread the word that everyone should "take the Fifth," (cite the Fifth Amendment to the U.S. Constitution, which guarantees the right not to incriminate oneself). Tony Accardo "took the Fifth" 150 times, Marcello 152. Both men refused to answer even the most anodyne question. Humphreys refused to divulge the names of his daughters. Although many of the witnesses who refused to answer were cited for contempt, these citations were for the most part later dismissed as unconstitutional. At the end of the hearings the Committee had amassed 11,500 pages of testimony and made 19 legislative recommendations, none of which were enacted.

When summing up the conclusions of his investigations, Kefauver concentrated on the "Mafia," stressing the fact that it was an "alien" (meaning largely Italian) importation rather than a home-grown phenomenon. From then on in the public mind organized crime was synonymous with the Mafia. This was a simple and comforting conclusion. In fact, the investigation actually revealed a much more complex situation. Police, politicians, and government officials were forced to admit involvement in bribery and patronage. Between 1953 and 1959, partly as a result of the Kefauver Hearings, the Department of Justice prosecuted 134 people for labor racketeering. Only 15 percent were of Italian descent. The proportion was about the same in the government-published list of "Convictions of Known Racketeers, Gamblers, etc. Under the Tax Laws," where 16 percent were of Italian background. Nobody, it seemed, had a monopoly on crime.

Kefauver Committee
Senator Estes Kefauver of Tennessee (center) is flanked by Senator Charles Tobey (left) and U.S. Attorney Irving Saypol (right). The investigation into organized crime revealed widespread corruption in the political institutions and structure of New York City.

> **"...There is a sinister criminal organization known as the Mafia operating throughout the country in the opinion of this committee."**
>
> U.S. Senator Carey Estes Kefauver

INSIDE STORY

SQUEALERS AND STOOL PIGEONS

One of the most famous police informers (or "stool pigeon" in Mafia slang) was Abe Reles, whose testimony exposed Murder, Inc. (see p151) and led to the execution of Louis Buchalter, the only high-ranking organized crime figure ever to die in the electric chair. Despite 24-hour police protection in a hotel on Coney Island, Reles was killed when he fell or was pushed out of the window.

Reles had implicated Mafia members in order to save his own life. Another informer was Joe Valacchi who, in 1963, exposed the inner workings of the New York Syndicate. No one was convicted on his testimony, but for the first time an insider described the day-to-day workings of the New York crime families. Valacchi broke the code of *omertà* because he thought Vito Genovese, with whom he shared a cell at Atlanta State Penitentiary, was going to have him killed. Genovese, he claimed, had given him the "kiss of death" to indicate that he did not have long to live. Valacchi described to the McClellan Committee the ceremony of initiation into the Mafia and the organization of the Five Families. Valacchi appeared to have almost total recall, but he was never high-ranking enough to know anything about the relationship between the New York families and the rest of the country. His description of the hierarchic structure of authority in the New York Mafia had a tremendous influence on law enforcement agencies, which drew up organizational charts based on his testimony.

MAFIA "RATS" AND THE PROTECTION PLAN

Vincent Teresa was a high-ranking member of Raymond Patriarca's New England crime family. He became an informer because his own people had not looked after his family when he was in prison. More than 50 people were convicted on his testimony. He even testified against Meyer Lansky. Lansky was tried and acquitted, and, with a $500,000 price on his head, Teresa wisely joined the Federal Witness Protection Plan. The U.S. government later withdrew its protection when Teresa and his family were charged with trading in endangered species. Teresa vanished in 1990 and it is unlikely that he is still alive today.

Abe Reles   **Jimmy Fratianno**   **Sammy Gravano**

The informers
Three key witnesses (left) gave a valuable insight into the workings of the mob. Informer Joe Valacchi (circled above) provided details on the structure of Mafia families, displayed on the rear wall at the McClellan Committee hearings.

Another Mafia gunman who informed for the Federal Bureau of Investigation (FBI), at least when it suited him, was Jimmy "The Weasel" Fratianno. He was a lieutenant in the Los Angeles family of Jack Dragna, even for a time acting boss. His most fascinating revelation was a description of the Central Intelligence Agency (CIA) plot to kill Cuban leader Fidel Castro, and the role of gangster Santo Trafficante in the plan. According to Fratianno, Trafficante, while ostensibly helping the CIA, kept Castro informed of their every move.

More recently, Mafia underboss Sammy "The Bull" Gravano decided to save his own skin by informing on his chief, John Gotti. In 1990, Gotti was convicted of murder on Gravano's evidence. Gotti died in jail in 2002. Gravano went into the Federal Witness Protection Plan and outlived his former boss.

Perhaps the most famous "squealer" of all is Henry Hill, whose story was told in Martin Scorsese's 1990 hit movie *Goodfellas*. Hill informed on Lucchese family *capo* Paul Vario and secured his conviction for extortion.

out of the estate. Since they had committed no crime, they could not be held. When asked what they were doing there, they claimed they had come to visit a sick friend, Joe Barbara having had a recent heart attack.

This was a terrible humiliation for the National Syndicate. Their cover had been blown, and those who had derided the idea of its existence, like J.Edgar Hoover, were forced to admit that they were wrong. The humiliation was even worse for Genovese. Since he was responsible for calling the meeting, he was discredited in the eyes of his peers. It is difficult to believe that the

fiasco of Apalachin was not orchestrated by Luciano, Lansky, and their friend Frank Costello. Luciano was in exile, but spent most of his time in Cuba, and could probably have arranged to attend to conference had he wanted. Lansky and Costello were invited but did not come. There were other notable absences, almost all of them regional bosses and well known supporters of Luciano and Lansky. In later years, Luciano claimed that Sergeant Edgar Croswell had been tipped off about the meeting. The point of the whole setup was to discredit Genovese.

For Vito Genovese, worse was to follow. Six months after Apalachin, Genovese and a number of his close associates, including Vincent Gigante, the man who shot Frank Costello, were arrested on a narcotics charge on evidence supplied by a heroin dealer known to have worked in the past for Luciano. Again, Luciano later claimed the dealer had been paid $100,000, plus a pension of several thousand dollars a month for life, to set up Genovese for the conviction. In 1959 Genovese began a 15-year stretch in Atlanta State Penitentiary, where he died in 1969.

The Transnational Mafia

In 1946, Luciano was deported to Italy (*see p157*). Established in Naples, he seamlessly took over Vito Genovese's black marketeering business. He often visited Sicily, and in 1949 he opened a candy factory there in partnership with the head of the Sicilian Mafia, Calogero Vizzini. It was almost certainly a heroin-processing plant.

While in Naples, Luciano met Tomasso Buscetta, a respected member of the Sicilian Mafia. In 1957, Luciano asked Buscetta to organize a meeting in Palermo with the leading Mafia families. From October 10 to October 14, 30 delegates from the United States and Sicily met to discuss the drug trade.

Luciano's plan was simple. First, he had to get the Sicilian Mafia families to stop killing each other. He suggested they form a commission, as in America, that would deal with territorial conflicts and that would be the only authority to sanction killings. The idea was instantly adopted, and the commission was called the Cupola. His second idea was that the New York Syndicate would franchise the entire narcotics business to the Sicilians for an agreed cut of the take. The system set up by Luciano operated well for 30 years. It was only broken up in 1987 when the Pizza Connection case was cracked (*see p170*).

A month after the meeting in Palermo, the Apalachin Gangland Conference was called (*see p159*). to inform the delegates of the results of the Palermo conference and that they were now part of a transnational business. Luciano had created the first criminal multinational.

Celebrity gangster
Mickey Cohen was a big gangland figure in Las Vegas and Hollywood in the 1950s. He loved the limelight, as can be seen from this photograph taken for *Life* magazine in 1950.

CASE STUDY

Cuba under Batista

Even when not actually in power, Fulgencio Batista y Zaldívar was the most powerful man in Cuba for more than 30 years. Born in Banes in 1901, Batista was educated in an American Quaker school and joined the army when he was 20. By 1932, he had reached the rank of sergeant. The following year he took over the government in the so-called "Revolt of the Sergeants," which overthrew the liberal government of Gerardo Machado. Between 1933 and 1934, Cuba had four different governments. Under the last of these, that of Carlos Mendieta, Batista appointed himself chief of staff of the army. Batista then ruled from behind series of puppet presidents, while publicly committing himself to "a new, modern democratic Cuba."

In 1952, Batista ran for president, but realizing that he could not win, staged a military coup and took power by force. His government was recognized by the United States soon afterward.

BATISTA'S PLAN FOR HAVANA
It was now that Batista determined to turn Cuba into a tourist and gambling destination. He asked Meyer Lansky, whom he had met in the 1930s, to do all he could to overcome the corruption in Havana's casinos. Lansky imported his own crews from Florida and Las Vegas, and made Havana famous for its honest gaming. Even the horse races, traditionally fixed, were run fairly. Lansky set up schools to train local dealers, pit crews, and casino staff. Tourists and gamblers began to flock to Cuba from the United States and beyond. Commercial air travel was now affordable, and Cuba was one of the first countries to encourage mass tourism. Throughout the 1950s, Cuba had the fastest growing economy in Latin America.

Wealth was concentrated in the hands of Batista and his cronies, and as opposition grew, Batista's regime became increasingly repressive. There were constant executions of dissidents, and Fidel Castro's communist guerrilla army began to strike back. Eventually, the United States withdrew its support for Batista. On January 1, 1959, Batista fled the country, just as Castro's ally Che Guevara took the capital city, Havana.

The face of Cuban capitalism
Fulgencio Batista, president of Cuba, with the help of crime boss Meyer Lansky, brought tourists flocking to the island's casinos,

Elegant surroundings
The central square in Havana, is dominated by the Supreme Court of Justice. Havana is rich in architectural heritage.

"The revolution is a dictatorship of the exploited against the exploiters."
Fidel Castro

High life in Havana
Night clubs and casinos throbbed to rhythms of native Cuban rumba bands such as this one in 1950s' Havana.

The Senate Labor Racket Committee
Teamster president Jimmy Hoffa (right) confronts Robert Kennedy of the Senate Labor Racket Committee, on September 17, 1958.

Cuba and the Mob

Since the 1920s, when gambling was largely outlawed in most U.S. states, wealthy Americans had visited Cuba's casinos. Serious gamblers, however, were put off by the prevalence of crooked games and fixed horse races. Meyer Lansky had ambitions to change all that.

Since the 1930s, Lansky had specialized in setting up "carpet joints." These were illegal yet luxurious gambling houses designed to attract wealthy gamblers. By providing a safe environment and honest tables, Lansky changed the public perception of gambling. He perfected his formula in Florida and in Las Vegas, Nevada, which gained a reputation as one of the safest cities in America. He realized that, since the advantage was always with the house, there was no need to cheat the customers. Also, carpet joints were ideal for laundering money.

In the late 1940s, Lansky cultivated the acquaintance of the ex-Cuban president Batista, then temporarily out of power and living in Florida. When Batista came to power for the second time in 1952, he planned to turn Cuba into a tourist paradise and attract wealthy tourists to the casinos. He hired Lansky as a consultant.

Batista's secret police arrested and expelled card sharps and crooked casino employees, while Lansky hired competent floormen and dealers from his Florida carpet joints. He opened the Montmartre Club in 1954 and it was a great success. Havana was easy to get to from Florida, and the good climate and lively night life had much to offer visitors.

Castro Comes to Power

In 1955, after the renovation of the Hotel Nacional, Lansky opened a new casino there, the Gran Casino Nacional. Lansky installed his brother Jake as floor manager and the new casino boomed. Lansky took advantage of a Cuban law that granted tax exemptions to places providing accommodation for tourists. He began to build a huge new hotel and casino complex, the 21-storey Riviera. It was completed in 11 months and opened in early 1958. It was an immediate success. However, a year later, revolutionary Che Guevara took Havana. Batista fled back to Florida and his regime crumbled before Guevara and Fidel Castro. Lansky tried to work with the new regime, but business was ruined by the political uncertainty. Lansky suffered estimated losses of $10 million.

The Rise and Fall of Jimmy Hoffa

James Riddle Hoffa was one of the most controversial figures in the history of the American labor movement. Born in 1913 in Brazil, Indiana, Hoffa went to work in a warehouse in Detroit when he was 17. Soon he was organizing strikes to improve working conditions. By 1933, he was involved in the Teamsters Union and, in order to get a better deal for the rank and file, Hoffa made a deal with the Chicago Outfit. In 1952, in exchange for their backing, he promised them access to the Teamsters' pension fund. The Outfit then secured Hoffa the Union vice-presidency.

The mob used low-interest loans from the fund to buy banks, oil wells, and real estate. Hoffa was duly elected Union president in 1957. In the same year Robert Kennedy, chief counsel for the Senate Rackets Committee, began investigating Hoffa. As the 1960 U.S. presidential election drew near, Hoffa feared that if Democrat John F. Kennedy won, his brother Robert would become attorney general. Hoffa instructed union members to vote Republican. In spite of this, Kennedy won.

In 1967, Hoffa was convicted of pension-fund fraud and sent to prison for 13 years. However, Hoffa refused to resign the Union presidency. In 1971, he was released by a pardon from new Republican president Richard Nixon, on condition that he did not take part in union activities for 10 years.

Hoffa disappeared on July 10, 1975. His body was never recovered, and in 1982 he was declared officially dead. Many believe that he was murdered by government agents, while others are certain his killers were linked to organized crime. Even more persistent is the rumor that Hoffa died because he knew too much about the assassination of president John F. Kennedy 12 years previously in 1963.

The Gallo–Profaci War

In 1962, the heads of the New York families were Joseph Bonanno, Carlo Gambino, Vito Genovese, Gaetano Lucchese, and Joe Profaci. Profaci was the only boss to continue to collect "tribute" from his membership, following an old Sicilian practice. Although this was only $25 per month, it was deeply resented and led to a revolt by the younger members of the Profaci family. It had begun in 1960, led by Joseph Gallo, his brothers Larry and Albert, and Joe Gioelli. The Gallos had killed Albert Anastasia (see p159) and felt they had not earned the status they deserved for the murder. The Gallos began the rebellion by kidnapping Profaci's brother Frank, and three other members of the Profaci family. The Gallos held the hostages for two weeks, threatening to kill them if their demands were not met. Profaci managed to secure their release and then began killing Gallo allies. Profaci also began wooing Gallo supporters by offering them important territories.

In 1961, Joe Gallo was sent to prison for 10 years for extortion. Profaci then died of natural causes, and the leadership of his family passed to his underboss Joseph Magliocco. Lucchese and Carlo Gambino threatened Magliocco, who turned to Joe Bonanno. He suggested they kill Lucchese and Gambino. Joe Colombo was offered the contract, but immediately informed Lucchese and Gambino of the plot. Magliocco was called to the Commission where he admitted everything. He was fined

The end of Crazy Joe

Umberto's Clam House in Lower Manhattan (below) was the scene of the death of Joseph "Crazy Joe" Gallo (inset) on April 7, 1972. Gallo and his two brothers fought a bloody battle for control of the Brooklyn underworld in the 1960s. He was gunned down by an unknown assailant.

Joe Colombo

Joe Colombo became the youngest Mafia boss and also the youngest to be killed by the mob. He gained his reputation as a killer with Joe Profaci's hit squad, and in the early 1960s he was approached by Joe Bonanno, who wanted to take control of New York's underworld. Bonanno planned to murder several of the Syndicate's board members and asked Joe Magliocco to take the contract on Carlo Gambino and Tommy Lucchese. Magliocco in turn passed on the job to his underboss, Colombo. Colombo saw the odds were against Bonanno and told the intended victims of the contract. Colombo was rewarded for his loyalty with the

leadership of the Profaci family. However, what he did next was to seal his fate.

Colombo founded an organization called the Italian–American Civil Rights League, the idea being to improve the public image of Italian–Americans, whom the media portrayed as nothing but gangsters. Other Mafia bosses were upset by the publicity he attracted and Colombo was shot three times in the head at close range at a League rally in 1971. He survived in a coma for seven years and died in 1978.

The most powerful Mafia boss in America, Carlo Gambino, is thought to have ordered the hit, with the help of Joe Gallo.

Dates (1914–1978)
Details Colombo was the first of the modern Mafia bosses. He saw the importance of a good public image, but in the end it cost him his life.

$50,000 and forced to retire as boss of the Profaci family. He was replaced by Joe Colombo, and the family took his name.

The Colombo–Gallo War

When Joe Gallo got out of prison in 1971 he saw that things had changed. Former Italian neighborhoods were now run by black and Hispanic gangs, and he decided to bring these newcomers into his operation.

Meanwhile, Colombo had alienated the Commission by going public. He had formed the Italian–American Civil Rights League to correct the public impression that all Americans with Italian names were criminals. In 1970, he organized a rally in New York. It was a huge success and was attended by 50,000 people. The Commission was very

worried about the publicity. When Colombo announced that he was going to hold another rally in 1971, Carlo Gambino told him to cancel it. Colombo refused. As a result, on June 28, the day of the rally, Colombo was shot three times in the head by one of Gallo's men, a black gunmen named Jerome Johnson. Johnson himself was then gunned down by Colombo's bodyguards.

Incredibly, Colombo survived, but he suffered massive brain damage. He died seven years later. After the shooting, Joe Gallo went into hiding, but on April 7, 1972, he ventured out to supper at Umberto's Clam House in Little Italy, New York. A gunman walked in and emptied his revolver into Gallo as he tried to escape. He just made it to the street, where he died.

Carlo Gambino

Between 1957 and 1976, Gambino built the old Mangano family, which he inherited after the assassination of Albert Anastasia in 1957, into the richest of all New York Mafia families. When Frank Costello was forced to retire by Vito Genovese, Meyer Lansky transferred his support to Carlo Gambino, giving Gambino access to the nationwide network of the National Syndicate. Lansky, Gambino, Luciano, and Costello were almost certainly the ones who framed Genovese on the drug charge that sent him to prison. Gambino then expanded his operations at the expense of the Genovese family.

Gambino adroitly evaded a series of plots to assassinate him in Joe Bonanno's attempt to win recognition as "the boss of bosses." When his health began to fail in the early 1970s, he came up with a complex plan to ensure the continued power of his family. He wanted the leadership to pass to his brother-in-law, Paul Castellano, whose weakness he

recognized. To offset it, he made a deal with Aniello Dellacroce, Gambino's logical successor. If Dellacroce would agree to act as underboss to Castellano, Gambino would grant him the most lucrative territory in New York: Manhattan. Gambino died of natural causes in 1976. The uneasy relationship between Castellano and Dellacroce, in fact, lasted for nine years, although Castellano was viewed with increasing disquiet both by members of his own family and by other Mafia bosses. This suspicion turned to active hatred when, during a trial for racketeering, tapes of Castellano's phone taps showed that he systematically disparaged the bosses of other families. When Dellacroce died of cancer in 1985, Castellano lost his protection. He was gunned down by three masked assailants outside a restaurant two weeks later. Leadership of the Gambino family passed to 45-year old John Gotti (*see box, p*170).

Dates 1902–1976
Details Although Gambino had a fine house on Long Island, he preferred to go shopping in his old neighborhood in Little Italy. This was the world he had grown up in and where he felt most comfortable. He insisted on formality and in many ways was the most traditional of the generation that had produced Lansky and Luciano, whom he had befriended when they were all in their teens.

The Structure of Mafia Families

The New York Mafia families have always shared a similar structure of boss, underboss, a counselor (*consigliere*), lieutenants (*capo* or *caporegime*), and soldiers (*soldati*). A *capo* might be responsible for between three to ten or more soldiers, referred to as a "crew."

These were the core members of the organization, the "made men" whose enviable status as members of one of the Mafia families made them respected and feared and gave them license to operate with virtual impunity, thanks to their network of connections with lawyers, policemen, judges, and politicians.

Candidates for membership serve long apprenticeships, during which time their behavior is monitored. If considered suitable, their names are circulated for approval among the other families. Some Mafia families still make use of traditional

During the next few weeks, a dozen men from both sides were killed. Then members of the Lucchese and Bonanno family began to be killed. Only one man was profiting from the thinning of the ranks of the New York families: Carlo Gambino. He had stood by, waiting while potential rivals killed each other. One by one the survivors went to Gambino, seeing him as the only one who could put a stop to the killing, which had

badly affected business and profits. Gambino halted the war and the families then recognized him as "the boss of bosses," the first mob chief to hold that position since the killing of Joe Masseria in 1931 (*see p*147).

Family business

Paul Castellano lies dead in the street on December 16, 1985, after being shot by three gunmen hired by his rival, John Gotti.

INSIDE STORY

MAFIA NICKNAMES

Most underworld nicknames are self-explanatory, usually based on some notable physical or mental characteristic or inspired by their real last name, like "Tony Pro" (Anthony Provenzano). In the case of Murray Llewellyn Humphreys, the "Hump" and "The Camel" are both a play on the first syllable of his last name and the fact that he always wore camel hair overcoats. "Happy" Maione was a dreaded killer who never smiled. Sam "Golf Bag" Hunt carried his favorite weapon, a semi-automatic shotgun, in his golf bag. He was also a very good golfer. The "Gurrah" in Jacob Shapiro is simply Brooklynese dialect for "Get out of here," which Shapiro used to say to resident union officials when taking over their local branch. Tony "Ducks" Corallo somehow always ducked convictions. "Scarface" was a nickname bestowed on Capone by the media. It would not have been wise to address him as such. His friends called him "Snorky."

induction ceremonies. Al Capone swore in members on a valuable 10th century Greek New Testament, probably brought to America from a monastery in Calabria. It is now in a university collection.

An oath of *omertà*, or "manliness," was taken, which meant that the oathtaker would never speak of the family or its affairs to outsiders. This secrecy extended to not identifying assailants to the police, even when dying. Revenge would be taken by the family. As in Sicily, *omertà* extended to the community at large, and very few witnesses have been so foolish as to testify against a Mafia member. However, *omertà* has never stopped Mafia bosses from eliminating rivals by giving them up to the police or federal government. Some high ranking *mafiosi* have written their memoirs. Joseph Bonanno's autobiography, *A Man of Honor*, famously led to his indictment. Vincent Teresa wrote two fascinating books on his life in the Mafia; and the informer Jimmy Fratianno wrote a bestseller, *The Last Mafioso*. All of these books are self-justifying and discreet, but nevertheless filled with information which, under the rule of *omertà*, should not have been divulged.

CASE STUDY

The Banana War

In the mid-1960s Joseph Bonanno was head of the most powerful of the New York crime families. Fiercely ambitious, Bonanno expanded from New York to the West Coast, Colorado, Arizona, and the Caribbean.

The Banana War, as the press dubbed it, was a direct result of Bonanno's expansionist policies. His cousin Stefano Magaddino was based in Buffalo, New York. When Bonanno began moving into upper New York State, Magaddino was incensed. Bonanno's ambitions were not only territorial. He wanted to be "boss of bosses." The only way to achieve this was to eliminate his rivals. When his friend Joe Profaci died in 1962, Bonanno made his move. He approached Profaci's successor, Joseph Magliocco, and divulged his plan to kill Stefano Magaddino, Carlo Gambino, Thomas Lucchese, and boss of Los Angeles, Frank DeSimone. Magliocco asked Joe Colombo to organize the killing of Gambino and Lucchese, but Colombo revealed the plot to them. Magliocco and Bonanno were summoned to appear before the Syndicate Commission. Bonanno refused, and was replaced as head of his family by Gaspar DiGregorio.

In 1964, Bonanno was kidnapped by Magaddino. He was released after promising that he would retire. He then disappeared for 19 months, while his son Salvatore "Bill" Bonanno waged an inconclusive war with DiGregorio in order to claim control of the family his father had founded. Between 1962 and 1966, 15 or 16 men from both sides were killed, and the war was attracting unwelcome press attention.

After suffering a heart attack in 1968, Bonanno retired to Arizona, where he wrote his memoirs, *A Man of Honor*. In the book he revealed the existence of the Syndicate Commission, which was enough for the federal government to successfully prosecute and jail him. He died in 2002.

Retired boss
Joseph Bonanno in 1977, after he had retired from the New York underworld.

Mafia "Soldiers"

The word "soldiers" is misleading. These are not simply the brainless torpedoes beloved of thriller writers, but the family's interface with the street. They are the moneymakers. They supervise the extortion, loan sharking, labor racketeering, hijacking, and drug dealing that are the life-blood of the family. They also lead the army of "mob associates," often of non-Italian origins, who make the actual physical contacts on the street. This world is beautifully evoked in Henry Hill's *Wiseguy*, the most accurate depiction yet of Mafia dealings at street level.

The McClellan Committee was fascinated to learn from Joe Valacchi (*see p163*) that Mafia family members are unpaid. What the family offers is not a salary, but an opportunity. What they earn depends entirely on their own energy and ability. They are responsible for any losses, and must make them good. Incompetence and dishonesty are not tolerated. A portion of all profits are turned over to their lieutenant or *capo*, but the amount varies according to their take. In other words, the Mafia is essentially a franchising operation, the bosses providing protection in return for a percentage.

The Mafia is not a corporation, but it is not dissimilar to any trade association, in which the members have agreed not to infringe each other's territories, and to unite over matters of common interest. Neither is the Mafia really interested in expanding its membership. In this, it is closer to a medieval guild than to a large modern corporation. Luciano "closed the book" on new memberships in the early 1930s

> "You live by the gun and the knife and you die by the gun and the knife."
>
> Joe Valacchi, the first "supergrass"

John Gotti

BIOGRAPHY

John Gotti was the media darling of New York for years. Immaculately dressed, he treated women with courtesy, but was otherwise foul-mouthed and violent.

Gotti was born in the South Bronx in 1940. He quit school at 16 and joined a gang of car thieves. Later he became an associate of the Gambino family. Gotti made his name in 1972, when Carlo Gambino's nephew was killed by Jimmy McBratney. Gotti led the hit squad that executed McBratney. He was arrested for the murder in 1974 and served two years in prison. On his release, he was made a lieutenant in the Gambino family.

Gambino died of a heart attack in 1976 and was replaced by Paul Castellano. Gotti thought his friend Aniello Dellacroce should have succeeded Gambino, but Dellacroce counseled patience. Gambino learned that Castellano planned to appoint Thomas Bilotti as his successor. In 1985, Dellacroce died of cancer. Two weeks later Castellano and Bilotti were shot and killed. Gotti then took over the Gambino family. The same year Gotti was indicted for racketeering, but beat the charges. The press began to call him "the Teflon Don" because no charges seemed to stick. Gotti was finally convicted of racketeering on the testimony of informer Sammy "The Bull" Gravano. In 1992, John Gotti was sentenced to life without parole. He died in prison on June 10, 2002.

Dates 1940–2002
Details Gotti's cultivated a sophisticated image, wearing hand-tailored suits and eating in exclusive restaurants, but underneath he was from the old-school: brutal and cold.

---

and it was not until 1954 that it was opened again. Albert Anastasia, Vito Genovese, and Frank Scalise even sold memberships, often to unsuitable recruits, reportedly for between $50,000 and $100,000.

The End of the Mafia?

In the early 1980s, Syndicate control of the infrastructure of New York was almost total. In 1981, Associate U.S. Attorney General Rudolph Guiliani convinced President Ronald Reagan that the time was ripe for a concerted attack on organized crime. In 1983, he became U.S. attorney for the Southern District of New York, a post he held until 1989. During this time Guiliani mounted the heaviest assault on the Syndicate since the days of Thomas Dewey.

Guiliani prosecuted the New York Mafia Commission itself for racketeering and won 100-year sentences against eight bosses from four of the five New York families. In the same year, 1986, convictions were won against leading members of the Colombo family for running a concrete cartel. Two years later it was the turn of the Genovese family, convicted for their part in the same cartel. Convictions were won against Mafia members and associates for the systematic looting of cargo at John F. Kennedy Airport, which had gone on for years, mostly at the hands of the Gambino family. Guiliani's suit against the Teamsters Union resulted in a trusteeship being set up that made free elections of officials possible for the first

time in many years. Guiliani became mayor of New York in 1994, and he began to purge the Mafia's influence from the waste haulage industry, refusing to grant licenses to haulers with known Mafia connections.

All of these initiatives, and the ongoing civil and criminal trials that were carried out under the auspices of the Racketeer Influenced and Corrupt Organizations Act (RICO), put enormous pressure on the New York families, and produced a series of informers seeking to get reductions in their sentences by incriminating their associates.

With the bosses of all five families serving long prison sentences and many of their *capos* and soldiers either in jail or under indictment, it began to look as if the power

of the New York Mafia was finally broken. The blows to their union powerbases were particularly serious, probably more so than the imprisonment of any individual.

The combined membership of the New York families in 2002 was thought to be 570, down from 634 in 2000 and 940 in 1986. In 1986, federal agencies estimated the number of Mafia associates at about 10,000. The figure is now probably only half that. The Genovese was still the largest family, with 152 members, including nine new recruits. The Gambino family numbered 130, having lost a surprising 33 members the previous year. The Lucchese family had 113 members, including three new recruits. The Colombo family came next, with 90 members, having lost 26 in the previous year. The Bonanno family is the smallest, with only 85 members.

The Sicilians Return

The elimination of the upper echelons of the New York families by Rudolph Guiliani was a serious blow, but at the same time freed top positions for younger men, many of whom had for years been dissatisfied with their leadership. Many of these are a throwback to the early 1900s – illegal immigrants from Sicily, often fleeing indictment in their home county. They are said to be taking over the streets from American-born family members. Since they have no police records in the United States,

---

CASE STUDY

The Pizza Connection

In the 1970s, the Sicilian Mafia formed an alliance with heroin suppliers in Turkey and established a network of refineries in Sicily. They formed alliances with South American suppliers of cocaine and then moved into the lucrative market of the United States.

They had the ingenious idea of using a nationwide network of pizzerias to market the drugs and to launder the profits. The Sicilians came to a franchise arrangement with American organized crime groups and brought in thousands of their own people to work in the pizzerias. By 1985, there were 100 pizzerias controlled by organized crime in the Washington DC–Maryland–Virginia area alone. The ring was run by two mob bosses, Gaetano Badalamenti and Salvatore Catalano. The FBI did not begin to investigate the network until 1980 and no convictions were made until 1987, when undercover FBI agent Joseph Pistone (known as Donnie Brasco) secured enough evidence to have Badalamenti and Catalano imprisoned for 45 years each.

Gaetano Badalamenti
Badalamenti was the main supplier to the Mafia drug network in the United States, smuggling narcotics from Sicily by way of Canada.

they can operate invisibly in a way that is impossible for the heavily compromised members of the New York families, almost all of whom have been identified and are under constant surveillance.

New Market Opportunities

Like other businesses, the Mafia has in the past adapted successfully to changing circumstances. Already the families are heavily engaged in stock market fraud, cyber crime, forged telephone cards, and Internet pornography, banking fraud, and gambling. The drug trade, however, remains too large and diversified to be controlled by any one organization. The American Mafia families

realized this long ago, and confine themselves to financing drug deals and laundering money for drug cartels, leaving production and distribution to specialists from Sicily or South America.

Globalization has opened up new market opportunities as well as reviving trades like white slaving and people smuggling. The sudden appearance of car-jacking in the United States and Europe was a direct result of globalization, supplying markets as far afield as China with cars stolen in New York or Canada. There are now markets that would have astonished men like Capone: organized crime groups in South America and India are involved in the growing trade

in human organs. There are thriving global trades in endangered species, forged airplane parts, fake pharmaceuticals, and a wide range of counterfeit consumer items.

The huge volume of imports and exports through the New York and New Jersey ports and airports have greatly facilitated the contraband trade, particularly in drugs, counterfeits of all kinds, and weapons. As long as the Mafia families retain some control over these ports of entry, their future is assured, but only if they can either resist or come to an accommodation with the increasing number of competitors from China, Russia, Japan, and Mexico who are now moving into their markets.

CELLULOID CRIME

The Mafia on the Modern Screen

Mario Puzo's 1969 novel *The Godfather* sold 21 million copies before it was made into a film. Puzo collaborated with director Francis Ford Coppola on the script of the movie version. Coppola's *The Godfather* came out in 1972. It was followed by two sequels and a host of imitators. Although Mario Puzo admitted that before writing the book he had never actually met a member of the Mafia, Don Vito Corleone, as played by Marlon Brando, is what he felt a traditional Mafia don should be like. Although it is sometimes claimed that the Corleone

character was modeled on Carlo Gambino, he is in fact much closer to the traditional Sicilian "godfathers" like Don Calogero Vizzini or Joe Masseria than he is to more recent dons like Carlo Gambino. Puzo summed up his feelings about latter-day dons when he said; "A guy like John Gotti wouldn't last a day in Sicily."

The most interesting thing about *The Godfather* movie was the public response to it when it first appeared. The combination of a closely knit family, united against the outside world, ready to defend its territory with violence, and ruled by a tough but caring patriarch obviously struck a deep chord in an America in the midst of the Vietnam War and still reeling from the inter-generational strife of the 1960s. Lots of people in the United States wished there was a Don Corleone to sort things out. The political implications of this may be disturbing, but nostalgia for an

earlier and seemingly simpler society seems to increase with the pace of modernization.

Joe Colombo's Italian–American Civil Rights League (*see* p167) succeeded in getting the words "Mafia" and "Cosa Nostra" removed from the script, but this only increased the universal appeal of the film. Joe Bonanno saw this clearly, saying: "This work of fiction is not really about organized crime or about gangsterism. The true theme has to do with family pride and personal honor. That's what made *The Godfather* so popular."

THE SOPRANOS

The TV series *The Sopranos* brilliantly follows the process of acculturation to its logical conclusion. The threads that tie Tony Soprano to his cultural past are so thin they are almost invisible in the world of middle-class domesticity, and his efforts to keep spinning them are truly heroic.

Gangsters on TV
The Sopranos (left) has proved popular with American and worldwide TV audiences since it first appeared in 1999. James Gandolfini (center) plays Tony Soprano, the head of a New Jersey crime family.

The Godfather
Marlon Brando starred as Mafia boss Don Corleone in the first of the *Godfather* movies in 1972. The film gave the world its image of the modern American Mafia.

"I'm gonna make him an offer he can't refuse"

Don Vito Corleone in *The Godfather*

NORTH AMERICA

GANG COLORS

Membership in a motorcycle gang is proclaimed by displaying the club's "colors" on the back of a short-sleeved denim or leather jacket. The name is embroidered on the top crescent-shaped patch, or "rocker," the city of origin on the bottom rocker, and the club insignia in the middle. Only full members may wear the complete colors, which are club property and considered sacrosanct.

TERRITORIES

Canada

Montreal
Minneapolis •   • New York
Oakland •   Chicago •

USA

• Corpus Christi

BANDIDOS: 28 chapters in Mississippi, New Mexico, Wyoming, Nth & Sth Dakota, Washington State, Texas. Founded: 1966, Galveston Country, Texas.

OUTLAWS : 43 chapters in U.S, 8 in Canada, 4 in Australia, 1 in France. Founded: 1959, Joliet, Illinois.

HELLS ANGELS: 100 chapters worldwide. Founded: 1948, San Bernardino, California.

The major outlaw motorcycle gangs have their own sayings or mottoes that succinctly encapsulate their shared philosophy:

Hells Angels	Three can keep a secret if two are dead.
Bandidos	We are the people our parents warned us against.
Outlaws	God Forgives, Outlaws don't.

Outlaw Motorcycle Gangs

" The government is waging a smear campaign against us. It is a Hollywood image and a government image, but it is not the truth. "

SONNY BARGER, HELLS ANGEL

The first and best known of the biker gangs, the Hells Angels (the apostrophe was dropped many years ago) was founded by disaffected World War II veterans in 1947 in Fontana, a steel town 50 miles from Los Angeles. The veterans felt alienated from a society that expected them to return after the conflict in Europe and the Pacific as if nothing had happened.

The Hells Angels changed all that. Until 1947, motorcycle rallies had been orderly events sanctioned by the American Motorcycle Association. Accounts differ slightly but it is generally accepted that the group first came to prominence that year over Independence Day weekend in the small town of Hollister, California. On July 4, 4,000 motorcyclists rode into town on a spree that left 50 injured and, following the call-out of the Highway Patrol, 100 bikers in prison. Two months later a ride into Riverside, California, on Labor Day weekend brought havoc again. This time 6,000 bikers turned up.

The term Hells Angels was first adopted by the San Bernardino ("Berdoo") chapter (group) of the club in 1948. Again, accounts vary. The name may have come from the prewar film of the same name by Howard

Gathering of the bikers
A Hells Angels' chapter meet on the street before taking to the highway for a motorcycle run.

Hawks but it certainly brought with it the winged deathhead insignia worn by World War II fighters. The Angels liked to refer to themselves as the One Per Cent, indicating that while 99 percent of motorcyclists in the United States were well mannered, in no way did this squeaky clean tag refer to them.

"Sonny" Barger Joins the Angels

Barger dropped out of high school in 1955 when he was 16 and forged his birth certificate in order to enlist in the army. He served 14 months stationed in Honolulu, Hawaii, before the army discovered that he was underage. He was given an honorable discharge and returned to Oakland, where he briefly joined the Oakland Panthers before founding his own motorcycle club in 1957, which he named the Hell's Angels (with apostrophe!), unaware that other clubs with this name already existed in

California. Barger made contact with these other Hell's Angels clubs and gradually built the Oakland chapter into the largest and best-run motorcycle club in California, with by-laws and elected officers. He consolidated it by appointing the most intelligent Angels as his lieutenants, providing them with the most vicious of the remainder as foot soldiers. Barger moved on to San Bernardino and the Berdoo chapter became the central headquarters of the Angels. Barger then began to target smaller rival clubs for forcible takeovers. They were, in fact, mutually beneficial transactions because the smaller clubs, once absorbed, received finance, advice, and additional membership if required.

By the mid-1960s, the Angels were holding press conferences and doing well out of two unpaid publicists: Marlon Brando in *The Wild One*, the 1952 biker movie, and Hunter S. Thompson, the writer and wild man of West Coast literature, whose rides with the Angels produced *Hells Angels — A Strange and Terrible Saga of the Outlaw Motor Cycle Gangs*. The Angels gained more publicity from their Labor Day turn-out in Monterey, California, when two girls alleged they had been gang-raped by bikers. Forty-six Angels were

Concealed weapon
A Hells Angel at a rock concert carries a cosh in his waistband. Weapons of all kinds are used by outlaw motorcycle gangs, including automatic weapons and rocket-propelled missiles.

arrested and four charged. They were released when a doctor found no evidence of an assault, and because one of the girls refused to testify while the other was deemed unreliable after a lie-detector test. The trial left the Angels short of money. The Angels turned to the manufacture of illegal amphetamines. They are now said to control the majority of the drugs market in the United States. Under Barger's guidance they took steps to protect themselves from imitators

"Three can keep a secret if two are dead..."

Hells Angels motto

in order to franchise the Angels "brand"; the Angels were legally incorporated in 1966 with an issue of 500 shares and the drawing up of a memorandum and articles of association, all with the wholly laudable aim of the promotion and advancement of motorcycle riding, motorcycle clubs, and highway safety. A patent on the flying Death's Head emblem was taken out in 1972. Revenue from breach of copyright cases has been used to establish defense funds for Angels charged with offenses from murder to racketeering. The Angels have also been able to secure tax-exempt status with the formation of the Church of the Angel, of which there are numerous pastors.

Joining the Gang

Prospective members must first undergo serious scrutiny. Although considerable knowledge of motorcycles is required, the ability to ride a Harley-Davidson is now of secondary importance. Members are still

Funeral procession
European, Australian, and U.S. members of the Bandidos gang ride in formation to the funeral of their Danish comrade Uffe Larsen in the village of Stenloese, Denmark, on March 20, 1996. Larsen died in a shootout with rival Hells Angels.

required to take part in four or five mandatory "runs" annually. Such runs are undertaken with military precision. The President and Road Captain lead the ride, followed by full color-wearing members with, behind them, probationary members, associates and honorary members. At the rear are an assistant road captain and

INSIDE STORY

OUTLAW MOTORCYCLE GLOSSARY

1%ers The 1% symbol is the Hells Angels' response to a statement by the American Motorcycle Association (AMA) that 99% of the country's motorcyclists belong to the AMA and are law-abiding individuals. The 1% symbol has thus become the mark of the outlaw bike rider and they display it on their colors. Many also have it tattooed on their bodies.

13 A patch worn on a gang member's colors, symbolizing that the biker either smokes marijuana, deals in it, or has contacts in the world of illicit drugs.

666 Patch worn on a member's colors, or a tattoo, symbolizing the mark of Satan.

Citizen A A motorcyclist who belongs to the AMA who is not a member of the 1% club.

Class To show "class" is do something extraordinary, usually an act that is violent or is shocking to the public.

Colors The official uniform of all outlaw motorcycle gangs. The colors consist of a sleeveless denim or leather jacket, with a club patch on the back and various other patches and pins. Colors are worn by male members only and are treated with reverence by the gang.

Crash Truck A van, truck, or converted school bus that follows the motorcycle gang's road trips and picks up broken down bikes. It can also be used to carry the club's weapons, drugs, food supplies, and camping gear.

Cross An emblem worn by 1%ers, as an earring, patch or as a pin attached to the colors.

Biker wars in Europe
A fireman amid the wreckage of what used to be the headquarters of the Bandidos motorcycle gang in Drammen, Norway, in June 1997. At least one person was killed in what was thought to be an attack mounted by the Hells Angels. In Denmark, a similar turf war led to 11 murders.

CASE STUDY

Hells Angels v. The Rock Machine

The essentially acquisitive nature of the Hells Angels has led to a long-running war between their elite chapter, the Nomads, and the rival biker gang the Rock Machine for control of the lucrative drug market in Montreal, Canada, estimated to be worth $1 billion per annum. The ongoing war has its roots in the late 1970s, when the Angels adopted their aggressive policy of absorbing smaller motorcycle gangs.

In 1979, the original Quebec chapter split and two Montreal Hells Angels chapters were formed. Discipline had previously been tight but former Hells Angel Yves Trudeau told a coroner's jury in 1984 that, after the split, things become lax and at least 12 members were executed for breaking the agreed code. The Laval chapter, which included Trudeau, had carried out the killings.

On March 25, 1985, they were summoned to a meeting at the Lennoxville clubhouse where five were shot dead. Two weeks later a sixth was beaten to death in a motel. Trudeau escaped the slaughter because he had checked himself into a detox clinic. On learning what had happened he gave himself up to the police. Over the years the turf war escalated,

and in August 1995 alone there were eight bombings. Twenty-one people were later killed in Quebec City and another nine in Montreal. Innocent bystanders included 12-year-old Daniel Desrochers, who was killed when a bomb planted in a jeep exploded. By the end of 1995 there was a temporary truce but it ended the next year with the Dark Circle, said to be the death squad of the Rock Machine, facing up to the Angels.

In 1998, Maurice "Mom" Boucher, the leader of the Montreal Hells Angels, was acquitted of charges that he had ordered the murder of two prison guards. That night he attended a boxing tournament where the crowd applauded his appearance at the ringside but, in October 2000, the Quebec Court of Appeal ordered a re-trial. Boucher was arrested on October 10 as he left a Montreal restaurant. Now he was charged with ordering a total of 13 killings, including the prison guards.

Throughout the summer Boucher had conducted a PR campaign, possibly to create an image which would be more acceptable when he faced a jury the second time around. In September he met with

Frederic "Fred" Faucher, a leading member of the Rock Machine. The men agreed a truce and then dined together along with 20 guests in the Bleu Marin, a fashionable Montreal restaurant. However, in April 2003 the 48-year-old Boucher was found guilty of ordering the deaths of the prison guards and sentenced to life imprisonment with no chance of parole before serving 25 years. It was thought that Mike McCrea, a leading member of the Halifax Hells Angels, would take his place. In September 2003 nine other Montreal gang leaders were jailed for up to 20 years.

Police presence
The house of Angels leader Maurice "Mom" Boucher (above) in Quebec, Canada, is watched over by a police unit in 2001.

enforcer and a crash car. The road captain ensures that there are enough spare machines, parts, and weapons. Before the ride he will have mapped out a route and pinpointed refueling and refreshment sites. He is also required to organize security for the ride. Probationers are carefully scrutinized to avoid gang infiltration by undercover police, and are usually recruited by existing members. Once accepted at the lowest level, a would-be Angel must serve a term of up to three years, during which time he will clean the clubhouses and wash existing members' machines. He will work security duty and is likely also to undertake criminal assaults.

On successful completion of his probationary period the new member will be given his colors. He may now vote in the weekly "chapel" meetings and may become a club officer. Among other duties, these officers are used for gathering information about law enforcement agencies who may be taking too close an interest in the chapter. A member is required always to place the group before his family and business

interests. Those who breach the rules can expect severe punishment and expulsion from the organization.

Worldwide, the Hells Angels complain that they have been victimized by society and that they are now a lawful organization. Gone are the filthy uniforms and anti-social and criminal behavior; instead there are business suits and, in Vancouver, Canada, there is a 6,000-strong annual ride bringing Christmas presents for underprivileged children. The Angels accept that there are criminal members within their ranks, but vehemently deny that they are a criminal organization.

There are more than 230 active chapters of the Hells Angels, of which about a third are spread across the United States, with other groups now established in Canada, Europe, South America, and South Africa. Other American biker gangs include the Outlaws, with 50 chapters, including four in Australia, and the Bandidos, with 28 chapters across the United States, and an increasing number in Europe.

Tooled up
Arms dealing has joined drug dealing as a major source of income for outlaw biker gangs.

MEXICO

THE MEANING OF "LA EME"

The Mexican Mafia is known as "La Eme," which is Spanish for the letter "M." The American mafioso Jimmy Fratianno has suggested that "La Eme" was formed in Folsom Prison, California, in the 1950s, by an Irishman named Joe Morgan. Morgan was a fluent Spanish speaker who gathered a dozen Mexicans around him. A more accepted origin for La Eme is the banding together of Mexican youths at the Deuel Vocational Institute in Tracy, California in 1957. Since then, La Eme has grown into one of the most powerful gangs in the world.

TERRITORY

Tracy
Fresno
Los Angeles
Otay Mesa
Tijuana
USA
New York
Cuidad Juárez
Houston
Brownsville
Durango
Matamoros
Monterrey
MEXICO CITY
Mexico

The Mexican Mafia's primary activities are trafficking drugs and illegal aliens into the United States. The long border order between Mexico and the United States offers many opportunities for Mexican gangs to gain entry to the major cities of North America.

- **TIJUANA**
  A major junction for drug and people smuggling.

- **CUIDAD JUAREZ**
  Base of one of the leading Mexican cartels.

- **TRACY, CALIFORNIA**
  The place where Mexican prison gangs originated.

Recent cocaine seizures made by the authorities on the Mexican–U.S. border:

1998	30.4 metric tonnes
1999	37.2 metric tonnes
2000	21.3 metric tonnes
2001	20.3 metric tonnes
2002	22.3 metric tonnes

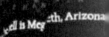

The Mexican Cartels

" These sophisticated drug syndicate groups from Mexico have eclipsed organized crime groups from Colombia as the premier law enforcement threat facing the United States today. "

THOMAS CONSTANTINE, DIRECTOR OF THE U.S. DRUG ENFORCEMENT ADMINISTRATION

Mexico took over as the leading heroin exporter in the world in the early 1970s. Turkey had been an important global supplier of heroin since the 1920s but, in 1973, the Turkish government banned the growing of opium and the country ceased to be a major drug power.

Mexico was already a significant drug producer. The leading Mexican drug baron of the 1960s was Jaime Herrera Navarez, who controlled much of the distribution of heroin cultivated in Durango in the Sierra Madre mountains of Mexico. So successful was he that, in 1969, U.S. president Richard Nixon tried to put a halt to his activities with a plan codenamed Operation Intercept. Over three weeks guards stopped and searched five million U.S. and Mexican citizens at border crossings. Not one single worthwhile seizure was made. Towns just inside Mexico, such as Tijuana, were declared off-limits to U.S. service personnel.

Mexico responded angrily to the effects of the clampdown on Mexican citizens and the United States backed down. Instead, it offered Mexico $1 million to wipe out the drug plantations. The Mexican efforts failed. By the mid-1980s, the farmers were growing

Drug bust in progress
A special unit of the Mexican police arrests suspected drug dealers in Mexico City in 2000. Mass poverty in the country means that many people see the drug trade as an opportunity.

drugs not only in the Sierra Madre but in other areas, including Veracruz, Sonora, and Baja California. By the 1990s, Baja California had become a principal point for smuggling drugs into the United States from Mexico and Colombia. The importance of the route was underscored by the discovery in April 2003 of two tunnels running beneath the border between Tijuana in Mexico and Otay Mesa in California. One tunnel was 520 ft (160 m) long and was equipped with electricity and an air-conditioning system.

America's Most Wanted

In March 1995, the U.S. Federal Bureau of Investigation added Mexican–American Juan Garcia Abrego to its list of Ten Most Wanted criminals. As a suspected link to the Cali drug cartel in Colombia (see p185), Garcia Abrego had been indicted by a Houston jury in 1993, in connection with a drug-trafficking and money-laundering scheme.

Confiscated drug mountain
Mexican government officials show off a massive haul of illegal drugs that police seized from traffickers trying to cross the border into the United States in June 1990.

He also faced charges of conspiracy to smuggle large amounts of marijuana and cocaine to the United States through Mexico. According to the U.S. Justice Department, he was the head of the Gulf cartel. He was also believed to be linked to the death in 1994 of Francisco Ruiz Massieu, a member of the Institutional Revolutionary Party.

In 1996, Garcia Abrego was captured near Monterrey, Mexico. He had no bodyguards and there was no gunfire. As a U.S. citizen, he was deported to Texas where his trial began in Houston in September 1996. On October 16, he was convicted of smuggling huge amounts of marijuana and cocaine into the United States. In January 1997, he was given 11 life sentences.

The Three Drug Rings

Garcia Abrego's Gulf cartel was just one of three cartels that have dominated the drug trade in Mexico since the mid-1990s. The other two are based in the border cities of Tijuana and Cuidad Juárez. The Mexican cartels had almost completely replaced the Colombian Cali cartel in controlling cocaine distribution by 1997. The Mexicans were also moving into traditional Colombian markets such as New York City. The change

came after several incidents. The first was the death of Pablo Escobar (*see p185*), the second the arrest of the Cali boss Miguel Rodriguez Orejuela. The Colombian cartels fragmented into smaller, lower-profile operations as a result.

The New Drug Barons

One of the new breed of Mexican drug barons was the 42-year-old Amado Carrillo Fuentes, head of the Juárez cartel. At its peak, Carrillo's empire was making an estimated $200 million a week from drug routes into California and the West. Although indicted in Texas and Florida, Carrillo had only minor weapons charges against him in Mexico before his death in July 1997. A turf war immediately broke out in which dozens were killed and Carrillo's brother Vicente took control of the Juárez cartel.

The U.S.–Mexican border remains one of the key areas of operations for the drug cartels, as it provides access to the biggest drug market in the world. The cartels now use a variety of carriers known as "mules," including senior citizens with motor homes, who take the risk on the basis that they are unlikely to be stopped. Mules can earn up to $400 for a run, the equivalent of several weeks' wages in Mexico.

By 2000, police estimated that almost half of the 15 to 20 international drug cartels were Mexican, the largest of which were now based in Tijuana and Cuidad Juárez, with cells operating in the United States. By the beginning of 2003, there were signs that all three major cartels had been affected by the crackdown by the Mexican authorities. Their control of the 1,940-mile (3,100-km) border with the United States was under threat. Osiel Cardenas, head of the Gulf cartel, was ambushed and captured after a firefight in Matamoros across the border from Brownsville, Texas. It was the culmination of a six-month investigation by the Mexican authorities into the

group, which was shipping hundreds of tons of drugs to the United States every year. Ramon Arellano Felix of the Tijuana cartel was shot dead in February 2002 in a battle with the police, and his brother Benjamin was captured. Control passed to their sister, Enedina, the first "godmother" of the cartel. She was thought to be under threat not only from the authorities but also from dissident elements inside her own organization and from a rival gang run by Ismael Zambada, known as "El Mayo."

As for the Juárez cartel, early in 2003 one of its top enforcers, Arturo Hernandez Gonzalez, known as "El Chaky," was arrested. With Gonzalez in custody, law enforcement officers hoped that inroads could be made into that organization. There were, however, signs that Colombian crime families were taking advantage of the situation by looking at the possibilities of setting up rival organizations in Mexico.

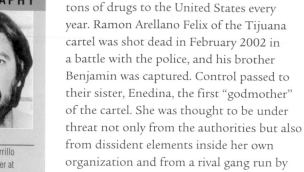

The hitman hit
Eudelio Lopez Falcon, a hitman and drug smuggler for the Juárez and Gulf cartels, slumps dead on a restaurant table on May 6, 2003, the victim of Mexican drug wars. Police say Falcon employed a network of gunmen to sneak narcotics into the United States.

CASE STUDY

Mexican–American Prison Gangs

Mexican street gangs have operated since the 1930s in towns in the southwest of the United States, but Mexican prison gangs probably originated in 1957 with the banding together of Mexican youths at the Deuel Vocational Institute in Tracy, California. Membership spread as prisoners were transferred across the state, and by the mid-1960s La Eme had almost complete control of the drug distribution inside Californian prisons. Since then it has grown into one of the four most powerful gangs operating both inside and outside U.S. prisons.

THE GANG MENTALITY

Recruits had often been leaders of street gangs who showed their loyalty, or fear, in prison by killing another inmate. Membership followed the maxim "In by blood, out by blood," allowing only those who had killed or assaulted a prison officer or another prisoner to join. La Eme has now established a business relationship with various Chinese criminal gangs, which has facilitated the sale of heroin on the streets of U.S. cities. Like other gangs, La Eme has taken advantage of projects offering government grants, which it has appropriated for its own use.

La Eme's principal rival is La Nuestra Familia ("Our Family"), another Mexican–American gang. Formed 10 years after the Mexican Mafia, the LNF initially sold protection to those under attack from La Eme. Then it moved into the extortion racket

for itself. When it challenged the Mexican Mafia for heroin trafficking inside the Californian prison system, the gangs became bitter enemies. By 1972, 30 prisoners had died as a result of the war. By 1975, LNF had developed beyond the prison walls, with a regiment established in Fresno, California.

Membership of La Nuestra Familia is based on the principle "Once in, never out," an oath that puts the gang's interests first. By 1982, there were 800 members and the leadership had begun to stress the importance of discipline and profit-making. To this end it drew up a constitution and reorganized. One general commands all the prison groups, while another controls the gang's street activities. Each general has up to 10 captains who control the lieutenants, who in turn command the rank and file soldiers.

> ## "We want to live *la vida loca* – the crazy life."
> Mexican gang member.

Allied to La Nuestra Familia in its war with the Mexican Mafia is the Black Guerrilla Family, begun in 1966 in San Quentin Penitentiary. Over the years the Black Guerrillas has been the most politically motivated prison gang. By the mid-1980s there was a clear division between the Black Guerrillas' political faction and the recruits who had joined to share in the criminal profits.

Less well known is the Texas Syndicate, a Mexican–American gang founded in California in 1974 with an all-Texan membership. Once released from Californian prisons, the members returned home and were soon rearrested and imprisoned in Texas. Initially their motive appears to have been self-preservation but, as their members became increasingly violent, they expanded to become the biggest single gang in the Texas prison system. Another group originating in Mexico, the Juaritos, are a violent street gang who are involved not only in drug trafficking but also in smuggling illegal immigrants from Mexico into the United States.

Hispanic crime gangs are likely to become more dominant in the coming decades as the Hispanic population of the United States grows. Already Hispanics are the majority ethnic group in many cities in the United States; for example, Hispanics now comprise about 29 percent of the population of New York.

Gang line-up
A police photographer takes a picture of three members of a street gang in Juárez, Mexico. On the table are the weapons police confiscated during the arrest.

After the riot
A lone police officer surveys the damage to a cellblock at the New Mexico State Penitentiary in February 1980. The riot cost the lives of 33 inmates and was one of the worst in the state's history. Gang warfare can be just as intense inside prisons as outside.

JAMAICA

TERRITORY

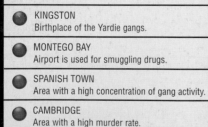

- Montego Bay
- Cambridge
- Spanish Town
- KINGSTON

The Jamaican Yardies and Posses were originally based in the poorer districts of Kingston and nearby Spanish Town. From these areas they spread out to other parts of the island. In the 1980s, the Jamaican gangs moved into illicit drug smuggling and developed a worldwide network, particularly into the United States and Britain from the early 1990s. The gangs benefited from Jamaica's convenient geographical location between the drug-producing countries of South America and their most lucrative market in North America.

●	**KINGSTON** Birthplace of the Yardie gangs.
●	**MONTEGO BAY** Airport is used for smuggling drugs.
●	**SPANISH TOWN** Area with a high concentration of gang activity.
●	**CAMBRIDGE** Area with a high murder rate.

The annual murder rate in Jamaica is one of the highest in the world and is frequently gang-related.

1998	953
1999	1,038
2000	887
2001	1,139
2002	1,045

Yardies and Posses

❝ The UK became an attractive destination for Yardies because of its long-standing association with its former colonies in the Caribbean. ❞

ROY RAMM, SCOTLAND YARD

The Yardies and Posses emerged in Jamaica in the 1960s and 1970s as urban armed gangs recruited by politicians to organize local constituencies, enforce party loyalty, and bring out voters at elections. The gangs were originally based in the districts of the capital, Kingston, and also in Spanish Town. The gangs later moved into illicit drug smuggling and developed an international network. The spread of the Posses or Yardies to the United States and Britain came in the early 1980s, when a number of groups fled Jamaica after the defeat of Michael Manley's People's National Party, which they had supported in the 1980 national elections. When the more moderate Labor Party toppled Manley's government, many gang members, who had been blamed for up to

Kingston, Jamaica
A soldier patrols the rundown back streets of the Jamaican capital Kingston. These streets were the breeding ground for the Yardies, who sought a quick way out of poverty.

500 murders during the campaign, and other arson attacks, fled to New York and Miami in the United States, and then moved further afield to the cities of Britain.

Gang Structure

Jamaican gangs are largely based on neighborhood associations and political affiliations. The members who arrived in the United States in the 1980s, often as illegal immigrants, and soon formed their own Posses or linked up with U.S. street gangs. In the early years the gangs were large and the membership readily identifiable. As a result, U.S. law enforcement agencies were able to mount successful prosecutions for illegal activity. Imprisonment, deportation, and murder by rival gangs weakened a number of the Posses. However, they grew again, and this time the leaders established a hierarchy to insulate themselves from street-level drug dealing but retain control of the profits. Underbosses supervise the gang's daily activities. The position of underboss is a risky one. It is usual for rival gangs to deal out violence not to the boss but to a second-in-command, as a demonstration of what will happen if the boss does not cooperate. It is difficult to determine to what extent, if any, Jamaican gangs are organized in a way comparable to other crime groups, such as the U.S. Mafia.

Dealing in Crack

At first the Posses dealt in marijuana, but soon moved into other drug markets, such as cocaine and its highly addictive derivative, crack cocaine, which were controlled in the United States by black and Hispanic gangs (see *Drugs and the Jamaican gangs, right*).

The Posses have never been slow to turn to violence to protect their interests. One often cited incident concerns a Jamaican gang

known as the Spanglers, who had taken over a couple of blocks in Edgecombe Avenue in Harlem, New York, peddling crack on 142nd and 144th streets. A policeman noticed a group of young men playing soccer, but with a human head. Inquiries showed that a rival drug dealer had been caught stealing from the Posse. As a punishment and warning to others, he was killed and dismembered in a bathtub.

Subsequent investigation by the police showed that at least 14 other victims had been dismembered in the same bath.

Illegal Guns

A similar disrespect for human life and willingness to use guns distinguishes Posses in Britain, where, in addition to narcotics trafficking, Jamaican gangs have become masters of obtaining firearms. They are bought through a straightforward purchase or by using a dummy buyer on behalf of a gang member; otherwise they are stolen from homes, military bases, and gun dealers. Other activities include marriage, immigration, and green card fraud, and counterfeiting.

It is almost impossible to estimate the number of Posse members at any one time in the United States or Britain but the figure must run into thousands.

Make: SF FIREARMS
Model: MAC 10
Type: sub machine gun
Calibre: 9 millimetre PARABELLUM

Make: IMI
Model: DESERT EAGLE
Type: self loading pistol
Calibre: .357 MAGNUM

Make: ENGLISH
Type: sawn off shotgun
12 bore

Yardie gun haul
On display at New Scotland Yard, London, an array of weapons, including shotguns and pistols, used in some of Britain's Yardie murders. The prevalence of gun crime means that there are few gang members over the age of 35.

CASE STUDY

Drugs and the Jamaican Gangs

The Posses have become heavily involved in drug trafficking since the 1980s, especially in crack cocaine. With its well placed location, Jamaica has become a major transshipment point for cocaine from South to North America.

At street level the Posses operate crack houses known as gatehouses, which are often managed by women protected by low-level gang members. A gatehouse may be an apartment, a store, a restaurant, or an office that has been taken over and heavily defended. The exchange of money and drugs is done through plexi-glass shields, and the drugs are then delivered to street dealers. The benefit is that the amount of drugs found by the police on any gang member is likely to be small.

A crack transaction may typically go through the following stages: A kilogram of cocaine is purchased from a Colombian

trafficker and then moved to New York. It is then transformed into up to 20,000 "rocks" of crack. The profit can be around eight times the initial purchase price. The Colombian trafficker who sold the drug originally will merely treble his money.

The profits from drug trafficking are laundered in a variety of ways, not all exclusive to the Posses. One is through the street trader who, financed by the Posse, buys goods in the United States and then sells them in Jamaica. Other methods include using corrupt or intimidated airline employees either to carry the money through themselves or to allow 55-gallon drums stuffed with cash onto planes bound for Jamaica. Amounts of money under $10,000 can simply be sent through Western Union. Drugs profits are also invested in legitimate businesses, such as grocery stores and nightclubs.

Crack cocaine
One of the drugs most commonly peddled by the Yardies is crack cocaine. This highly addictive drug became popular in the 1980s because it is inexpensive to produce and to buy. In Britain and the United States Yardies have almost total control of the crack cocaine market. The trade in crack is closely linked to gun crime, with rival Yardie gangs using firearms to guard their territories.

COLOMBIA

THE MODERN COLOMBIAN CARTELS

In the 1990s, a new generation of Colombian drug traffickers emerged. These groups are more sophisticated than the traditional Medellín and Cali cartels, operating in a much less hierarchical fashion, and using the Internet to pass on instructions and to transfer funds. Most Colombian cocaine is now sold in bulk to Mexican organizations, who assume the risks involved in smuggling the drug into the United States, by far the world's biggest market. Smaller and less visible, the modern cartels are much harder to detect.

TERRITORY

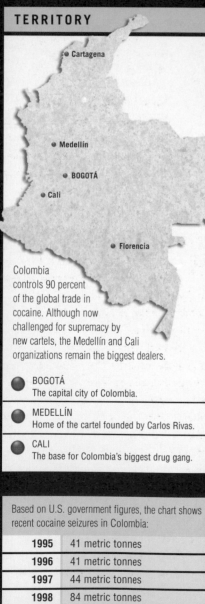

- Cartagena
- Medellín
- BOGOTÁ
- Cali
- Florencia

Colombia controls 90 percent of the global trade in cocaine. Although now challenged for supremacy by new cartels, the Medellín and Cali organizations remain the biggest dealers.

- **BOGOTÁ**
  The capital city of Colombia.

- **MEDELLÍN**
  Home of the cartel founded by Carlos Rivas.

- **CALI**
  The base for Colombia's biggest drug gang.

Based on U.S. government figures, the chart shows recent cocaine seizures in Colombia:

1995	41 metric tonnes
1996	41 metric tonnes
1997	44 metric tonnes
1998	84 metric tonnes
1999	32 metric tonnes

Medellín and Cali Cartels

" There is a whole new generation of traffickers in Colombia who have carefully learned from the mistakes of the groups that went before them. They are much harder to fight because they are much harder to find. "

GENERAL ROSSO JOSE SERRANO, DIRECTOR OF THE COLOMBIAN NATIONAL POLICE

Before the advent of the international drug trade, Latin America did not feature greatly on the world crime scene. There was some traffic in European women to the brothels and cabarets of the capital cities, and some counterfeiting gangs dealt in forged cheques across the U.S.–Mexican border. Until the early 1970s the only real Colombian presence in organized crime was in the smuggling of consumer goods and the training of teams of pickpockets. They toured Europe and many were arrested at the time of the soccer World Cup in London in 1966. The Colombian crime scene changed dramatically within a decade.

The Colombian Drug Connection

Colombia is well situated for the drug trade. There is access to coca (the plant from which cocaine is extracted) from other South American countries and Colombia has a long coastline on both the Pacific and Caribbean for easy shipment to the United States. The east of the country is sparsely populated, with vast forests that can conceal both airstrips and cocaine laboratories.

From this background, individual drug traders began to form cartels – groupings of

Up in smoke
A soldier stands guard over a bonfire of cocaine seized from drug traffickers in Colombia on May 10, 1990. The fight against the smugglers becomes ever tougher.

A mountain of poverty
An infant competes with scavenging crows and vultures for anything recyclable on a rubbish dump in Bogotá, Colombia. The drug trade is seen as an easy way out of this endless cycle of grinding poverty.

illicit narcotics "entrepreneurs," who fixed prices and eliminated any non-cartel competitors. The Medellin and Cali cartels (named after the cities they were based in) rose to prominence, partly thanks to Colombia's unstable political situation. On April 9, 1948, the Liberal leader, Jorge Eliecer Gaitan, was shot. Outrage at the assassination gave rise to a wave of looting and destruction. For the next 17 years Liberal and Conservative factions fought a civil war, marked by atrocities on both sides. At the same time, the city of Medellín was prospering. Smuggling had always been prevalent in the region and the routes that had been established for bringing in guns, gunpowder, and brandy were ideal for the growing industry of drug trafficking.

Until 1973, the South American cocaine trade had been small and based in Chile.

When General Augusto Pinochet overthrew the Chilean government of Salvador Allende in September 1973, he destroyed the trade by jailing or deporting drug dealers. The Colombians stepped in to take over the lucrative business.

The principals of the main Medellín cartel were Carlos Enrique Lehder Rivas (*see p184*), Pablo Escobar-Gavira (*see p185*), Jorge Luis Ochoa Vasquez, and Jose Gonzalo Rodriguez Gacha. By the mid-1980s, the four controlled more than 30 percent of the cocaine going into the United States. They had thousands of employees and were said to be earning $2 billion annually. Ranged alongside them, for a time their associates and then their enemies, was the Cali cartel led by the Orejuela brothers and Jose Santacruz Londono.

Cartel Bosses Under Pressure

In 1979, the United States and Colombia, already collaborating in the war on the drugs traffickers, signed an extradition treaty that permitted smugglers to face trial in the United States for offenses committed there. The agreement collapsed in June 1987, but in the early 1980s the Colombian

Carlos Enrique Lehder Rivas

Born to a Colombian mother and a German father, Carlos Enrique Lehder Rivas spent much of his childhood in the United States, where he began his criminal career by stealing cars and dealing in drugs. In 1973, he was sentenced to five years in a U.S. federal prison, having been caught in possession of a large amount of marijuana. While behind bars he met George Jung, a drug trafficker, and the two hatched a plan to transport large amounts of cocaine into the United States by plane. On his release, Rivas set up a distribution network using aircraft. He then struck a major deal with established trafficker Jorge Ochoa Vasquez, catapulting

himself into big-time drug smuggling. He became so successful that he was able to buy an island in the Bahamas as a staging post for his trafficking routes.

Rivas developed a penchant for his own product – cocaine – and became increasingly difficult to work with. This led him into conflict with Pablo Escobar, the leading member of the Medellín cartel.

In 1987, Rivas was captured by police at his Colombian jungle stronghold. He was extradited to Miami in Florida, where he was found guilty of smuggling cocaine into the United States. He received a sentence of life imprisonment plus 135 years.

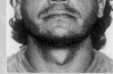

Dates 1949–

Details A major international drug smuggler, Carlos Rivas surrounded himself with bodyguards. Even they could not save him from prison.

government made a number of efforts to tackle the Medellín cartel, but with little success. In 1984, the cartel organized the assassination of the justice minister. After the murder and the resulting government reaction, the drug barons sought exile with General Manuel Noriega in Panama for a price said to be between $4 and $7 million. The ill-judged act of hospitality led to Noriega's imprisonment for 40 years in the United States after he was snatched from Panama City by U.S. military forces in 1990.

On November 15, 1984, Ochoa Vasquez was found in Spain with the Cali cartel boss,

Gilberto Orejuela. They had moved to Madrid, from where they continued their dealings and were laundering large sums of money. Ochoa Vasquez was wanted in Colombia for illegally importing fighting bulls and in the United States for running cocaine through Nicaragua. After many court appearances, in which the United States and Colombia battled over Ochoa Vasquez's extradition, Colombia won. He was returned there but was subsequently acquitted of the charges.

On February 4, 1987, Rivas (*see above*), many of his assets already having been

seized by the government, was arrested at a ranch in Antioquia. He was extradited and flown to Tampa, Florida, where on July 20, 1988, he was given a sentence of life without parole plus 135 years for conspiracy to smuggle cocaine. It was the last extradition of a top dealer before Colombia's treaty with the United States broke down.

In 1987, too, Ochoa Vasquez was arrested at a roadblock near Palmira, possibly at the behest of the Cali cartel. His offer of a bribe was refused and he was imprisoned on an army base. The cartel's response was the threat of open warfare on the authorities. Ochoa was released on December 30.

Against this background, in 1988 one of the other Medellín bosses, Jose Gonzalo Rodriguez Gacha, began to expand his empire aggressively, visiting New York with a view to taking over the Cali distribution network there. The move simply fueled the ongoing quarrels between the Medellín and Cali dealers in the city. One thing of which Gacha felt he could be proud was that his name featured for the first time in *Forbes* magazine's annual list of billionaires, next to those of Escobar and Ochoa Vasquez. He did not have long to savor his triumph. On December 15, he and his son Fredy were caught near the Colombian port of Covenas.

Gracious living
The palatial dining room in the mansion owned by drug baron Camilo Zapata, who was a leading member of the Medellín cartel.

Living the life
Some of the "drug soldiers" belonging to the Medellín cartel, seen relaxing. These are the men who control the street dealers and oversee the processing of raw coca leaves into saleable cocaine.

Fredy was shot and according to reports, either Gacha blew himself up with a grenade or he was shot as he tried to escape.

In 1991, two of Ochoa Vasquez 's sons, Jorge Luis and Fabio, agreed to a plea bargain and went to prison in Colombia. On release in 1996 they claimed the court cases and personal security expenses had erased all their drug profits. After these reverses the Medellín cartels were forced to reduce their operations. Much of their trade was taken over by the Cali cartels.

Extradition Reinstated

In 1997, extradition from Colombia to the United States was reinstated. Any earlier immunity did not apply to crimes committed since then, and Fabio Ochoa Vasquez was re-arrested in 1999. In August 2001, the Colombian Supreme Court ruled that Fabio could be extradited and President Andres Pastrana Arango confirmed the decision. It was seen as the most significant extradition from Colombia since that of Rivas in 1987. The decision was a severe blow to the Ochoa Vasquez family, who had been running an advertising campaign and a website aimed at freeing Fabio. The family claimed the charges were brought because Fabio had refused to become a government informer.

Fabio first appeared in court in Miami, Florida, in September 2001, amid high security. He was convicted in May 2003 and sentenced to 30 years in prison. As the verdicts were read out he knelt and made the sign of the cross.

The Cali Cartel

The Cali cartel – the biggest, most powerful crime syndicate in Colombia – was founded in the 1970s by Gilberto Rodriguez Orejuela and Jose Santacruz Londono, initially to smuggle cocaine from Peru into the United States. By 1980, the enterprise was worth millions of dollars annually. Never as violent as their Medellín counterparts, the operation was run almost on a commercial franchise basis. The cartel was built around a cell-like structure, with each

CASE STUDY

The Rise and Fall of Pablo Escobar

The most violent member of the Medellín cartel was Pablo Escobar-Gavira. Born in 1949, he was suspected of the 1971 kidnapping and killing of Diego Echavarria, a leading industrialist, for whom a ransom of $50,000 was paid before he was murdered. He moved on to contract killing and then began smuggling cocaine to be sold in Panama. He followed this by going into partnership with the Ochoa drug family. Along with him went his cousin Gustavo and his brother-in-law Mario Hanao.

In 1976, Escobar, Gustavo, and Hanao were arrested over the transportation of cocaine. It was now that Escobar began to display the ruthlessness that would characterize the Medellín cartel. Over the next few years the arresting officers, their regional chief, and the judge who ordered the arrest were all shot dead. Meanwhile the case became snarled up in the Colombian legal system until the trio were discharged.

Escobar then began to wage a full-scale war against the Colombian government in which 1,000 judges and officials were killed. At the same time he was engaged in a struggle with the rival Cali cartel.

At this time the Colombian Army stepped up its attempts to capture Escobar. Aware that he was wanted on drugs charges in the United States, Escobar chose the lesser of two evils. In 1991, in a carefully negotiated deal, Escobar agreed to surrender to the Colombian authorities. He was imprisoned in a low security compound. The arrangements suited everybody. Colombia could say that its top drug dealer was behind bars, while Escobar had not only avoided extradition to the United States, but was still able to control his cocaine empire.

An outcry against Escobar's soft prison conditions followed and, in July 1992, a move to a military prison was planned. Escobar learned of his impending transfer and escaped. A substantial reward was offered for his capture. On the run, Escobar could not stay more than a few hours in any one place and his bodyguards deserted him, were captured, or were killed.

On December 1, 1993, his birthday, Escobar spoke to his family on the telephone. The call was traced to a house in Medellín and troops took up positions outside. Escobar tried to escape over the rooftops but died after being shot three times. He was just 44 and had often said that a Colombian grave was better than an American prison.

Pablo Escobar
Born in 1949 and initially a small-time crook, Escobar had a gang outside Envigado, Colombia, working the usual scams of street swindles and selling fake lottery tickets. He worked for Mario Cacharrero Garces in the stolen car trade and for Gilberto Saldarriaga, an emerald smuggler. For a short time Escobar was also a cigarette salesman for Philip Morris in Panama, where he learned how the U.S. markets worked. From these beginnings, Escobar rose to become the most feared drug baron of his time.

The death of Escobar
Colombian drugs officers examine the dead body of Pablo Escobar after he was shot trying to evade capture in December 1993. He had been on the run for 15 months after escaping from a Colombian jail.

Gangsters and Plastic Surgery

An extreme way to cheat the authorities is to have a facial and body makeover. Colombian drug magnate Jose Santacruz Londono was known as "Mil Rostros" (many faces) because of the number of times he underwent plastic surgery before he was shot and killed in March 1996. On July 3, 1997, gangster Amado Carrillo Fuentes died of a heart attack during liposuction surgery in Santa Monica Hospital, Mexico City. Initially reports of his death were met with skepticism – he would not have been the first gangster to fake his own death – but fingerprints and a DNA analysis confirmed his identity. Further confirmation came in early November when three tortured bodies, including that of Jaime Godoy Singh who was thought to have led the team of surgeons, were found in oil drums dumped on the Mexico City–Acapulco highway.

Londono and Fuentes were by no means the first gangsters to have tried to change their appearance and fingerprints. In 1934, American hoodlum John Dillinger almost died when he underwent plastic surgery. Nor was Jaime Singh the first doctor to pay the price for failure. Dr Joseph Patrick Moran also died at the hands of his gangster patients. Moran had started life well enough, qualifying with honors from Tufts Medical School but, convicted twice of performing illegal abortions, he went to work for Chicago crime boss Al Capone. Also in 1934, the bank robbers Fred Barker and Alvin Karpis, one time Public Enemy No. 1, paid Moran $1,000 to change their appearances. Moran

was drunk and botched his work, leaving the men in extreme pain. When the bandages came off, Karpis was even uglier than before, and Moran had merely burned away the top skin on the men's fingers. He was taken to Toledo, Ohio, where Barker and Karpis shot him and dumped his body in a lake.

Some doctors simply end up in prison. In February 1997, 69-year-old Dr Jose Castillo was convicted in Philadelphia of harboring a fugitive and obstructing justice. He had been the confidante of Philadelphia drug lord Richie Ramos, whose face he had successfully altered in 1990. Ramos was not found until 1992, when he was offered 30 years in prison instead of life without parole if he agreed to give evidence against Castillo. Ramos did what he could for his doctor by failing to recognize him in an identification parade where the choices were Castillo, a 39-year-old lawyer, and a young woman. Castillo went to jail anyway.

Open coffin
The body of Amado Carrillo Fuentes (*see box, p178*) is displayed to the media by Mexican police on July 7, 1997. Carrillo was recovering from plastic surgery when he died at a hospital in Mexico City.

---

cell consisting of six to ten trusted employees. This facilitated supervision of all aspects of the drug-running business, from the coca farms of Bolivia and Peru through the processing to the street dealers. The cells also provided a protective layer between the workers and the kingpins, who remained in Colombia.

One of the early barons to split off from the Orejuela–Londono partnership was Helmer Herrera Buitrago, who had run part of their New York operation. He and his brothers were believed to have set up their own distribution networks in Texas, Florida, and California. The level of profit can be gauged by the seizure in 1991 of $16 million from Herrera's properties, mainly in the Queens/Jackson Heights district of New York. Over the years, importation and

transportation techniques have been refined and improved. Shipments made by the Cali cartel have entered the United States under such diverse covers as frozen broccoli and ceramic tiles.

The End of the Cali Cartel?

The destruction of the Cali cartel began on March 2, 1995, with the arrest of Jorge Eliecer Rodriguez Orejuela, the youngest of the brothers. On June 9, the authorities also arrested Gilberto Rodriguez Orejuela at his apartment. The same day, a bomb exploded in Medellín, killing 29 people and injuring 200 others.

Four other senior members of the cartel surrendered. On August 6, the police in Cali arrested Miguel Rodriguez Orejuela, whom they believed to be No. 2 in the administration, along with No. 3, Jose Santacruz Londono. In between came the surrender of Henry Loaiza Ceballos, who gave himself up at an army base in Cali on June 19. He was accused of planning the

Jungle drug factory
Colombian troops examine cocaine in its purest form in a crude processing shack deep within the jungle. Troops are directed to these hideouts by sophisticated satellite technology.

Medellín bombing and the massacre of 107 peasants in Valle de Cauca, who had refused to cooperate with the drug barons.

As a result of the arrests, the street price of cocaine in New York rose by 50 percent. Killings in Colombia dropped to 1,653, a reduction of 117 on the previous year. For a short while things seemed quieter but, with Colombian president Ernesto Samper coming under suspicion of collusion with the drug cartels, former public prosecutor Felipe Lopez was gunned down in January 1996. It was thought that he was about to give evidence against either politicians or cartel leaders or both. The following month Samper faced corruption charges, and the U.S. government announced that it considered him guilty of accepting financial contributions from drug dealers.

On January, 11, 1996, Jose Santacruz Londono escaped from jail but his end came on March 5, 1996, when he was killed in a shootout with the police. Samper, clinging to office, proclaimed that the killing "ratified" his government's "unbreakable" will to fight against drug trafficking.

The Orejuela brothers continued their incarceration in La Picota Prison, Bogotá, but were able to run their businesses from a public telephone. Despite government protests, Gilberto was released on a judge's orders in November 2002. He had served less than half his sentence. Miguel remained in prison after being found guilty of the additional charge of bribing a judge.

The drop in the level of killings in 1995 did not last. In 1996, vigilante groups (a

"The Cali Mafia has spread poison around the world."

Thomas A. Constantine, U.S. Drug Enforcement Administration

powerful force within Colombian society) resumed unofficial action against criminal gangs and ensured the regular total of 70 deaths per day or 25,000 per year was maintained. The contract price for these killings was around $20 and the killers were the drug soldiers who had been left leaderless when the barons were arrested the previous year.

There was, however, good news for President Samper. Although most opinion polls, along with the Catholic Church, thought Samper was guilty, a Colombian congressional panel recommended that he be cleared of all charges. Pedro Rubiano, Archbishop of Bogotá, dismissed Samper's claim that he did not know that millions of dollars of drug money were in his campaign coffers as "like saying an elephant walked through your living room and you never noticed."

By September 1996, the drug dealers were back on the offensive, and, in a series of attacks, 100 government officials were killed. The blame was placed on the Revolutionary Armed Forces of Colombia, one of the country's oldest rebel groups. The complaint this time was that the government planned to destroy coca, and the peasants, who scraped a living from growing the plant, and the rebels were resisting violently.

The temporary defeat of the largest Cali cartel has meant only that Colombian targets are now harder to see, let alone hit. Unlike the centralized Cali cartel, smaller drug rings that have emerged in recent years have spread widely. Two of note are the North Atlantic Coast group, which has moved into cocaine trafficking, and the Bogotá cartel, which has developed links with the Mafia in the United States.

Casualty of the drug wars

The body of one of the 29 people killed by a bomb that exploded in Medellín, Colombia, on June 11, 1995. The bomb was allegedly planted by rival Cali "soldiers" in enemy territory as a response to the arrest of their leader "El Señor" Rodriguez Orejuela (right) in August 1995. He was believed to be No. 2 in the Cali drug cartel, and his capture was a major blow against Colombian drug crime.

Index

Page numbers in **bold** denote the main reference. Page numbers in *italics* indicate an illustration or its caption.

Picture Credits

(b = below, r = right, l = left, c = center, t = top)

SOURCE KEY

AA = The Art Archive AL = Archivi Alinari Milano AP = Associated Press BAL = Bridgeman Art Library, London, New York BJ = Bejaye BR = Brown Reference CO = Corbis GN = Grazia Neri HA = Hulton Archive/Getty Images HE = www.hemera.com KN = Kyodo News KOB = Kobal Collection MA = www.mayang.com MEPL = Mary Evans Picture Library PA = Press Association Picture Library PN = Peter Newark REX = Rex Features RH = Robert Hunt Library SW = Smith and Wesson TO = Topfoto TOC = TalesOfOldChina.com VM = Vin Mag Archive

RUNNING HEADERS: 8–17 (left–right): All pics CO: /Royalty-free/ Dave Bartruff/Steve Raymer/Dave G. Houser/Bettmann/John Springer Collection/Arne Hodalic/Dennis Galante/Hulton Deutsch-Collection/ H. Armstrong Roberts; 20–51 (left–right): All pics CO: /The Purcell Team/Corbis/Bettmann/Christine Spengler/Corbis/Darrell Gulin/Andrew Brookes/Corbis/Patrick Robert/Corbis; 54–187 (left–right): All pics CO:/ Bettmann/Aaron Horowitz/Walter Hodges/Peter Blakely/Scott Houston/Brooklyn Production/Henry Diltz; 188–192 (left–right): RH/SW/HE/BJ/HE/BJ/BJ

1 BJ (passport); 1 CO/Bettmann (Al Capone); 1 HE (pills); 1 SW (gun); 2–3 main pic CO/E.O. Hoppé; 2–3 background MA; 4 CO/Bettmann (mug shot); 4 REX (mug shot); 4 SW (gun); 5 CO/David Turnley (border patrol); 5 CO/V. Velengurin/R.P.G./Sygma (Russian police); 5 REX (Hells Angel jacket & Russian prostitute); 5 SW (gun); 6 BR ('Ancient Map Book' map); 6–7 CO (opium den); 6 HE (coins); 6 Library Of Congress, Washington, D.C.(wanted poster); 7 HA (pirate); 8 AA/Domenica del Corriere/Dagli Orti; 9 CO/Underwood & Underwood; 10 b CO/Steve Starr; 11 l AP; 11 r CO/Gideon Mendel; 12 b PA; 12 t REX; 13 t CO/Jacques Langevin/Sygma; 13 b John R. Jones/Papilio; 14–15 b CO/Bettmann; 14 b CO/Jacques M. Chenet; 14 t CO/Shaul Schwarz; 15 t CO/Richard T. Nowitz; 16 b CO/Bettmann below; 16 t AA/National History Museum, Mexico City/Dagli Orti; 17 CO/Hulton-Deutsch Collection; 18 BJ (calling card); 18–19 CO/A&E/Sygma (van X-ray); 18 CO/Micheline Pelletier/Sygma (prostitutes); 18 HE (lighter & pills); 18 REX (mug shot & prostitute in bar); 19 BJ (passport & passport photo); 19 SW (gun); 20 CO; 21 REX; 22 CO/Micheline Pelletier/Sygma; 23 c, t PA; 23 b, l REX;

24 b PA; 24 r REX; 25 b CO/David Turnley; 25 r CO/Royalty-free; 26 b, c, t REX; 27 b CO/A&E/Sygma; 27 t CO/Shura Davidson/Sygma; 28 CO/Ed Kashi; 29 CO/John R. Jones/Papilio; 30 t CO/Bettmann; 30 c CO/Philippe Eranian; 30 b REX; 32 r CO; 32 l REX; 33 b CO/ V. Velengurin/R.P.G./Sygma; 33 t REX; 34 b REX; 35 b CO/Robert Patrick/Sygma; 35 t CO/Ron Sachs; 36 t CO/R.P.G./Roman Poderni/Sygma; 36 b CO/R.P.G./Yevgeny Kondakov/Sygma; 37 bl Corporation of London; 37 br REX; 38 CO/Bettmann; 39 CO/Bettmann; 40 cl CO/Earl & Nazima Kowall; 40 bl CO/Royalty-free; 41 b CO; 41 tl CO/Bettmann; 42 br CO/Carl & Ann Purcell; 42 bl CO/Michael S. Yamashita; 42 t REX; 43 b CO/Bettmann; 43 t CO/Mark E. Gibson; 44 CO/Bettmann; 45 CO/Alan Schein Photography; 46 t CO/Bettmann; 46 br CO/Neil Rabinowitz; 46 bl CO/Royalty-free; 47 b AP; 47 t REX; 48 CO/Houston Scott/Sygma; 49 bl AP; 49 br CO/Viviane Moos; 50 CO/Najlah Feanny/SABA; 51 tr AP; 51 cr CO/Annebicque Bernard/Sygma; 52 CO/Bettmann (Al Capone & murder in restaurant); 52 CO/Gideon Mendell (Mafia arrest); 52 REX (Hells Angels); 52 SW (gun); 53 AP (wanted poster); 53 CO/David Turnley (prisoner with tattoos); 54 REX; 55 CO/Hulton-Deutsch Collection; 56 b CO/ Archivo Iconografico, S.A; 57 b CO/Bettmann; 57 t CO/Hulton-Deutsch Collection; 58 t, b CO/Bettmann; 59 cl, cr, tr CO/Bettmann; 60 b HA; 60 t, b TO; 61 b AP; 61 t REX; 62–63 b AL /Grassi, Giuseppe, Touring Club Italiano; 62 t HA; 63 br GN/Team; 63 t TO; 64–65 HA; 66 t AL/Team; 66 bl AP; 66 br CO/David Lees; 67 t CO/Bettmann; 67 b TO; 68 t AP; 68 b CO/Origilia/Ongaro/Sygma; 69 b AP; 69 t REX; 70 cr AP; 70 tl CO/Origlia Franco/Sygma; 70 b CO/ËPizzoli Alberto/Sygma; 71 REX; 72 t AP; 72 –73 b REX; 73 br, tr AP; 74 AP; 75 CO/Michael Maslan Historic Photographs; 76 b AP; 76 t CO/Nogues Alain/Sygma; 77 t CO/B. Vaillot/Galaxie Presse/Sygma; 77 b REX; 78 RH; 79 MEPL; 80 b, c, tr HA; 81 tr CO/Rune Hellestad; 81 bl HA; 81 cr VM; 82 bl CO/Hulton-Deutsch Collection; 82 bc VM; 83 b AP; 83 c CO/ Steve Starr; 83 cl, tr REX; 84 CO/Peter Blakely/SABA.; 85 CO/Hulton-Deutsch Collection; 86 REX; 87 t AP; 87 b CO/Marc Garanger; 88–89 CO/V.Velengurin/R.P.G./Sygma; 90 r CO/David Turnley; 90 l REX; 91 b CO/Gideon Mendel; 92 CO/Patrick Robert/Sygma; 93 b CO/Nogues Alain/Sygma; 93 b Reuters; 94 CO/ Gideon Mendel; 95 CO/Asian Art & Archaeology, Inc; 96 b CO/Horace Bristol; 96 c CO/Tom Wagner/SABA; 97 CO/Bettmann; 98 b, c, tr KN; 99 t AP; 99 b CO/ B.S.P.I; 100–101 CO/Peret Franck/Sygma; 102 b CO/Michael S. Yamashita; 102 c KN; 103 b, t KN; 104 l CO/James Leynse; 104 t CO/Royalty Free; 105 br CO/Tom Wagner/SABA; 105 t KOB; 106 CO/Jacques Langevin/Sygma;

107 BAL/National Palace Museum, Taipei; 108 AP; 109 b CO/Bettmann; 109 cr REX; 110 t CO/Hulton Deutsch Collection; 110 b HA; 111 b CO/Bettmann; 111 t TOC; 112 CO/Roger Garwood & Trish Ainslie; 113 b CO/Hulton-Deutsch Collection; 113 t CO/Underwood & Underwood; 114 b, tr CO/Bettmann; 114 cl REX; 115 b CO/Bettmann; 115 t CO/Photo Collection Alexander Alland, Sr; 116 b CO/Dallas and John Heaton; 116 tl PA; 117 b AP; 117 t CO/Annie Griffiths Belt; 118 CO/Bettmann; 119 CO/Bettmann; 120 b CO/Bettmann; 120 cr KOB; 121 b, t CO/Bettmann; 122 t, c CO/Bettmann; 123 b CO; 123 t CO/Bettmann; 124 bl, br CO/Bettmann; 124 t CO/Hulton-Deutsch Collection; 125 b CO/ Alinari Archives; 126 cr CO; 126 bl CO/Underwood & Underwood; 126 br, t CO/Bettmann; 127 CO/ Underwood & Underwood; 128 CO/Bettmann; 129 b, t CO/Bettmann; 130 b, l CO/Bettmann; 131 b, t CO/Bettmann; 132 l, r CO/Bettmann; 132–133 (main) CO/Bettmann; 134 CO/Bettmann; 135 b, t CO/Bettmann; 135 cr KOB; 136–137 CO/Bettmann; 138 b, t, CO/Bettmann; 139 b, l CO/Bettmann; 140 CO/Bettmann; 141 br, cl1, cl2, cl3, cl5, cl6, t CO/Bettmann; 141 bl KOB; 142 b, t CO/Underwood & Underwood; 143 bl CO/Richard T. Nowitz; 143 cr, tr CO/Bettmann; 144 b CO; 144 cr, tl CO/Bettmann; 145 CO/Bettmann; 146 bl, br, t CO/Bettmann; 147 l CO/Bettmann; 148 b, t CO/Bettmann; 149 tl CO/Bettmann; 149 c HE; 149 tr PN; 150 CO/Bettmann; 151 b, t CO/Bettmann; 152 cr CO; 152 bl CO/Bettmann; 152 br CO/Richard Bickel; 153 br, l, tr CO/Bettmann; 154 l, r KOB; 155 CO/Bettmann; 156 b, tr CO/Bettmann; 157 b, t CO/Bettmann; 158 b, tr CO/Bettmann; 158 cl CO/MacFadden Publishing; 159 b, br, t CO/Bettmann; 160–161 Getty Images/Timelife; 162 CO/Bettmann; 163 tr AP; 163 c CO; 163 cl CO/Bettmann; 163 cr CO/Norcia/New York Post/Sygma; 164 bl CO/Underwood & Underwood; 164 br, cr CO/Bettmann; 165 Getty Images/TIMELIFE; 166 CO/Bettmann; 167 bl, b, tr CO/Bettmann; 168 CO/Bettmann; 168–169 b CO/Doerzbacher Cliff/Sygma; 169 t CO/Arthur Rothstein; 170 br CO/Bettmann; 170 t CO/Robert Maass; 170 bl HE; 171 b, l KOB; 172 bl, cl AP; 172 cl, (main) REX; 173 CO/Bettmann;174 t AP; 174 b PA; 175 cr AP; 175 tr CP/Montreal Gazette/John Mahoney; 175 br REX; 176 REX; 177 REX; 178 b, t AP; 179 b CO/Bettmann; 179 t CO/Lichenstein Andrew/Sygma; 180 AP; 181 t PA; 181 b REX; 182 CO/Stone Les/Sygma; 183 REX; 184 t CO/ Bettmann; 184 bl, br REX; 185 b CO/Rovar Willy/Sygma; 185 t CO/El Espectador/Sygma; 186 t AP; 186 b CO/Philippe Eranian; 187 bl CO/Sygma; 187 br CO/ El Espectador/Sygma.

Index by Indexing Specialists (UK) Ltd